FROM DEATH
TO LIFE

To: Pastor Jesse,

May God Bless

you

Janita Dominguez

FROM DEATH TO LIFE

Experience the Power of God Within You

ESTHER O. KING

Library of Congress Control Number: 2018912705
ISBN: Hardcover   978-1-9845-6189-3
               Softcover   978-1-9845-6190-9
               eBook   978-1-9845-6264-7

Print information available on the last page.

Rev. date: 06/17/2020

To order additional copies of this book, contact:
Xlibris
1-888-795-4274
www.Xlibris.com
Orders@Xlibris.com
777335

REVELATION 1:10-11

On the Lord's Day I was in the Spirit, and I heard behind me a loud voice like trumpet. Which said: "Write on a scroll what you see and send it to the seven churches: to Ephesus, Smyrna, Pergamum, Thyatira, Sardis, Philadelphia, and Laodicea.

PSALM 136:12

With a Mighty Hand and Outstretched Arm

ACTS 4:30

Stretch out Your hand to heal and performs miraculous signs and wonders through the name of Your holy servant Jesus.

THE STORY ABOUT THE PICTURE FROM THE BOOK COVER

One day, I heard the voice of the Lord saying that He was going to appear to me. I was very excited that God Himself was going to appear to me. I waited expectantly for a week, but did not see Him appear.

Then, two weeks later, I heard the news that the Solar **Eclipse** was going to cross the USA from the West Coast to the East Coast. I was ready for the Eclipse to come. On August 21, 2017, I saw a lot of people outside my window, and they were all looking up. I went outside excitedly to see the Eclipse and I took several pictures of the Solar **Eclipse.** I studied the pictures afterwards, and was amazed at how the Solar **Eclipse** changed and in its shape something different. I asked God about this and it took me two weeks to understand what the shape meant. Finally, I heard the voice of God speaking to me about the Solar **Eclipse.**

He said to me, "My daughter, the shape of the Solar **Eclipse** is My Outstretched Arm."

I was amazed with His beauty, His love, and His power over me, for allowing me to see His wonders and miracles in my life and for God to be able to appear to me in the form of the Solar **Eclipse,** in the shape of

His "Outstretched Arm." The promise that God gave me about wanting to show Himself to me is fulfilled through the form of the Solar **Eclipse** in the shape of His "outstretched Arm." God is an Awesome God.

God spoke to me again and He told me that He wants His Solar **Eclipse,** the "Outstretched Arm of God's picture" to be put on the cover of the book. He said that whoever looks at the book, touches, and reads the book "From Death to Life" will be Blessed, will be Healed, will be Restored, will be Revived, will be Refreshed, will be Renewed and will be Delivered, and it will be a new beginning for all of them.

> *"This move of God will be unlike anything that we've seen before, so powerful and far reaching, visible across the globe."*

ECLIPSE;

I was so glad to be able to know Smith Wigglesworth Prophecy on 1947, and for him to mention about the **ECLIPSE.** The similarity of the message about the Eclipse from him and my story about the Eclipse that the Lord laid upon my life gave me hope, courage and confidence in Him. God wants to pour out His Spirit to me and to you for His glory.

SMITH WIGGLESWORTH PROPHECY ON 1947,

> *"When the word and the spirit come together, there will be the biggest movement of the Holy Spirit that the nation, and indeed the world, has ever seen it will mark the beginning of a Revival that will* ***ECLIPSE*** *anything that has been witnessed within these shores."*

REVIVAL ECLIPSE IS IN GOD'S MIND;

LET THE MIRACLES BEGIN IN YOUR LIFE.....

It is not coincidence that the book From Death to Life is in front of you, God wants to talk to you, and He wants to encounter you through this book. May God overwhelm you with His love and with His outstretch arm, and open your heart to receive Him. God loves you.

1 JOHN 5:13

I write these things to you who believe in the name of the Son of God so that you may know that you have eternal life.

1 CORINTHIANS 15:4

That He was buried, that He was raised on the third day according to the Scriptures.

1 JOHN 3:14

We know that we have passed from death to life, because we love our brothers.

JOHN 5: 24

Very truly I tell you, whoever hears My word and believes Him who sent Me has eternal life and will n ot be judged; but has crossed over from death to life.

Jesus Christ Nazareth

The Finger of God

LUKE 11:20

But, if I drive out demons by the FINGER OF GOD, then the kingdom of God has come upon you.

CONTENTS

DEDICATION

I dedicate this powerful book to my Lord and Savior Jesus Christ of Nazareth. Lord Jesus, You are My Immanuel, my God who is always with me. You are my God who rejected by men who gave me favor and freedom. You are the lover of my soul who created me. You are my suffering God who healed me. You are my humble servant who helped me. You are my powerful Messiah who showed mercy for me. You are my resurrection power who gives life for me. You are my conquering Almighty God who fights for me. You are victorious in battle who wins on my behalf. You are my Creator who gives me love and peace into my soul. You are my anointed One, my King. You are my incredible, indescribable, unexplainable, unsearchable, unshakeable, and uncontainable Prince of Peace over me. You are my God, my Savior, My Jesus, my Husband and my KING. Thank You for everything that You have done in my life. You have transformed me and created me into Your Image. Lord Jesus I LOVE YOU, and thank You.

To my greatest gifts that God ever gave to me. The love of my life, they are my two Amazing Children and my grandchildren.

I want to thank God for my wonderful, and my beautiful first born (Mary), she is the one who made me pursue God to climb up higher, to have the passion, the knowledge of God, and through her I learned how to search for God, to be able to find Him and to be able to present her to our Creator. I asked God, if He is real, then I wanted Him to come and be with her, I am so glad that God answer my prayers. My daughter found God in the most intimate way in her life. I love her so much, that I thanked God for touching her heart, creating and making the new things in her life. She brings love and joy into my life. She is a great daughter and the best mom for my grandchildren, and for those to come. I thank God for my precious grandchildren, they mean a lot to me, and I love them.

I want to thank God for my great daughter (Elizabeth), she lights up my life. She is an intelligent child. She can spin the whole world upside down and knows it completely, I am so proud of her. She always has the patients and love, to teach me about all the things that I don't know. But yet she knew them, I thank God for her for being my child and I love her.

I want to thank God for my granddaughter (Ruth), she is my pride and joy I thank God for her bringing joy in to my life. She is my precious granddaughter the flower of many colors that God sent for me. She is my rock that keeps me grounded. I love her.

I want to thank God for my grandson (Elijah), the fire in my heart, He bring joy into my life. He is a blessing to me. He is my precious grandson that I love, and I thank God for Him. He makes my whole life spin with his beautiful smile. He is my inspiration. He is the winds of fire over me and he is my prince that moves my heart, I love him.

I want to thank God for my new born grandchild "Moses." The day he was born, he turned our world upside down, from his beautiful smile and the sounds from his lips, our hearts are melted. He is the river flowing in our lives.

For my Dad who is already in heaven, I thank God for him guiding me, disciplining me, and loving me while he is here on the earth with us.

Dad without you by my side I knew I would have been lost. I love you with all my heart.

Your loving daughter,

Esther.

For my Mom, thank you for loving me, correcting me, and teaching me. Thank you for your love and passion towards me. Thank you for being my mom. Thank you for showing me how to love and be kind to others. Without you in my life I would not be the woman I am today. I love you with all my heart,

Your loving daughter,

Esther

ACKNOWLEDGEMENT

I want to thank God for everything He has done for my life and for all the love and cares over me, and for the passion of His heart to teach me for the unseen and for the seen over my life.

I want to thank God for the FORERUNNER SCHOOL OF MINISTRY and to all my teachers, my mentors and my leaders for being with me, loving me, encouraging me, believing in me, and for their dedication and passion for pursuing me to do the task that I could not do on my own. There are no words that can explain, how my heart melted with their compassion and determination and perseverance towards me. "Lord Jesus Christ, thank you for bringing them into my life."

I want to thank God for all of them, for always being beside me, taking me to the higher levels where God wants me to go. I want to thank God for them being with me, and loving me. Their words are the power of life coming from God. My heart arose with compassion, love and perseverance for two years in that season of my life with them.

The passion and dedication that my leaders brought into my life compelled me to get to know God even greater than I had before. In my weakest moment I found myself surrendering all to God who created me. I will not be who I am right now without my teachers, mentors, and leaders pursuing me, so I could get to know God even greater, so I could be blameless and spotless before Him. I thought that I knew God not until I went to Forerunner School of Ministry, my eyes were open and I saw the brightness and understanding of God's word in my life.

By the word coming from them and with their powerful teaching coming from the Holy Spirit brought me to my knees in prayers, as I pray the word of God became alive to me. The words that came from my leader's lips bring my soul to be righteousness before God. The teaching and the word of God penetrate into my soul and touched my heart and it changed my life completely. I want to thank God for them and I feel blessed for everything that God had done in my life. My God and my leaders are my heroes. I want to thank God for my wonderful leaders for giving me the insight for the things that was hard for me to understand. Their passion and dedication towards me brought courage in my life.

I want to thank God for all of them, from the bottom of my heart. They are all my inspirations, and they bring laughter into my heart and joy of healing to my mind, body, and soul. They are my abundance of joy and through their teaching I got to know God even greater. They turned my world upside down by sharing God to me accompanied with power, laughter, happiness and their joy with God.

I want to thank God for all of them they are wonderful chosen vessels of God. I will not be who I am if was not for their powerful words coming from the Holy Spirit. I want to thank God for their passions, dedication, and willing hearts for wanting more of my testimony concerning the wonders of God over my life. Their love and their encouraging words towards me brought love and peace into my heart. They are the answer to my prayers. Their dedications, passions, caring, patients towards me brought encouraging and positive thinking in everything I do. I want to say; they are my Guardian angels, they always brought words of love into my life. I love them and I thank God for all the good things that they have done for me and for God's children.

FOREWORD

PSALM 45:1

My heart is stirred by a noble theme as I recite my verses for the king; my tongue is the pen of a skillful writer.

DANIEL 4:2-3

It is my pleasure to tell you about the miraculous signs and wonders that the most High God has performed for me.

PSALM 139:13-16

For You created my inmost being; You knit me together in my mother's womb. I praise You because I am fearfully and wonderfully made; Your works are wonderful, I know that full well. My frame was not hidden from You, when I was made in the secret place. When I was woven together in the depths of the earth, "Your eyes saw my unformed body." All the days ordained for me were written in Your book before one of them came to be. How precious to me are Your thoughts, God! How vast is the sum of them! Were I to count them, they would outnumber the grains of sands. When I awake, I am still with You.

MY STORY

My life is full of stories, is about the love of God, in awe of God, with signs, wonders, miracles, of God, with resurrection power's of God, healing, deliverance, restoration of God, and the supernatural divine connection from our God who built the universe.

My stories will inspire the whole nations for the manifestation of His love and glory and to the whole level of God's Divine Power through His mighty acts in my life.

My stories is about God's glory of what God has made, created and done in my life, and I'm delighted for every Encounter with the Lord Jesus Christ, the Manifestation of God's power and glory, and every spoken word and the move of God, in every Healing, every deliverance, every breath of God and every manifestation of Jesus Christ's Mighty power of His scepter with His crown and prayers over my life.

My stories have been revealing God's reality of His love and faithfulness and to making, creating, and shifting from the act and the move of the Holy Spirit within my soul.

My stories can bring the people to have courage, strength, boldness, encounter, awe, and power to have a supernatural divine faith in their life.

My stories will bring confidence and assurance to the people's faith, and I will share and act the greatest legacy for being blameless, spotless and having a pure heart and being faithful to my creator and to be able to participate in the essence of His wonders for His kingdom.

My stories will be able to give the new possibilities to have hope, joy and faith to every situation and challenges in people's lives.

My stories are about how God reveals Himself to me, His love, His faithfulness, and His goodness that makes me to be the unshakeable and Immovable one.

My stories are an example of how God can make all things from the restoration, healing, blessings, deliverance, and faith within my soul.

My stories are the one that shows that it is only when I die is when I truly find life.

This is my life changing testimonies and it is a story's of a greater dimension that will lead God's people to their destiny and purposes in their lives.

This is my CREATOR, my GOD, my SAVIOR, my HOLY SPIRIT, my KING, my HUSBAND and my LORD "JESUS CHRIST OF NAZARETH" who CREATED ME!

My burning desire is that this book will take you to the highest dimension and a level of God's promises in your life. I pray that by sharing my testimony it will bring love, peace, hope, joy, faith, courage, boldness, healing, blessings, restoration, deliverance, assurance and confidence in your life. And may you walk in His path of revelation in your life.

REVELATION 1:1-11

The Revelation from Jesus Christ, which God gave Him to show His servants what must soon take place.

He made it known by sending His Angel to His servant John, who testifies to everything He saw – that is, the word of God, and the testimony of Jesus Christ.

Blessed is the one who reads aloud the words of this prophecy, and blessed are those who hear it and take to heart what is written in it, because time is near.

John, to the seven churches in the province of Asia:

Grace and peace to you from Him Who Is, and Who Was, and who is to come, and from the seven Spirits before His throne.

And from Jesus Christ, who is the Faithful witness, the Firstborn from the dead, and the Ruler of the kings of the earth. To Him who loves us and has freed us from our sins by His blood, and has made us to be a kingdom and priests to serve His God and Father, - to Him be glory and power forever and ever. Amen. Look, He is coming with the clouds, and every eye will see

Him, even those who pierced Him. And all peoples on earth will mourn because of Him. So shall it be! Amen.

"I AM the ALPHA and the OMEGA," says the Lord God, "WHO IS AND WHO WAS AND WHO IS TO COME, THE ALMIGHTY."

I, John, your brother and companion in the suffering and kingdom and patient endurance that are ours in Jesus, was on the island of Patmos because of the word of God and the testimony of Jesus. ¹ On the Lord's Day I was in the Spirit, and I heard behind me a loud voice like a trumpet, which said: "Write on a scroll what you see and send it to the seven churches: to Ephesus, Smyrna, Pergamum, Thyatira, Sardis, Philadelphia and Laodicea."

God has given John the vision and the revelation to write about what is to going to happen. How beautiful it is to know about God's beauty. God is letting John know that God is infinite and there is nothing that can compare Him.

REVELATION 22:16

"I, Jesus, have sent My angel to give you this testimony for the churches. I AM the root and the offspring of David, and the bright Morning star."

REVELATION 1:19

"Write, therefore, what you have seen, what is now and what will take place later."

WRITING ABOUT MY STORY

On 2012, I heard the voice of God saying that He wanted me to share my testimony to the whole world. He told me to write a book, and the book was about the story of my life. God wanted me to share my testimony throughout the Nations. My heart was pounding as to what God wanted me to do. I have never written a book before in my entire life. I started to have fear and defeated just for me to think about writing a book. Being a Woman from a poor country and not knowing English very well, I felt as though my English was not good enough. I felt like I needed help God to teach me of what I needed to do. At that moment I thought I misunderstood God. I could not understand why He wanted me to write a book. Was I hearing God wrong? My poor mind was not able to comprehend as to what God really wanted me to do. So the word from the Holy Spirit to write the book about my life was delayed. Therefore I did not write the book for two years. At that moment I felt like I put God in the box.

On 2014, God spoke to me again, and this time He sent people to tell me about their visions seeing me writing a book. I tried my best to listen to God. I decided to write down the things that I could remember about my life when I was a child, I remembered thinking about all the things that was happening to me and what would it be like also in my future. As I was trying to remember all those things I asked God to reveal to me about my life from the beginning and to the ending of my life. And what is happening to me at this hour. When God showed me what happen to me in my past life. I found myself being broken down and I started to cry. I realized that my story was very pain full for me to remember or even to write it down. There was so many question that I want to ask God. In my heart, I was feeling shattered, broken and full of fear and trying to find God at the same time. I was lost, and I found myself asking God is to how and where He was while all those bad things was happening to me.

Because of all the pain and hurts that I was experiencing, I develop confusion. I decided to stop writing about my story all over again. I had put God back in the box again.

On 2016 God spoke to me again about the book and my story. This time I realized that God really wanted me to write my book. I was so glad for all those years that had passed in my life, that I have actually had found God's love and compassion towards me. God healed, restored, delivered and redeemed me. I can now say that I am ready to write my story and to share it to the whole world, that God is real and alive within my soul. God fulfilled all the promises over my life. He gave back my joy, love, faith, and strength.

I remember, before I gave my life to my Lord and savior on 2007, I was reading this powerful book from a powerful man of God, I was so glad that the book that I was reading had scripture in it.

Because of that, I now love to read the Bible. At that time in my life I had never read the Bible and I did not know how to start reading the Bible, God gave me the opportunity to have the knowledge, wisdom, vision, provision, understanding and revelation about the scriptures and to be able to find them in the Bible, also the Bible is the only book that God gave me for direction and guidance to navigate my life. Through the Bible and the Holy Spirit, my life was given back to me. Through the bible I began to have confidence and the confirmation as to what God was saying about my destiny and my future. When I hear the voice of God speaking to me, God backs it up with His scripture. The Bible inspired me to understand that God is even greater. Now with the Holy Spirit in my life, I am able to read the Bible with confidence, assurance, revelation, wisdom, knowledge, and with His power within me.

God's word has Spirit and it has life. It is God's desires for me to read His diary. It is because of that, I included the scriptures in my book. It is because of God's words, that I have life, love, power, strength, healing, restoration, direction, blessings over me.

As you read this book I know without any doubt that your life will be transform for God's glory.

I pray that you will find God, as you read this book that your life will change completely for His purpose, His will, and for His glory in your life.

HUMBLE IN HIM

I am sharing my life with you, as a servant of God being humbled, obedient, and not to gain anything. Instead is to bring glory to God. To be able to protect the people and to have peace now and in the future, I did not use the real names of the people in this book and in my life. I am writing my story to let you know that God, the Creator of the universe is higher than I could ever imagine. God is with me and performing miracles in everything that has happened in my life.

As I started writing my story, I saw the glory of Jesus Christ in my life that I actually experienced everything that happened to Him while He was here on earth. Because of His love over me I embrace and adore

Him. I follow His word and the path of righteousness upon my life. I thank God for giving me an opportunity to know Him and to be able to experience His beauty, love, and power over my life. As I got to know Him, I wanted more of Him. As I seek His face, I encountered Him. I can see His glory in everyday of my life.

Jesus story is about being humble, meek, and love from the beginning and to the ending of His life. He was despised and rejected from the moment of His birth and until His last breath on this earth. His story is about Signs, wonders, and miracles. It is about Suffering, His Blood, His Death, His Tomb, His Resurrection, and is about Him being the "KING" from heaven, earth, and under the earth. Jesus experienced the waves of life here on the earth and through His blood and through His death that human kind also conquered death. Jesus Christ the anointing One who carried the whole world accompany with Signs, Wonders and Miracles, the ONE WHO SITS ON THE THRONE, the LAMB WHO WAS SLAIN, the One who Is, and who Was, and Is, to Come, the Almighty God. The Nations worships Him and through Him that we are "Saved."

As Jesus Christ walked with me, I saw the incredible and unique power that brought me onto my knees. I saw His beauty and love that melt my whole being. His nature inspired me so much. I realize that I have experience the same things He did while He was walking here on the earth. I experience to be humble and to die daily with Jesus. I experience to be poor, homeless, suffer, rejection and crucified by men. I also experience Death to Life. I experienced to be the servant of God by helping and sharing the Gospel, praying, and prophesy for God's people, accompanied with signs, wonders, and miracles. Truly God is real within my soul. Jesus Christ is real and He is alive.

As I went deeper about knowing Jesus Christ in my life, my whole life changed completely and when I found Him my heart started to sing with joy. The more I became drawn to Him, my eyes were open. The more I knew Him my mouth became full of revelation. The more I loved Him my understanding grew bigger. The more I hunger for Him, the more my ears became alert for His voice. The more I longed for Him my body shook with His presence over me as the years go by, the wisdom, revelation, and the knowledge, of Him manifested in my life. Knowing God in my life, I realized that JESUS AND I ARE ONE.

PRAYER,

As I shared my story to you, I prayed that you will experience God's love and greater power than you could ever imagine in your life. I prayed that my story will bring comfort, hope, joy, healing, restoration, blessings and deliverance into your soul. May God take you to the whole level of His righteousness and His faithfulness and may you walk worthy of your calling, In Jesus' name. Amen.

PREFACE

ABOUT YOUR STORY

When you believe in Jesus Christ of Nazareth

You have a story to tell to the whole world. Your story was just beginning. God loves to writes and rewrites the story from your past and your future, your story are awesome it is from the finger of God, there is more of your story because there is more of Him and there is more to come. Your story has the ability to change and to light up the world for God's manifestation of His glory. Your story is about how Jesus Christ's creativity transformed your life into His Image. Your story is special and unique it is about God making and creating a new thing in your life. Your story will touch someone's life. Signs, wonders and miracles will follow wherever you go. You are precious to God, and God takes the broken pieces of your story and makes it to be beautiful, magnificent, and marvelous into His ears, eyes and heart. The love of God will rise up in you and they will see the goodness of God in your life. The people will be impacted by your powerful story. You have the ability to speak and to have courage and to be boldness to share what God has done in your life. You are God's favorite and He is writing your name in the Palm of His Hands. When God is writing your story it is not secondary to God's will, it is His will and nature. God in His word and action will tell you who He is and what you can expect from Him. Writing everything about you is a door and the window into the heart of our Creator and part of radiance of His glory. You are His possession, you are His inheritance, you are His treasures, you are His jewel and everything about you is His because He made you, He molded you and created you into His Image and you are important to Him. He knows every detail of your life, He knows every number of your hairs, He formed and fashioned you in your mother's womb, and you are what God says you are. The end of your story is a triumph of victory of the Lord Jesus Christ in Your life.

God loves you!

ISAIAH 53:3-5

He was despised and rejected by mankind, a man of suffering, and familiar with pain. Like one from whom people hide their faces He was despised, and we held Him in low esteem. Surely He took up our pain and bore our suffering, yet we considered Him punished by God, stricken by Him, and afflicted. But He was pierced for our transgressions, He was crushed for our iniquities; the punishment that brought us peace was on Him, and by His wounds we are healed.

As I take you through the journey of my life. I hope that you will see the power of God. When I experience death, resurrection, pain, suffering, persecution, rejection, hardships, challenges, sickness, disease, love, peace, strength, joy, faith, healing, restoration, redemption, deliverance, for the first time in my life, I saw God's love and Mighty act of the Holy Spirit over my life. By Him giving me strength to conquer the brokenness of my life and bringing me back to one piece all over again. When I saw the broken pieces of my life, God made me whole again, all I can say is that I won the triumph of victory of God over me. And I overcame the works of the enemies. God is at work within my soul. And I thanked God for Him being with me.

SEEK HIM FACE TO FACE

PSALM 27:8

My heart says of You. "Seek His face" Your face, Lord, I will seek.

As you seek God's face to face, you will experience God's Power in your life, you will be healed, you will be restored, you will have freedom and you will be blessed. You will experience God's love, His power, and manifestation of His glory, that you have never experience before in your life.

When I experience the power of God, I stand in awe of Jesus Christ. And I knew without any doubt that you will experience the same way, because He is God and He created all things, He created you, you are His child and He is your "ABBA", FATHER.

I invite you to seek God and find Him in your heart. God will lead you and fulfilled all the His promises for His purpose and for His glory over your life. You will see God as you embraced His love and peace. God will unlock the hidden treasures from heaven that is already ordained for you to have, and you will be blessed.

The God that I know is the only one who can bring life and encouragement to me, and without Him by my side I know that I will be lost and be broken. Yet through prayers and believing in God, I conquered all things from this falling world. I would never have been here on the face of this earth if it was not for the Almighty God that I serve. God's power has been revealed not only to me but also to the people around me. I saw His power, signs, wonders and miracles in my life. His loves and presence takes over me and brings love, assurance and confidence into my life, and His people. His presence is very tangible in my heart and it brings awe within my soul.

The only reason I' am alive today is because of God's love, grace and mercy and His ability to perform miracles for me. I will be in the eternal fire without God in my life. But God wins all. To God be the glory.

GOD HAS SPOKEN

JOHN 14:14

You may ask Me for anything in My name, and I will do it.

NUMBERS 23: 19-20

God is not human, that He should lie not a human being, that He should change His mind. Does He speak and then not act? Does He promise and not fulfill? I have received a command to bless; He has blessed, and I cannot change it.

ISAIAH 46: 9-10

Remember the former things, those of long ago. I Am God, and there is no other, I AM God, and there is none like Me. I make known the end from the beginning, from ancient times, what is still to come. I say, My purpose will stand, and I will do all that I please.

PSALM 33:9

For He spoke, and it came to be, He commanded, and it stood firm.

ISAIAH 40:8

The grass withers and the flowers fall, but the word of our God endures forever.

ISAIAH 26:3

You will keep in perfect peace Him whose mind is steadfast, because He trust in you.

GOD IS REAL, AND HE IS ALIVE

REVELATION 1:1–3

The Revelation of Jesus Christ, which God gave Him to show His servants what must soon take place. He made it known by sending His angel to His servant John, who testifies to everything He saw-that is, the word of God and the testimony of Jesus Christ. Blessed is the one who reads aloud the words of this Prophecy, and blessed are those who hear it and take to heart what is written in it, because the time is near.

PSALM 77:10–15

Then I thought, "To this I will appeal: the years when the Most High stretched out His right hand. I will remember the deeds of the LORD; yes, I will remember your miracles of long ago. I will consider all your works and meditate on all your mighty deeds." Your ways, God, are holy. What god is as great as our God? You are the God who performs miracles; you display your power among the peoples. With your mighty arm you redeemed your people, the descendants of Jacob and Joseph.

INTRODUCTION

SALVATION

Since the foundation of this world, God already had an eye on you. He knew you before you were born. He watches over you, and He never leaves you or forsakes you. He nurtures you until you grow up to become a beautiful child. You did not choose God. But God chose you. The question is? do you know Him? Are your eyes fixed on God? Or are you focusing on things that are not of God? Which are called sins?

EZEKIEL 16:1–14

The word of the Lord came to me: Son of man, confront Jerusalem with her detestable practices and say, This is what the Sovereign Lord says to Jerusalem; your ancestry and birth were in the land of the Canaanites; your father was an Amorite and your mother a Hitite. On the day you were born your cord was not cut, nor were you washed with the water to make you clean, nor were you rubbed with salt or wrapped in cloths. No one looked on you with pity or had compassion enough to do any of these things for you. Rather, you were thrown out into the open field. For the day you were born you were despised.

Then I passed by and saw you kicking about in your blood, and as you lay there in your blood I said to you "live!" I made you grow like a plant of the field. You grew up and developed and become the most beautiful of jewels. Your breast were formed and your hair grew, you were naked and bare.

Later I passed by, and when I looked at you and saw that you were old enough for love, I spread the corner of My garment over you and covered your nakedness. I gave you My solemn oath and entered into a covenant with you, declares the Sovereign Lord, and you become mine. I bathed you with water and washed the blood from you and put ointments on you. I clothed you with an embroidered dress and put leather sandals on you. I dressed you in fine linen and covered you with costly garments. I adorned you with jewelry. I put bracelets on your arms and necklace around your neck, and I put a ring on your nose, earrings on your ears and a beautiful crown on your head. So you were adorned with gold and silver, your clothes were of fine linen and costly fabric and embroidered cloth. Your food was fine flour, honey and olive oil. You became very beautiful and rose to be queen. And your fame spread among the nations on account of your beauty, because the splendor I had given you made your beauty perfect, declares the sovereign Lord.

Before we were born, God knew us. God takes care of us and gives us our new life. God loves us so much, and He is willing to give His Son to give us eternity. But sometimes we don't see the way God sees; instead, we see ourselves being opposite of what God sees in us. Our eyes become blind; and we can't see the love, acts, beauty, and glory of God anymore. We don't feel satisfied with what God has for us; instead we find ourselves sinning against God. And when we sin against God, the Bible says that it separate us from God. Then we will no longer be called children of God; instead, we will be called His enemies.

PSALM 51:4

Against You, You only have I sinned.

ROMANS 5:10

For if, while we were God's enemies, we were reconciled to Him through the death of His Son, how much more, having been reconciled, shall we be saved through His life!

EPHESIANS 2:1–22

As for you, you were dead in your transgressions and sins, in which you used to live when you followed the ways of this world and of the kingdom of the air, the spirit who is now at work in those who are disobedient. All of us also lived among them at one time, gratifying the cravings of our sinful nature and following its desires and thoughts. Like the rest, we were by nature objects of wrath. But because of His great love for us, God, who is rich and mercy, made us alive with Christ even when we were dead in transgressions—it is by grace you have been saved. And God raised us up with Christ and seated us with Him in the heavenly realms in Christ Jesus, In order that in the coming ages He might show the incomparable riches of His grace, express in His kindness to us in Christ Jesus. For it is by grace you have been saved, through faith—and this not from yourselves, it is the gift from God—not by works, so that no one can boast. For we are God's workmanship, created in Christ Jesus to do good works, which God prepared in advance for us to do.

With Jesus Christ, there is hope . . .

ROMANS 4:7–8

Blessed are they whose transgressions are forgiven, whose sins are covered. Blessed is the one whose sin the Lord will never count against them.

GOD

JOHN 3:16–17

For God so loved the world that He gave His One and only Son, that whoever believes in Him shall not perish but have eternal life. For God did not send His Son into the world to condemn the world, but to save the world through Him.

Because God loves you so much, He thought about giving you His Son Jesus Christ over anything of this falling world. He is the one who died and shed His blood for you. He is the one who will remove every sin you've committed. He is the one who holds the key for your destiny in the heavens. He is the one who can save you. God is full of grace, mercy, and compassion toward you. And you are blameless and spotless before His throne. And with His resurrection, God put your name in the Book of Life; and in heaven, you will be satisfied.

JESUS CHRIST OF NAZARETH

HE SUFFERED, DIED, WAS BURIED AND RESURRECTED

He is our suffering servant, yet He is our king. He was bruised, oppressed, and afflicted; yet He is our healer. He was rejected by men, and He was cut off from the land of the living, yet He is our hope. He was crushed for our iniquities, yet He is our redeemer. He died, yet He gives life. He is the light of life. He is satisfied, and He is our redeemer and provider. Through it all, He released freedom and life for us all, and His blood set us free for all eternity.

Jesus died and shed blood for all of us; He was the one who gave it all. In Him, we may have life and have it more abundantly. Jesus is the only one who can take away our sins so we can be righteous and be able to have a pure heart. The glory of God's kingdom is the suffering of Jesus Christ, and through His death, we became children of God.

Jesus love is the way that can and will change your life. His suffering, death, and blood wash away your sins, which will bring confidence in the way you walk with Him. With His blood, you will know, believe, and proclaim with boldness, confidence, and courage that He is your King and Savior.

Jesus Christ is the living Word. He is God, and He is also man in the flesh with full of wonders. When He came to this world, the world changed, full of glory. He saved, forgave, blessed, restored, healed, raised the dead, changed lives, and liked sinners. He came not to destroy the world but to save the world. *He is our King from heaven.*

GOD SAVES

If you have not given yourself to our God, and to our Savior Jesus Christ, this is a good opportunity to have a new starting point in your life to give and surrender yourself to the one who created you.

The scripture says in . . .

ROMANS 10:9

If you declare with your mouth," Jesus is Lord" and believe in your heart that God has raised Him from the dead, you will be saved.

Every sin that we committed in our life is a sin that will take us to the burning fire, but know this: Jesus Christ's love, blood, death, and resurrection is the way to our salvation for us to have eternal life. Jesus will wipe away all of our sins, and He will create a new heart within us. God is our Creator. He created us, and we are made in the Image and likeness of Him.

PRAYER FOR SALVATION

PRAY THIS PRAYER TO INVITE JESUS INTO YOUR LIFE

My Lord Jesus Christ, I acknowledge that I am a sinner. Please forgive me for the things that I have done wrong, knowingly and unknowingly. I ask you to wash me, to cleanse me, and to mold me into your scarred hands. I confess with my mouth, and I believe in my heart that You are the Son of God who died and rose again to be my Savior. Thank You for hanging on the cross for me. Thank You for Your blood, which washed away all my sins. Thank You for saving my soul and for giving me the gift of eternal life.

Lord Jesus, fill me with Your Holy Spirit. Lord, I accept You, I receive You, and I want You to come and be the Lord of my life. Make and create a new heart within my soul. Thank you for touching my heart and changing me completely. Lord Jesus, help me to know You more and more. Lord Jesus, please keep me, train me, equip me, and teach me Your ways so that I may walk worthy in Your sight. Thank you for giving me the wisdom, the knowledge, and revelation of You.

Lord Jesus, show and reveal Yourself to me that I may go right with You. Lord Jesus, open my eyes to see You. I want to be near You, and I want to see You face-to-face. Open my ears to hear You and open my heart to receive You into my life. Lord Jesus, I want to see Your glory within my soul, In Jesus Mighty name. Amen.

DID YOU JUST PRAY THIS PRAYER?

Congratulations! Your name is guarantee that is written in the Book of Life. You are in the right path for His kingdom, you have been given the key for His mansion, and the angels are rejoicing over you in heaven. I encourage you to surround yourself with people who love God and fellowship with them. God is with you, and He loves you.

1 JOHN 5:1–5

Everyone who believes that Jesus is the Christ is born of God, and everyone who loves the Father loves His child as well. This is how we know that we love the children of God, by loving God and carrying out His commands. In fact, this is love for God: to keep His commands. And His commands are not burdensome, for everyone born of God overcomes the world. This is the victory that h as overcome the world, even our faith. Who is it that overcomes the world?

Only the one who believes that Jesus is the Son of God.

Jesus is the man who died for you and He took every beating people can't even imagine. He is the only One who suffered. He made a huge sacrifice, doing the will of His heavenly Father, just for you. Jesus suffered for your sins so that through Him, you will have access to heaven. You will have access to the key of His mansion, which has many rooms. You have access to His kingdom. You have access to His authority and power for dominion over this earth. Jesus Christ surrendered all so that in Him, you may have eternal life and have it more abundantly. The blood of Jesus is the only way to heaven.

JOHN 14:6

Jesus answered, "I AM the Way and the Truth and the Life." No one comes to the Father except through Me.

HEBREWS 8:10–12

This is the covenant I will establish with the people of Israel after that time, declares the Lord. I will put my laws in their minds and write them on their hearts. I will be their God, and they will be my people. No longer will they teach their neighbor, or say to one another, 'Know the Lord,' because they will all know me, from the least of them to the greatest. For I will forgive their wickedness and will remember their sins no more.

2 CORINTHIANS 6:16–18

What agreement is there between the temple of God and idols? For we are the temple of the living God. As God has said: "I will live with them and walk among them, and I will be their God, and they will be my people." Therefore, "Come out from them and be separate, says the Lord. Touch no unclean thing, and I will receive you." And, "I will be a Father to you, and you will be my sons and daughters, says the Lord Almighty."

ROMANS 9:25-26

As He says in Hosea: "I will call them 'My people' who are not My people, and I will call Her my loved one' who is not My loved one," and, "In the very place where it was said to them, 'You are not My people,' there they will be called 'Children of the living God.'"

EZEKIEL 34:25–31

I will make a covenant of peace with them and rid the land of wild beast so that they may live in the wilderness and sleep in the forests in safety. I will make them and the places surrounding My hill a blessing "I will send down showers in season; there will be showers of blessing. The trees will yield their fruit and the ground will yield its crops; the people will be secure in their land. They will know that I Am the Lord, when I break the bars of their yoke and rescue them from the hands of those who enslaved them. They will no longer be plundered by the Nations, nor will wild animals devour them. They will live in safety, and no one will make them afraid. I will provide for them a land renowned for its crops, and they will no longer be victims of famine in the land or bear the scorn of the Nations. Then they will know that I, the Lord their God, AM with them and that they, the Israelites, are My people, declares the Sovereign Lord. You are My sheep, the sheep of My pasture, are people, and I AM your God, declares the Sovereign Lord."

EPHESIANS 2:19–22

Consequently, you are no longer foreigners, and aliens, but fellow citizens with God's people and members of God's household, built on the foundation of the apostles and prophets, with Christ Jesus Himself as the Chief Cornerstone. In Him the whole building is joined together and rises to become a holy temple in the Lord. And in Him you too are being built together to become a dwelling in which God lives by His Spirit.

Jesus is the only way, the truth, and the life; and through Him, you become God's children.

A NEW HEART

As I read the Word of God, it becomes alive to me, and it is actually manifested in every fiber of my soul. God is real, and He is alive in my life. I want to share with you of some of the scriptures that led me to be amazed and to walk in righteousness before God.

PSALM 51:7–12

Cleanse me with hyssop, and I will be clean; wash me, and I will be whiter than snow. Let me hear joy and gladness; let the bones you have crushed rejoice. Hide Your face from my sins and blot out all my iniquity. Create in me a pure heart, O God, and renew a steadfast spirit within me. Do not cast me from your presence or take Your Holy Spirit from me. Restore to me the joy of Your salvation and grant me a willing Spirit, to sustain me.

ANGELS

The angels are God's messengers from heaven and earth. The angels are listening and watching over you. The angels are your refuge, protection, blessings, comfort and deliverance during times of trouble. The angels want to give you hope, restoration, and they want you not to have fear but to have faith in God in all your ways.

PSALM 91

Whoever dwells in the shelter of the Most High will rest in the shadow of the Almighty. I will say of the Lord, "He is my refuge and my fortress, my God, in whom I trust." Surely He will save you from the fowler's snare and from the deadly pestilence. He will cover you with His feathers, and under His wings you will find refuge; His faithfulness will be your shield and rampart. You will not fear the terror of night, nor the arrow that flies by day, nor the pestilence that stalks in the darkness, nor the plague that destroys at midday. A thousand may fall at your side, ten thousand at your right hand, but it will not come near you. You will only observe with your eyes and see the punishment of the wicked. If you say, "The Lord is my refuge," and you make the Most High your dwelling, no harm will overtake you no disaster will come near your tent. For He will command His angels concerning you to guard you in all your ways; they will lift you up in their hands, so that you will not strike your foot against a stone. You will tread on the lion and the cobra; you will trample the great lion and the serpent. "Because He loves me," says the Lord, "I will rescue Him; I will protect Him, for He acknowledges my name. He will call on me, and I will answer Him; I will be with Him in trouble, I will deliver Him and honor Him. With long life I will satisfy Him and show Him my salvation."

LIVE AGAIN

In every dead, dry-bones situation or challenges in your life (e.g., sickness, poverty, brokenness, demons), knows this: you can trust God. He promises to breathe a new spiritual life in you. Never give up. Instead, have hope, faith, and joy in God because He is at work calling you into Himself to restore, revive, and renew you.

EZEKIEL 37:1–14

The hand of the Lord was on me, and He brought me out by the Spirit of the Lord and set me in the middle of a valley; it was full of bones, He led me back and forth among them, and I saw a great many bones on the floor of the valley, bones that were very dry He asked me, "SON OF MAN, can these bones live?" I said, "O Sovereign Lord, you alone know." Then He said to me, "Prophesy to these bones and say to them, 'Dry bones, hear the word of the Lord! This is the Sovereign Lord says to these bones: I will make breath enter you, and you will come to life. I will attach tendons to you and make flesh come upon you and cover you with skin; I will put breath in you, and you will come to life. Then you will know that I am the Lord.'" So I prophesied as I was commanded. And as I was prophesying, there was a noise, a rattling sound, and the bones came together, bone to bone. I looked, and tendons and flesh appeared on them and skin covered them, but there was no breath in them. Then He said to me, "Prophesy to the breath; prophesy, SON OF MAN, and say to it, 'this is what the SOVEREIGN LORD says: Come from the four winds, O breath, and breathe into these slain, that they may live.'" So I prophesied as He commanded me, and breath entered them; they came to life and stood up on their feet—vast army. Then He said to me: "SON OF MAN, these bones are the whole house of Israel. They say, 'Our bones are dried up and our hope is gone; we are cut off.' Therefore prophesy and say to them: This is what the SOVEREIGN LORD: O My people, I am going to open your graves and bring you up from them: I will bring you back to the land of Israel. Then you, My people, will know that I am the Lord, when I open your graves and bring you up from them. I will put my Spirit in you and you will live, and I will settle you to your own land.'"

GOOD SHEPHERD

The "Shepherd"—the King of heaven, earth, and under the earth—directs, leads, and guides the sheep, His children, on His pathway, direction, and destination. God's love, comfort, and protection for His sheep bring courage, assurance, boldness, and confidence for His children. The sheep will not be lost as they follow the Shepherd to direct, guide, lead and protect them from any danger.

Do not have fear, for He is your God . . .

DO NOT HAVE FEAR

PSALM 23

The Lord is my shepherd, I lack nothing. He makes me lie down in green pastures, He leads me beside quiet waters. He refreshes my soul. He guides me along the right paths for His name's sake. Even though I walk through the darkest valley, I will fear no evil, for you are with me; your rod and your staff, they comfort me. You prepare a table before me in the presence of my enemies. You anoint my head with oil; my cup overflows. Surely your goodness and love will follow me all the days of my life, and I will dwell in the house of the Lord forever.

GOD'S HAND

God creates ways to bring you to the promise land by performing signs, wonders, and miracles. His love toward you is beyond all things of this world. God and His Mighty acts of wonders show you that He is God and that there is no one and nothing like Him so that you can trust in Him.

EXODUS 14:21

Then Moses stretched out His hand over the sea, and all that night the Lord drove the sea back with a strong east wind and turned it into dry land. The waters were divided, and the Israelites went through the sea on the dry ground, with a wall of water on their right and on their left.

DANIEL 4:1–3

King Nebuchadnezzar, to the nations and peoples of every language, who live in all the earth: May you prosper greatly! It is my pleasure to tell you about the miraculous signs and wonders that the Most High God has performed for me. How great are His signs, how mighty His wonders! His kingdom is an eternal kingdom; His dominion endures from generation to generation.

CHAPTER 1

MY FAMILY

My mother shared with me about where they used to live and what happened to me after I was born. She told me that we used to live in a bungalow with six stairs; the roof was made out of the palm leaves with holes all around it, and when it rained, the whole house was flooded. All sides of the house were made out of plywood, and it had one small window. The house was hot and dark because we didn't have any power.

My mother continued sharing with me of the time when I just started learning how to crawl. As I was crawling, my mother was too busy doing other stuff that she did not noticed that I was beside the door. I crawled out and I fell down the stairs. To her surprise, she did not hear me fall until I cried very loudly. That shocked her, and she immediately came and rescued me. By the grace of God, I was fine. Nothing in my body was broken. She thought that an angel was watching over me. My parents did not take me to the doctor because my dad believed that God already healed me, and also, they did not have a lot of money at that time. We were surrounded by fruits, vegetables, and also animals like chickens, pigs. My dad raised animals, and that was how my parents got our food every day.

As I grew up, our living situation changed. We didn't live in the same house anymore; instead, we lived in a house whose roof was made out of old metal. The metal had holes on it; and again, every time it rained, the water will go inside the house. Because the roof is made out of metals, the heat from the sun was very strong, and it was very hot and uncomfortable inside the house; everybody always felt hot in the house. The windows were open, and it was very humid outside; we found ourselves getting sick all the time because of the heat. We always had hot and rainy weather in the Philippines. My brothers, my sister, and I slept on the floor; we still tried to go to sleep even with water all around us.

The house also did not have electricity at that time; we lived in a house that was always dark, and we also didn't have any air-conditioning. When it got dark, we used an empty glass bottle with clothes and gasoline on it, and we made a fire out of it. We used that for light in the house and also outside. For light, we brought the bottle anywhere we went, and we held it while we walked on the streets so we had light while walking. Without the bottles used for light, we would not be able to walk on the street because it was very dark and dangerous at night.

Outside the house, my parents gathered all the rocks they could find to form something like a stove. They also found pieces of woods and sticks to make a fire out of it and they used the handmade rock stove for us to be able to cook food for us to eat. Even though our house was not perfect, I called it my home.

When I look back about my life as I was growing up as child, I realized that my life was not easy I was innocent, and not knowing the things of this world. I lived every day knowing that my dad, my mom, my brothers, and my sister were there for me knowing that we loved one another. That's all that mattered to me.

MY DAD'S STORY

My dad was always there to teach me of the things I needed to know growing up; He taught me how to plant fruits, vegetables, and other things from our beautiful acres of land. We also had a farm. My dad showed me how to raise pigs and chickens, and I was a very happy child.

PROTECTED BY GOD

One day, while my dad and I were sitting at the table, my dad started sharing his story with me. His story is about the Japanese soldiers trying to take over the Philippines many years ago. He told me that the Japanese soldiers tried to capture him and his family, but by the grace of God, the soldiers failed; they were hiding in a secret place where the Japanese soldiers could not find them. He told me that one day, he was walking by himself, and he saw Japanese soldiers from afar coming toward him; my dad had to think and move quickly so they would not capture him. A great relief came over him when he saw a river close by; it was a matter of life or death. My dad had to make an executive decision to jump in the river, and he stayed underwater for a long time. While He was underwater, he remembered that he had a bamboo shoot with him in his pocket, and he used it so he could breathe while underwater until the Japanese soldiers went past him without seeing him. I was so glad that God was with him and that my dad was not dead at that time because I would not be here if my dad didn't live. I thank God for protecting my dad. God is my Hero.

My dad always fascinated me; he was very creative, and he loved God. He loved to pray, and he loved to bring glory to God. My father's love brought me to a higher level of God's goodness over my life; my dad taught me how to understand God. But as I grew up, the word of God did not stayed in my heart very long because I was swayed by the things of this world. But there was one scripture I remember that my dad shared with me, and that scripture really touched my heart. And it has stayed in my heart until to this day. It is about Judas. My dad told me about Judas and how he was very hurt about what Judas did to Jesus, that Judas betrayed Jesus.

One day, my dad and I were at the lake, we were fishing, and he was sharing with me again about how Judas betrayed Jesus; he told me that Judas was the reason Jesus was hanged on the cross. I saw my dad's eyes in tears, full of hurt and pain; He was trying to find hope in God. He was waiting for the Lord to come and show him and his family a miracle as He was sharing Judas's story with me.

LAST SUPPER

One day, my dad found a picture of the Last Supper, and he showed me who Judas was. I was so glad that there was a picture of Jesus with His disciples because, at that time, I could only understand who Jesus was from the picture since I didn't read the Bible then. After my father showed me the picture of Judas, He told me that no matter what happens in my life, he always wanted me to show love, honesty, respect, and faith to anyone, especially the old people; he wanted me to respect the old people.

There was a day that my dad stared at me and told me that I would go far and that whatever I wanted, I would have them. Every word my dad said to me I keep in my heart. My dad told me that if I carried the word of God in my life, my life would always be right in the eyes of God and that God would always be with me.

As the years went by, I tried my best to keep God's Word in my life; but as I was just a child growing up, everything my dad taught me about God was forgotten.

WORD OF KNOWLEDGE

ROMANS 11:33–34

Oh, the depth of the riches of the wisdom and knowledge of God! How unsearchable His judgments, and His paths beyond tracing out! Who has known the mind of the Lord? Or who has been His counselor?

One day, at the age of nine years old, my dad asked me to go to the market to buy food to last us for at least three weeks because he said that it was going to rain. I said yes, and my dad gave me some money to buy food. While I was getting ready to go to the market, I thought about what my dad said to me about how it was going to rain, so I tried my best to go faster. On my way to the market, I noticed that the sun was burning my skin; it was very hot that day, and I thought that the rain was impossible to happen because when I looked up at the sky to see if there is any dark cloud, but I did not see any cloud. I knew it was not going to rain; the way it looked, rain would be impossible. At that time, I was thinking that my dad was wrong. I thought that it was not going to rain, but after I came back home from the market, it did rain.

I was amazed because I realized that my dad was right at that moment, and I was shocked at the same time. I thought *"how can it be?"* I thought to myself, *how can the rain come down when the sun was just burning my skin?* But I was so glad that I was already in the house when the rain fell, and I praised God.

I realized that I was wrong and my dad was right the whole time. It rained for a long time that the whole city flooded, and we couldn't even go anywhere. I saw a lot of people trying to go to the market, but the water was above them, and the markets were closed. I saw a lot people going hungry because they were not prepared for the bad storm. I saw some people trying to go to the other places, but they could not. I saw some people riding boats, but they ended up being stuck in the water. The water was above their heads, and the rain kept falling, and nothing could stop it. I could hear the sound of rain from our metal roof; it was very loud and aggressive, and the whole roof was shaking from the heavy storm.

I was amazed with how my dad knew that it was going to rain. I was so glad that my dad was able to know things from heaven, and I was very happy at the same time because I knew that we had plenty of food. We would not go hungry; our family was saved, and we were prepared for any disaster.

After the rain stopped, I saw my dad giving food to the people, especially to the women with children. God spoke to my dad and revealed hidden things to him. I love God. He always gave my dad a revelation and the knowledge of Him.

MIRACLES FROM GOD

One day, as a child, I saw a lot of people coming to our house; they were carrying bags and baskets full of vegetables, fruits, rice, live chicken, and other food. They gave it all to my dad as a sacrificial gifts, I saw many people who were very sick, and some of them could not walk; they were carrying canes with them. That whole time, I was just watching them coming to our house, but I didn't have any understanding as to why they did. I saw my dad praying and laying his hands on them, touching their heads all the way down to their feet, and God was healing them. I saw that healing was taking place on people. The miracles of God were happening in our home. People were being healed.

By the time they left our house, people were not the same anymore; the people that carried canes left the house walking. People that had sickness and disease were healed; signs, wonders, and miracles were taking place in our house. I saw people giving their life to the Lord Almighty. When my neighbors found out that my dad could heal, they also came to our house to be touched by God. God amazed me with what I was seeing. At that time, I, as a child, had no clue as to what was happening. I was just watching everybody. I kept everything that took place in our house in my heart.

MIRACLES OF GOD

ACTS 10:38

How God anointed Jesus of Nazareth with the Holy Spirit and power, and how He went around doing good and healing all who were under the power of the devil, because God was with Him.

MATTHEW 9:35

Jesus went through all the towns and villages, teaching in their synagogues, proclaiming the good news of the kingdom and healing every disease and sickness.

ACTS 5:16

Crowds gathered also from the towns around Jerusalem, bringing their sick and those tormented by impure spirits, and all of them were healed.

MATTHEW 4:24

News about Him spread all over Syria, and people brought to Him all who were ill with various diseases, those suffering severe pain, the demon-possessed, those having seizures, and the paralyzed; and He healed them

FIRE OF GOD

One day, when I was thirty-five years old, my daughter and I went back to the Philippines to visit my family. I remember my mom and my brother sharing with me about what was happening to my dad before I came back to the Philippines. They told me that my dad was sitting in the corner of the house, and my mom and my youngest brother saw my dad talking to himself; he was speaking in unknown tongue, and they told me that my dad was crazy because they could not understand the way he was saying. My dad was saying something, but they could not comprehend what he was saying. They thought he was speaking Hebrew, Spanish, or Italian. When my mom and my brother told me this, I realized that my dad was not speaking Hebrew, Spanish, or Italian. I realized now that my dad was speaking in "tongues of fire from heaven." It is the unknown language from heaven, and God is the only one who can understand the language. My father's prayers always reached the throne of God because of his pure heart devoted to the Lord.

ACTS 2:2–4

Suddenly a sound like the blowing of a violent wind came from heaven and filled the whole house where they were sitting. ³ They saw what seemed to be tongues of fire that separated and came to rest on each of them. ⁴ All of them were filled with the Holy Spirit and began to speak in other tongues[a] as the Spirit enabled them.

My mom and my brother did not understand the Bible and were also not saved at that time. They also didn't have an interpretation of the tongue from heaven, and that was why they didn't know what my dad was saying at then. My mom and my brother told me that after my dad finished praying, he would come out from the corner and go to the living room, where he would touch my pictures hanging on the wall. My dad would start crying and praying, hoping that God would answer his prayers for me to come back to the Philippines to visit them because he missed me so much. At the same time, God touched my heart here in America for me to come back to the Philippines.

BLESSINGS OF GOD

At that time, and I don't know why, I heard the voice of God telling me that I needed to come back to the Philippines. But I thought to myself that it would be impossible because I didn't have any money to buy plane tickets for me and for my daughter. I thought I was just dreaming; but little did I know, one week later, when I went back to work, all of my customers were giving me three times more than what I charged them. All of my friends are also started giving me some money; they said it was because they loved me and that was all. I was amazed by the generosity that I was receiving from everybody. Altogether, I received $3,000. One week later, I received a credit card that had $3,000 in it. I did not even apply for a credit card, and my credit score was not even good enough to be qualified to get a credit card.

The following night, my dad called me, and he was crying for me to come back home. I comforted my dad by sharing with him about the good news that I was coming back home. I felt so much joy knowing I would be with my family soon.

I used the credit card to buy plane tickets to go to the Philippines. Upon my return home to the Philippines, sadness came over me because I found out, that my dad was very sick. My dad was diagnosed with diabetes and a pancreatic disease. I tried to take him to the doctor, but there was no hope.

I remember one early evening, how my dad was looking right at me and telling me that he loved me. he told me that he didn't know when he was going to see me again; so he thought that it was time to pass on to me all the *blessings, talents,* and *gifts* that God had given to him. At that time, I did not understand what my dad was telling me because I did not understand what the word "gifts" meant. But later on, after I was saved. God spoke to me and showed me where is the gifts of the Spirit from the Bible.

1 CORINTHIANS 12:9–11

To another faith by the same Spirit, to another gifts of healing by that one Spirit, to another miraculous powers, to another prophecy, to another distinguishing between spirits, to another speaking in different kinds of tongues, and to still another the interpretation of tongues. All these are the work of one and the same Spirit, and He distributes them to each one, just as He determine.

After God showed me the chapter about the gifts of the Spirit, my heart was overwhelmed with joy because God gave me the understanding, wisdom, knowledge, and revelation of who He is my life.

IMPARTATION GIFT FROM GOD

I was amazed at how good God was in my life. I remember how my dad was looking right at me, and I was looking right at him. I noticed his right hand coming toward me and to my surprise, my dad put his hands on my head, and he prayed for me. He told me that it was time for the impartation of the gift that my father received from God, that I was highly favored by God. I immediately felt the presence of God when my dad prayed over me. I felt like the fire of God just enveloped me and that the Holy Spirit stayed with me.

After staying with my family for fifteen days, I felt like God rejuvenated me. I really needed God to rejuvenate me to be able to have a new beginning in my life. God answered my dad's prayer. I was amazed at how God moved and put together everything that was good for all of us.

After coming back to America three months later, my dad was getting worse and worse. One day—and I will never forget it—I decided to call my dad. As I was talking to him, I noticed his voice was very weak, and I could barely understand him, all I could say to my dad was that I loved him. I asked him if he wanted me to come back home for him, and he said yes. He wanted for me to come back home so that he could be with me. But due to not having enough money, I could not come to see my dad on his deathbed. I felt like the whole world was upside down for me. Tears poured down on my cheeks. I was very hurt that I could not see my dad.

In my moment of brokenness, I blamed God, I blamed the world, and I blamed the father of my daughter. I thought that he was the reason why my dad had to die. I thought that if I did not financially support my ex-husband, that my dad would still be alive because I would have had the means to provide for my dad and take him to the hospital while he was still young and strong when I could still provide for him with good food that he needed to eat. I felt like it was my fault that I wasn't there for my dad. I felt like I failed my dad.

After my dad died, I was sad and all alone. I felt like some part of me was gone. I loved my dad so much, and I missed him. I knew that he was always there in my heart.

One day, God spoke to me and told me that He was my Father. When God told me that, I found love and peace; and in the end, God healed, restored, and delivered me. It was a good feeling to have a Father from heaven. God set me free.

OVERCOMER

When someone you love passes away, it is not easy; it can be very difficult, intense, painful, unloved, overwhelming, and challenging. You may feel abandoned. But I want you to know that God will not leave you nor forsake you. God's love toward you will never fade away. God created you for His glory. God knows your heart and your mind and what you are going through. God knows you completely, and He is here to be with you. God wants to be with you through this time of sadness in your life. The promises of God are *right, truth, yes,* and *amen for you.*

Here are His promises for you. God wants to guide you and lead you from darkness to light.

PSALM 23:4

Even though I walk through the darkest valley, I will fear no evil, for you are with me; your rod and your staff, they comfort me.

ISAIAH 41:10

"So do not fear, for I am with you; do not be dismayed, for I am your God. I will strengthen you and help you; I will uphold you with My righteous right hand."

PRAYER

Dear heavenly Father,

I love You, Thank You that you are my refuge and my strength, an ever-present help in times of my trouble. Therefore, I will not fear. Lord Jesus, you are my hiding place. You protect me from trouble, and you surround me with songs of deliverance, and your righteous hand is with me. In Jesus' name Amen.

THE BLESSINGS OF THE LORD

GENESIS 22:17

I will surely bless you and make your descendants as numerous as the stars in the sky and as the sand on the seashore. Your descendants will take possession of the cities of their enemies.

GENESIS 27:28

May God give you heaven's dew and earth's richness— an abundance of grain and new wine.

PSALM 1:3

That person is like a tree planted by streams of water, which yields its fruit in season and whose leaf does not wither—whatever they do prospers.

2 CORINTHIANS 9:8

And God is able to bless you abundantly, so that in all things at all times, having all that our need, you will abound in every good work.

PHILIPPIANS 4:7

And the peace of God, which transcends all understanding, will guard your hearts and your minds in Christ Jesus.

PSALM 20:4–5

May He give you the desire of your heart and make all your plans succeed. May we shout for joy over your victory and lift up our banners in the name of our God. May the LORD grant all your requests.

MY MOM'S STORY

My mom is very sweet and thoughtful, and she has a pure heart, which is a priceless jewel. She loves to give her heart to people in need. I love her, and I owe all my life to her.

One early morning when I was a young child of four years, my mom was getting ready to go somewhere. But I didn't want her to go, so I started crying, hoping she would take me with her. But my mom did not really want me to go, so I cried harder, and it was very intense. I cried so hard for her to say yes for me to come with her. I would go wherever my mother would take me. I just wanted to be with my mom. So finally, she got tired of hearing me crying; my mom took me with her so I would no longer cry and give her a hard time. My mom was in a hurry that day that she forgot to feed me, and I was also wearing a dress with holes on it. She took me to a faraway place; it was so far away that I was losing my patience, and at the same time, I was very excited and couldn't wait to be wherever my mom would take me. I was just happy to be with my mom instead of staying at home.

We left very early that morning, and it was still dark. To get to the place where my mom was taking me, we need to ride two jeepneys (little buses) because the place was very far away. When we finally got there, it was still very dark. I saw this huge mountain, and it had a lot of people, especially a lot of children. Also, the mountain is completely dark and smelled really bad.

My mom just took me to this place called the garbage dump. It was a place where people threw their garbage and also dead animals. I saw a lot of adults and children on the top and the bottom of the mountain, with trash and sticks in their hands. They were trying to dig to the trash all the way to the bottom, hoping they would get something. I saw children who were very alert, and they knew what they were doing.

They were digging for food and other stuff that they may need. The children looked very hungry, tired, and dirty; but they were out there to have a mission and that is to find unwanted stuff. But to them, they were treasures. The children were not afraid; they were very strong and brave.

I did not understand why we were there, but I went along with it. I saw my mom starting to dig at the piles of the garbage as if like she was digging gold from the piles of smelly trash. The place had a very bad odor. I saw dead dogs, other animals, and flies everywhere in that place. It was a place that you didn't want to go. When I saw my mom and other children digging in that pile of smelly trash, in my weakest moment and confusion, I decided to do the same thing. I found a long stick, and I was excited to do the same thing like other children are doing, and I also started digging. As I was digging, I saw these things that looked like food; and at that time, I was very thirsty, tired, and hungry because I did not eat that morning. And without asking my mom if I could have the food that I found while she was not looking at me, I immediately put the dirty food in my mouth. I was so glad that my mom did not see me doing that. But then, at the same, I didn't think that my mom would care because she knew that I was hungry. And I don't remember if I spit it out or not either. So the food must have been good enough for me to eat, and at that time, I was so glad that I did not get sick that day. People called us scavengers.

Time passed by, and it was noon. The weather was changing, it was becoming very warm. I started to get sweaty, and it was very hot. We didn't have any water handy. I was very thirsty and very weak, and there was no shade for me to have shade. I saw my mom kept digging and digging from this dump; she never stopped, like she didn't want to miss out on anything. My mom really needed rest. I had never seen my mom work so hard while she was hungry; she was focusing on what she was doing. She managed to stay working in the heat of the day without hurting herself. My mom found a lot of metals, wires, cans, and more. My mom did not rest that day; she was digging since early morning and all through the late afternoon. I watched my mom work very hard, she was working all day long, but she never complained. Our clothes and our faces were very dirty, and we smelled really bad.

After we finished taking all the metals and other stuff, we put them in sacks and took them to the buyers, whom we sold to them. After the men paid us, my mom and I went to the market and used the money to buy food (e.g., rice, fish, chicken, vegetables, and other stuff). My mom would do whatever it took to make sure that she could put food on the table for the family. I learned that my mom did what she did to earn some money so she could feed her family; my mom just showed me that the real life is not about not have anything, but to have wisdom and have a willing spirit to do what necessary to have something by believing that we will eventually get everything. Through her eagerness to make some money and not being lazy to stay home, my mom get what she needs which is to have money to buy some food for all of us. I am very proud of my mom and her courage, dedication, and passion for all her children to provide to the best that she knew how.

I love being with my mom just to see what she is going to do next when she is not home. I love my mom, and I love being with her. As a young child, I have this passion to be able to help her, to help my dad, and help my brothers and my sister.

INCREASE OF GOD

God's blessings are the signs of His love and compassion toward us. He blesses, protects, and leads us to the path of His overwhelming joy in our lives. The Word of God gives us direction, and He walks with us toward our future and our destiny.

PHILIPPIANS 4:19

And My God will meet all Your needs according to the riches of His glory in Christ Jesus.

JEREMIAH 29:11–14

For I know the plans I have for You, declares the Lord, plans to prosper you and not to harm you, plans to give you hope and a future. Then you will call upon me and come and pray to me, and I will listen to you. You will seek Me and find Me when you seek Me with all your heart. I will be found by you, declares the Lord, and will bring you back from captivity.

I will gather you from all the nations and places where I have banished you, declares the Lord, and will bring you back to the place from which I carried you into exile.

GALATIANS 6:9

Let us not become weary in doing good, for at the proper time we will reap a harvest if we do not give up.

God's plan for you is good and full of hope, with a new beginning and a new purpose for His glory. You are not created to live your life with little to no goals, vision, dreams, hope, or renovation. God created you to live abundantly above all that you could ask or think according to His riches and glory. No matter what you are, who you are, and where you are, God created you to worship Him and to increase and multiply in this earth.

God does not want you to give up He wants you to keep moving forward, because you have a purpose in Him. God always been there for you and He has known you since the foundation of this world. God is good and He is perfect in all His ways, and He has complete knowledge of you. He knows the way you think and act, and He knows exactly what is in your heart. He chooses you to live in His kingdom. His mission on this earth is to love you, to bless you, and to serve you because you are precious in His sight. For Him, you are perfect, and He is pleased with you. God loves you.

PSALM 139

O Lord You have searched me and You know me. You know when I sit when I rise You perceive my thoughts from afar, You discern my going out and my lying down. You are familiar with all my ways. Before a word is on my tongue, You know it completely O Lord. You hem me in—behind and before, You have laid Your hand upon me. Such knowledge is too wonderful to me, Too lofty for me to attain. Where can I go from Your spirit? Where can I flee from your presence? If I go up to the heavens, You are there, If I make my bed in the depths, You are there, If I arise on the wings of the dawn, If I settle on the far side of the sea, Even there Your hand will guide me, Your right hand will hold me fast. If I say, "Surely the darkness will hide me and the light become night around me." Even the darkness will not be dark to You; The night will shine like the day, For the darkness is a light to You. For You created my inmost being, You knit me together in my mother's womb. I praise You because I am fearfully and wonderfully made; Your works are wonderful, I know that full well. My frame was not hidden from You, When I was made in the secret place. When I was woven together in the depths of the earth, Your eyes saw my unformed body. All the days ordained for me, were written in Your book before one of them came to be. How precious to me are Your thoughts, O God! How vast in the sum of them! were I to count them, They would outnumber the grains of sand. When I awake, I am still with You. If only You would slay the wicked, O God! Away from me, you bloodthirsty men! They speak of You with evil intent; Your adversaries misuse Your name. Do I not hate those who hate You, O Lord, And abhor those who rise up against You? I have nothing but hatred for them; I count them my enemies. Search me, O God, and know my hearts; Test me and know my anxious thoughts. See if there is any offensive way in me, and lead me in the way everlasting.

Sometimes life is not easy. But knowing God in your life will give you hope and courage to make it through. Don't be scared of what's in front of you, but knowing that God is always with you, you will find rest and peace in your soul. Don't let the opportunity pass you by. Just trust God; and He will move mountains, fear, and anxiety out of the way. He will carry you up to His throne. You will find courage and comfort to test the waters and fire, and you will not be afraid of God taking your life to a whole new level. No matter how big the mountain in your life is, know this: God will always be there to rescue and bless you in every area of your life.

I have three brothers and one sister: My younger brother is Joseph. My older brother is Manasseh. My older sister is Rebecca. My oldest brother is Peter.

MY BROTHER JOSEPH'S STORY

My youngest brother, Joseph, brings joy into my life. I love him, and he brings comfort to me. He's always there for me. I was always the only one that took care of Him when we were children. I felt like a mother to him every time I took care of him. I was just a young child who wanted to take care of him to make sure he was okay.

One day, when he was in first grade, he came to my class; he had so much pain in his stomach. I saw him touching his stomach. He was very hungry; but we did not eat breakfast that morning before we went to school because we didn't have any food to eat. So my brother was very hungry; he went to my class, and when he saw me sitting in my classroom, he started crying because of his stomach was hurting him so bad. So we left school and decided to ride a jeepney, which is a form of public transportation that can sit twelve people or more. We did not go home because I knew that we didn't have any food there, so we went to the market instead. My brother and I did not have any money to pay for the jeepney, but we rode it anyway; the jeepney driver just asked us to stand up so other people who were able to pay could sit down. So we were standing the whole time until we got to our destination.

When we got to the market, we started walking around, and my brother and I saw a restaurant. From the windows, we saw a lot of people eating, and my brother started crying for food. I felt very sad for my brother. I felt like I needed to help him. Because my brother was very hungry and was about to pass out, I was thinking that I needed to be strong and bold. I loved my brother so much; and I didn't want him to be hungry, hurt, or, worse, faint. He kept asking me for food, and that was why we were in the market in the first place.

So I decided to muster the courage to come into the restaurant and ask for food from the people who were eating there, and every one of them left food for us. I picked up the food from every plate and put them in the plastic bags until the plastic bags were full. And the people never asked me where my parents were. And I'm so glad that no one asked because I did not know how to answer them because I really didn't know where my parents were at that time.

As I was walking toward my brother with the food in my hands, I saw him being comfort and he was smiling and jumping with joy, seeing me with all the food. He came toward me really fast. I gave him the food, and he started eating like he never ate food all his life. After eating, my brother was very happy and satisfied. We left the restaurant and came back to school.

I don't know how we did that that day, but all I know is that God was with us and was watching over us. God showed His love and compassion toward us by helping us and giving us something to eat. I learned so much by being independent and courageous and believing in God. "How do people endures and perseveres in the poorest country?" For me, the way is through the spirit of wisdom and the love of God in my life to overcome fear and hunger. God blesses us and gives us strength and peace.

ISAIAH 41:10

So do not fear, for I AM with you; do not dismayed, for I AM your God. I will strengthen you and help you; I will uphold you with My righteous right hand.

PSALM 81:6–7

I removed the burden from their shoulders; their hands were set free from the basket. In your distress you called and I rescued you, I answered you out of a thundercloud; I tested you at the waters of Meribah.

PSALM 21:1–2

The king rejoices in your strength, O Lord. How great is His joy in the victories You give! You have granted Him the desire of His heart and have not withheld the request of His lips.

In Jesus presence, there's a time of victories and there's a time of being overcome; and in His presence, there is a time that He will test you and ask you questions like He did to His disciples. Jesus said, "Give them something to eat." The disciples said, but that they only had five loaves and two fish." Jesus love for you is beyond your understanding. His love is infinite and is a miracle that you cannot fathom. He performs miracles like multiplying the loaves of bread and fish, so He can bring glory to His name just for you.

God has the power to bless you and increase you. If you want to experience a life that is abundant with blessings and one that is filled with God's good, peace and abundance, then let your heart be at rest with Him as you let go of all your worries to your God who created you. When you believe and trust in Him, you will have confidence and assurance with His love and power over your life.

Do not have fear because you are the child of God.

MY STORY

My family called me Esther. I always wondered about the meaning of my name. So one day, I prayed to God, is to what is the meaning of my name, and God answered my prayer and He said to me that the meaning of Esther means is "life." I said to myself, is to why my name means "life" knowing that my whole life is about me experiencing death. It has always been a puzzle to me. I experienced dying and coming back to life twice. They were also so many times that I almost died. But I thanked Jesus Christ for giving me the name that is related to His nature. He brings signs, wonders, miracles, courage, boldness, and confidence in my life; and He always wins over me every time.

I'm the second youngest in the family; at the age of twelve, I always wanted to find my ways to make things happen for my family. I always wanted to know how I could help my parents and my brothers and sister because they didn't have that much money. My mom did not have an education, and she did not go to school. She washed clothes for people to make some money to support the family, and sometimes she didn't make enough money to put food on the table. My dad was a carpenter and also he is a chef, one day, he was sick with a disease, which weakened him. The disease slowed him down, and sometimes he even stopped working. Only my mom worked if she had a job; sometime she did not.

One day, at the young age of twelve, I found a way to help my parents. I decided to go to the market. The markets in the Philippines are like flea markets here in the America. I taught myself to sell grocery bags to the people and also carried their bags to their transportation, and they paid me at least 25¢. Sometimes I sold fish and vegetables. I would go around the market to find customers. I was working mornings and nights, and I was very tired and hungry; but even though I had a hard time selling all that food, I could not take a break because I didn't want to miss the customers. My customers were very important to me; they were precious jewels to me at that time as they were my source to bring food for my family. So I took good care of them.

One day, I was introduced to work at the fruit juice industry on the street. I was pushing a cart at the age of thirteen, selling fruit juice on the street, beside the high school, at the market, and also everywhere in the corner of the street. It was not easy for me to pushed the cart everywhere on the street daily in the heat of the day. It was very hard for me. Most of the time, I would be hungry because I was in the middle of nowhere and far away from other vendors, and there was no place to buy food around. I also did not have enough food with me. I saw myself weak and sick pushing the cart. I even fainted many times from the heat.

Even though I was very weak, I still continued selling the fruits juice, hoping that I would make a lot of money. By the grace of God, I sold enough fruit juice to give some money to my dad and buy food for my family. I was so happy just to be able to make $2 or $3 a day as my dad did not have a job at that time because he was always sick. And my dad used the money to buy food for all of us. I loved what I did. I learned to be strong and to have confidence in my life.

PHILIPPIANS 4:19

And my God will meet all your needs according to the riches of His glory in Christ Jesus.

DEUTERONOMY 8:7–9

For the LORD your God is bringing you into a good land—a land with brooks, streams, and deep springs gushing out into the valleys and hills; 8 a land with wheat and barley, vines and fig trees, pomegranates, olive oil and honey; 9 a land where bread will not be scarce and you will lack nothing; a land where the rocks are iron and you can dig copper out of the hills.

God is the source of all riches and wealth, and the hands of God are with you. You are the primary creation that God has made. You are blessed. God increases you with His love. God increases you with His hope. God increases you with His joy. God increases you with His compassion. God increases you with His power; and God increases you with His signs, wonders, and miracles. You are the one God increases. He created you and molded you into His Image, and you belong to Him.

MY BROTHER MANASSEH'S STORY

My brother Manasseh is the third child in the family, he was very independent and courageous, at a young age, he wanted to experience the way of life from this falling world. My brother wants to hang out with a wrong crowed and he found himself into disaster of his life. One day, I saw him sleeping with a broken cardboard outside the store. He realized that leaving home is a hard thing to do. But years later, He decided to come back home. I was very happy for him.

I remember my two brothers and I were outside our house in front of the fire that my dad made; we were playing with the fire, and suddenly, my brother Manasseh decided to pick up a long stick from the ground and put the plastic all around it. After he did that, he decided to put the stick on the fire; and the minute he did that, I saw the plastic stick was melting with fire. While the stick was on fire, my brother decided to throw it up on the air. The plastic stick on fire landed on my right arm. I was shocked seeing my arm on fire. It was a first-degree burn. When I saw my arm on fire, I passed out. I woke up inside the house, and I couldn't remember how the fire on my arm was put out. When I woke up, I felt so much pain even though my arm wasn't on fire anymore. My dad was praying for me, believing that God would heal me completely. God did heal me. But the fire left scars on my right arm, and I still have those scars until to this day. I love my brother; he is everything to me.

JOHN 15:5

"I am the vine; you are the branches. If you remain in me and I in you, you will bear much fruit; apart from me you can do nothing.

As you trust in Him and follow His way, you will see the fruits of His goodness in your life.

PSALM 34:19

The righteous person may have many troubles, but the LORD delivers Him from them all;

God's power is incredible. He is Mighty and nothing impossible for Him. The confidence we have in Him brings us into His knees. God's authority brings wonders and awe into our hearts. No matter how hard and difficult your problem's are, God will always be by your side if you seek Him. He will always make a way to get you out of the problem you're experiencing and give you peace and strength. God is your healer, and He is your deliverer. God wants to heal you and delivered you.

MY SISTER REBECCA'S STORY

When I was a child, I remember my sister Rebecca working as a live-in nanny and housekeeper for a wealthy family in the city. She was making a lot of money, and some of that money was used to buy a land close to our old house. That land stood on the huge rocks, and beside it was a long creek going up the mountain. My dad and my brothers helped one another dig out and remove the rocks little by little. Until one day, the land was big enough to build a house, and that land is where my dad built the house that I grew up in. Now we had a place to call home, and the house is still standing until to this day. My brothers and their families, including their grandchildren, still live together in the house.

I was thanking my sister for having such compassion toward us; my parents were blessed knowing that we had a place to live instead of just wandering the streets, not having a home.

One day, I had enough money to buy the house from my sister. I put the deed in my father's name. After I bought the house from her, I felt so much better because I was able to find peace within my soul knowing everything was going to be all right for my family. I felt relief for my sister and also for my parents and my brothers. I was feeling at peace.

My sister and I lost contact for many years. I love my sister; and I help her by sending her some money to buy medicine, food, and other things she needs. I started to minister to her, and I prayed over her. I was so glad that she listened to me as I shared the Word of God with her, and she gave herself to the Lord Jesus Christ.

I was hoping for God to heal her and give her peace. I believe that God will make a way in her life and heal her completely. I did not hear from her until two years later; she called me, and I was so glad to hear from her again. It gives me joy to be able to share with her about God again. I ministered to her again, and I told her about the goodness of Jesus Christ in her life; my sister found peace and love with Jesus, and she surrendered herself to Him. This time, she has complete hope in and understanding with God.

In 2017, she turned her life around, giving herself to the Lord all over again. My sister is now taking care of my mom, and when I found out that she was back home, I was so glad because I knew that everything was going to be good for my mom and also for my sister. I love my sister, and I want the best for her. God is good. He is exalted in all things. To God be the glory!

YOUR DESTINY

2 CHRONICLES 7:14

If My people, who are called by my name, will humble themselves and pray and seek My face and turn from their wicked ways, then will I hear from heaven and will forgive their sin and will heal their land.

When you seek God's face, you will see the manifestation of His glory in your life. God will perform miracles that will bring awe upon your lips. God is the one who can change you and turn the situation around. He is the one that holds the scepter of your destiny. God is the one who can pick you and sit you upon a rock and give you peace. God is your healer, provider, and deliverer; and He wants to build and mold you into His image.

You are full of love, faith, and joy with Him.

Continue to keep forward to the things of God, God wants to give you prosperity and ordained you and He wants you to go to the destination that God has empowered you.

God wants to increase you with His love and God wants to give favor that last for eternity, God wants to bless you and your family.

The spirit of wisdom and the spirit of compassion are working in your behalf.

Your life is an abundance of flowing oil to bring the manifestation of the Lord's glory.

The wealth and riches of the Lord are upon your hands from the throne of heaven.

Faith is your life to have assurance and confidence in the Lord.

You are the apple of God's eye and you are special, unique, you are operating with His love and excellence, power of gold purification, and perfection.

This is the hour and the season for you to shine. Let the whole world see the beauty of God through you.

You are born to be famous in the Lord and a blessing to the whole world.

PEACE WITH GOD

May the Lord bless you, may the Lord keep you, may the Lord make His face shine upon you and give you His love and peace. May you walk worthy and may you know His loving and sweet Spirit, may your heart filled with awe and comfort with the Lord as you give Him love and thank Him for all the kindness and goodness that He has shown into your life.

May He gave you the truth, assurance, confidence and desires of your hearts and filled your life with joy, peace, faith, healing, restoration, and the eternal love of God within your soul. God's favor is your hope, protection, shield, and healing; and you are surrounded with His flames of fire. He will take you higher and make the doors open for blessings and overflow over you. He will also protect you and your family, and He will keep you in His heart at all times. With His love, you will find peace and joy in every situation and challenges in your life.

God wants to get involved with you in every area of your life, making, creating, changing and molding you into His image. When the Lord Jesus Christ shows up, there is no fear, slavery, bondage or captivity that can remain to weigh you down. His love and His words declare that you are set free.

When God speaks it came to be. God speaks health, healing, restoration, and wholeness over you and your family and friends. God will touch every brokenness and conflict that exists and bring love and unity among your families. God increases your finances so that you can move from poverty to wealth, from destruction to peace, from bondage to freedom. God is always there for you for every hurt, pain, persecution, rejection, hardship, and stressful situation in your life. God will always fulfill what He promises in your life; in the very difficult times of your life, you will see the hands of God creating magnificent treasures from heaven. God will rend the heavens and come down for you. You are the overflow of His miracles. God loves you.

MY BROTHER PETER'S STORY

My elder brother, Peter, always made sure that I was okay. I felt loved and cared for from my brother Peter. One day, my brother took me to the mountain. The church was built on top of the mountain, and every woman wore a white robe and a blue veil, and every man wore a white robe. The church was open night and day, and there they prayed all night long and all day long. I have never really understood that place at that time. Initially, I enjoyed coming just to be around my brother and my friends, but I started coming more frequently as I got to know God. I was fifteen years old at that time. I love my big brother Peter; he was full of love toward me. He was very kind and respectful toward others. I am so proud of him.

One day, my big toe on my right foot was hurting me, and it started to get swollen. It was turning red, and it was getting infected. I was having a hard time walking because of the pain. I told my brother about it. My brother felt compassion for me, and he knew that I was very hurt; my brother believed that God could heal me, so he decided to pray and believe God for me. My elder brother decided not to take me to the doctor. After He prayed for my big toe to be healed, he decided to take a sharp knife and used it to open the skin from my infected toe and remove what was inside. While He was removing the infected skin, I was screaming very loudly because I was in so much pain. But by the grace of God, the swollen big toe was healed in the following weeks; there was no infection or bacteria in my foot. I was able to walk and be free. God is good. He used my elder brother to heal me.

MY BROTHER'S BLESSINGS

In 2010, it was Saturday night while I was at work. My elder brother, Peter, called me from the Philippines; he told me that his neighbor was selling a rice field, and he asked me if I could buy the rice field for him and his family. Their neighbor needed the money due to a family crisis; someone was sick, and they needed to go to the hospital, so they need the money immediately.

I was shocked with my elder brother. I thought to myself, *why would my elder brother ask me to buy them the land, knowing I don't have any money to give them?* I also didn't have any money to buy presents for my children at that time; it was almost Christmas, and I had not been shopping because I didn't have any money to buy gifts for my family.

So I asked God to give me wisdom. I knew I was not able to send him some money because I didn't have any money to give them at that time, and I didn't make a lot of money from my job either. I told my elder brother that I didn't have any money, but God could provide for him. I shared with him what was in the heart of God and what He said concerning him and his family. I told to my elder brother is to how God could bless them. I told him that even though I didn't have any money, but I knew the one who is, the God I knew was able to bless him. This reminds me of the following scripture:

ACTS 3:6

Then Peter said, "Silver or gold I do not have, but what I do have I give you. In the name of Jesus Christ of Nazareth, walk."

And I told my brother that God was the only one that could bless him and not me because I did not have anything to give. And God really wanted to bless them, so I asked my elder brother to read the following from the Bible:

JOHN 3:16

For God so loved the world that He gave His one and only Son, that whoever believes in Him shall not perish but have eternal life.

I asked my elder brother to forgive everybody that wronged him and also to repent for everything that he did wrong, knowingly and unknowingly. I asked my elder brother to have faith and believe that the blessings of the Lord were already in his hand, given to him by God. While he was on the phone with me, I asked him to lift up his hands and receive his blessings from God by faith. I start praying for him on the phone. I asked him to go to church and pray, and I also told him to ask God to have somebody give me some money so that I could send it to him. And I asked my elder brother to believe in God. And I also asked him to call me by Monday to see what God was going to do for him. We were expecting God's power to create a new thing for him and his family.

On Monday morning, when I came back to work, my boss had an envelope waiting for me. I was shocked because I didn't know what the occasion was that he would give me one. When the envelope was in my hands, I felt like it was already been ordained for me to have it. I was so excited, and I couldn't wait to open it to see what was in it. While I was opening the envelope, I was thinking that maybe it had some money in it, so I got even more excited. Before I opened it, I was thinking that maybe I should go shopping for my family and that I could also buy the children some Christmas presents. So much stuff was on my mind as to what I was going to do with the money.

For a moment, I forgot about my brother and what we talked about over the weekend. When I opened the envelope, I was shocked because the letter had a check with my name on it, and the amount was the exact amount that my elder brother was asking from me for him to buy the rice field. My whole body was starting to shake; the wonder of God was just revealed to me, and it was so beautiful. I was overwhelmed with God's goodness and faithfulness in our lives. I forgot about going shopping for my family. I knew it was God and that money was not for me, but for my elder brother and for his family. And I told God that I understood Him. I knew that He wanted to bless my elder brother. So I was not disappointed. I was so glad that God did not put me to shame toward my brother when I told him that God truly wanted to bless him and his family.

I remember the scriptures about Elijah asking a widow to bake him a cake even though the woman knew that she didn't have enough money to buy food for her and her son. But she believed that Elijah was truly the servant of God, so she decided to bake him a cake and gave it to him. Because of her being obedience to the Lord, the woman was blessed mightily; the Lord blessed her for three years. In the same way, God backs me up and never puts me to shame.

And that's what I felt about my elder brother and me, so I gave all the money to him and told him that it was from the Lord and that God wanted to bless him. He was thankful to God for all the blessings that he received. To God be the glory!

One year later, God blessed me. I received a check four times the amount of the one that I received for my elder brother. God is faithful; and His desire is to bless me, my brother, and our family. God is working wonders for all of us.

YOUR IDENTITY WITH GOD

AMOS 3:7

Surely the Sovereign LORD does nothing without revealing His plan to His servants the prophets.

The Spirit of God is upon you. He transformed you into His image, His wisdom, His likeness, His Face, His character and His glory. He blesses you in everything you do, and you belong to Him. You are precious to God, and He loves you. When the world was formed and there was nothing in it, God's spirit was hovering over you.

When God said, "Let there be light," and there was light, everything changed; there's no darkness, but only light in you. God expanded you to see His beauty. And God saw you, and it was good, and He was pleased with you. God is a God who sees, and He sees you as the anointed One, God bring confidence in everything you do. You are created for His purpose and will in His kingdom. You are fruitful in number. Multiply on the earth and increase upon it and increase of His goodness and mercy. God has granted you His treasures from heaven as you walk in His righteousness. You will have assurance and confidence with His faithfulness. God granted you His great passion of His offerings. You have found favor in the eyes of the Lord. You are the righteous one, blameless among the people of His time, and God walks with you and gives you more life abundantly. God built you an ark because you are worthy in His sight. God established His covenant with you; whenever God brings clouds over the earth and the rainbow appears in the clouds, God will always remember the covenant He had with you because you are righteous on the earth.

GOD is Mighty GOD. He wants to make your name great and fruitful. The covenant with you is to make you a leader to His people, kings, and nations. God will give you an everlasting possession for you and your descendants, and He will be your God. His presence will go with you and give you rest because He is pleased with you and knows you by name. God will show you His glory. He will cause all His goodness to pass in front of you, and He will proclaim His name in your presence. He will have mercy on you. He will have compassion for you. You will stand on the rock when His glory passes by. He will put you in a cleft in the rock and cover you with His hands when He passes by. God is a compassionate and gracious god, slow to anger, abounding in love and faithfulness to you alone because you have been chosen by Him. God is walking among His people, and you will see Him like a man sitting on the lamp stand.

God is the one who gave dominion that does not pass away, and you and everyone will serve Him. He is the King and Great High Priest, and great I am for you. He is girded and clothed with the garment of righteousness and truth in your life. He is above all and highly exalted just for you. He is mighty to say when you call out His name. He is the one who carries the authority on earth to forgive your sins. You shall be white as snow; when you see Him, you will be like Him. His eyes are like a flame of fire burning inside you. In His eyes, no darkness will prevail because His eyes are on you.

He is making a new covenant with you, and He is doing wonders beyond your understanding. You are the child of the King; you are famous in His eyes. You are an important, unique, and valuable creation of God. And God has found you favorable to His sight. You are loved, blessed, restored, and healed, In the Mighty Name of Jesus. Amen.

GENESIS 7:1

The Lord then said to Noah, "Go into the ark, you and your whole family, because I have found you righteous in this generation."

MY DAUGHTER MARY'S STORY

PSALM 139:13–16

For you created my inmost being; you knit me together in my mother's womb.

I praise you because I am fearfully and wonderfully made; your works are wonderful, I know that full well. My frame was not hidden from you when I was made in the secret place, when I was woven together in the depths of the earth. Your eyes saw my unformed body; all the days ordained for me were written in your book before one of them came to be.

One day, while I was nine months pregnant and the baby could come out at any time, I remember using the bathroom. Shockingly, my water broke, and my ex-husband rushed me to the hospital. I was amazed because I was not feeling sick on the way to the hospital. I remember even ordering fast food. I was so scared when the doctor told me that the baby was breech, and they needed to cut my stomach for my baby to come out. I had to have a C-section, and it was the worst feeling that I have ever experienced. I remember looking at the huge needle, and I thought, *Wow*. Fear came over me, especially when the nurse was about to inject the needle in the middle of my back. I thought about screaming very loudly on the top of my lungs. Suddenly, I screamed out my mom's name. I was in so much pain when the nurse injected that needle in my back.

In February, I saw my baby girl for the first time. When she came out of my womb, my heart jumped with joy. I fell in love with her right away; she filled my life with love and joy. She completed me with her tenderness and beautiful smile. I thanked God for her. I completed her with my love and affection. Her being sweet and huggable brought comfort to my heart. I forgot about the pain that I was going through by holding her and looking at her beautiful smile.

As the years went by, she was growing up stronger and more upbeat, trying to understand the way of life. My daughter experienced a lot of things before she found out that God was watching her. She was trying to see if God was real in her life. My daughter tested God to make sure He was near her. At one point, she was being rebellious toward God, and she was doing things that were not of God. She found herself experiencing sins, pain, hurt, sickness, and even near death.

I watched her grew up, I watched her rise up, and I also watched her fall as the years went by. She is a young teenager, and her life changed drastically; she had a mind of her own. I saw the changes in her life. She was not like what she was before, full of energy and love. She experienced falling away from God. And every time she wanted her way and was being disobedient to God, she will experience hardship in her life. And her path toward God was fading away; it seemed like God always intervened and showed Himself to her in a manner she could not understand. Sometimes she found herself in a dead-end situation and other obstacles without God in her life.

I remember telling her one day that we would be going to church, but she didn't feel like going. So she complained so much and became so aggressive that I had to let her have her way because I did not know what to do with her. But I gave her instructions not to go anywhere while we were in the church; little did we know that she had somebody pick her up, and they went downtown. She thought she got her way for not listening to me, but little did she know that God did not let her have her way. God was watching over her. On the way to wherever place she was going, God intervened by having them get into a little accident, and no one was hurt. By the time she knew it, she had to turn around to come back home safe. God made my day by bringing my daughter back home to me. Whatever this place that my daughter was going to, maybe it was not a good place for her to be, and I knew that God was protecting her. I was so glad that God was on my side and that He was watching my daughter and answering my prayers. Hallelujah!

At around 11:30 p.m. one night, we were upstairs. Little did we know that my daughter and her friend were at the basement, we thought they were sleeping in her bedroom, but they were expecting two boys to come in at the back door of the basement, we didn't have any idea because we were getting ready to go to bed. But not God—God was not going to bed. God was wide awake, and He is not going to sleep, (that's my God). He knew what was going on in my house. And God was watching over our house. God Himself called the police to let us know that there were two boys outside my house and that they were trying to come in, but they did not succeed because God intervened. We didn't know who called the police, but we believe that it was the Lord; the police knocked on the door in front of the house, and we were terrified and shocked. We didn't know what was happening in the basement. After talking to the police, we became alert and more concerned for her.

My daughter was just young and didn't know any better; she needed help from God. And I was so glad that God saw and heard the situation in our life. God was protecting us once again. He was just letting us know that His presence was with us. I got to saw the activity and the move of God upon our family. He is our protector.

One day, she got out of the house. At her young age, she was not allowed to drive yet and didn't have a driver's license. But she decided to drive her friend's car without knowing how to drive because her friend let her drive it. Little did she know that the police was behind her, the police pulled her over and gave her a ticket. Again, God is watching her. I was so glad that God was protecting my daughter again because she could have had an accident and hurt herself and others, or something worse could've happened to her. But God intervened in her life again. When I found out about her driving without a license, I started to pray hard to my core for my daughter's breakthrough, for the Lord to help her. God told me that it was better for her to get a ticket than for me to see her get hurt or die. God was protecting my daughter once again. Whatever place my daughter was going to, God knew that was not a good place for her to go. God wanted her to be safe again and she is home with us, God forgave and set her free.

I do not know what to do without God in our lives; we need God in our lives. We cannot live without Him. God is watching my daughter every day, every hour, every minute, every second seven times a week. Praise the Lord! God is awesome. He is faithful, loving, and kind; and He will never fail us.

As the years went by and she became old enough to understand the realities of life, she decided to have a family of her own. She had one child—my beautiful granddaughter, Ruth. At first, everything was good; my daughter's life was agreeing with her—until one day, she found herself with a form of darkness in her life, realizing that there was something void missing in her life. She was trying to find life on her own but was left disappointed. So she found herself moving toward the darkest moment of her life. She realized that nothing in this world could satisfy her; she tried everything and even listened to music that was not of God.

One day, I was in her car, and she was listening to hard-core and destructive music that brought pain to her soul. I remember telling her that if she continued listening to this kind of music, she would find herself in the area of brokenness. I asked her to stop listening to music that would hurt her soul in the future. I told her to listen to God's music instead. It would bring life, beauty, and light into her soul so that she would see and feel the love and power of God in her life. But she decided not to listen to me.

One day, she hit rock bottom; she thought the man who once loved her was going to be around forever, but little did she know that they would break up with each other. She found herself with darkness and loneliness within her heart. So she decided to come back home again to be with us. I love my daughter. I was delighted to have her back in my home. I knew that she was safe in my home. I knew that God would perform miracles for her. This time, God gave her a new beginning in life, a refreshing breeze to revive and renew her. God was creating a new thing for her. My daughter was in so much pain breaking up with her baby daddy.

One day, without her telling me, God spoke to me, and He said to me that my daughter wanted to kill herself because of all the pain, the affliction and rejection that the enemy created in her life. But God told me that He would never let that happen to her. I was so concerned for my daughter, but I knew God would perform miracles for my daughter because I knew that He was in control, and I trusted Him. I decided not tell my daughter about what God told me, that I knew that she wanted to kill herself. I trusted God that He would make a way in her life. That God will give her life back.

My daughter was trying to fight for her relationship from her baby daddy for them to get back together. But at the same time, God was also fighting for her. Two weeks later, I told her that she was a prophetess who would be spreading the Word of God to people and that God would use her as an instrument for His people because that was her calling. God would do a new thing for her, and He was protecting her.

Two weeks later, she met up with her high school sweetheart, and he took her to the church that he went to. She was surrounded by all the prophets and the prophetess, and they were all telling her of the Word of God, she went home full of hope and awe of God in her heart; she was asking me is to how the people knew her, knowing she never met them before. My daughter was now trying to understand that what I told her was true. God revealed Himself to her by introducing her to other prophets and prophetess in her life. God was letting her know that she was one of them and that she was a prophetess. Now my daughter is spreading the Word of God to her friends and other people who are broken. She was amazed by all the revelation she received from God for herself and other people. My daughter now has the knowledge, love, wisdom, and revelation from God; she now believes in God.

One month later, my daughter and her high school sweetheart got married. And lo and behold, they found out that she was pregnant. God spoke to them, telling them that the baby would be a boy and that they would name him Elijah (which means "fire"). Their baby boy was born on July 4. Truly, the baby was fire with God. My daughter came back to the Lord; she stopped listening to destructive music. She worshipped and praised God from then on, and she lifted her hands up as she worshipped God as a sign of victory in her life.

My daughter confessed to me later on that she had planned to end her life because she thought her life was over. Little did she know that her life was just beginning and she was glad that God came to saved her, and gave her another chance to have life God wins over Satan, my daughter and her family found favor in God's eye.

The wrath of God turned it by remembering mercy toward my daughter. My daughter continually sought God and loved Him. God gave her love and peace; she was restored, healed, blessed, and delivered. To God be the glory! Thank you, Jesus.

GOD'S VICTORY OVER YOU

ISAIAH 46:3–4

"Listen to me, you descendants of Jacob, all the remnant of the people of Israel, you whom I have upheld since your birth, and have carried since you were born. Even to your old age and gray hairs I am He, I am He who will sustain you. I have made you and I will carry you; I will sustain you and I will rescue you."

JEREMIAH 1:5

Before I formed you in the womb I knew you, before you were born I set you apart; I appointed you as a prophet to the nations.

HABAKKUK 3:2 *Lord, I have heard of Your fame; I stand in awe of Your deeds, O Lord. Renew them in our day, in our time make them known; in wrath remember mercy.*

JAMES 1:2–5

Consider it pure joy, my brothers and sisters whenever you face trials of many kinds, because you know that the testing of your faith produces perseverance. Let perseverance finish its work so that you may be mature and complete, not lacking anything. If any of you lacks wisdom, you should ask God, who gives generously to all without finding fault, and it will be given to you.

You are a masterpiece, craftsmanship, and workmanship of His love and beauty. You are the instrument, prophet, disciple and the voice of God. God is your beautiful, wonderful and magnificent Creator. You receive God's perfect wisdom and His presence, and His loving kindness; and you enjoy His beauty and perfection, and being nearness in your life. When you pray for repentance and you come back to the Lord, you will have a pure heart, and you will be as white as snow without blemish as you can be.

God's will has mercy on you, according to His unfailing love and His great compassion. He will blot out your transgressions. He will wash away all your iniquities and cleanse you of your sins. He will clean you with His hyssop, and you will be clean. He will wash you, and you will be whiter than snow. God will create a pure heart and renew a steadfast spirit within you. God will not cast you from His presence or take His Holy Spirit from you. He will restore you with the joy of His salvation and grant you a willing spirit to sustain you.

God is your refuge, shield, and strength—a very present help in times of trouble. Therefore, you will not fear even though the earth changes. God has a plan in your life, and He wants to show you great things. God never fails, and He will never turn His back on you.

And He is in control over your life. You are the abundance of God's glory; you are surrounded with His love. You are filled with the Holy Spirit. You are the robe of His righteousness, and you are crowned of His beauty. God is your refuge and fortress. In God, you can trust. God will come to you, and His glory will pass by. He will put you in the cleft of the rock and cover you with His feathers until He passes by.

For in the day of your trouble, He will conceal you in His tabernacle; in the secret of His tent, He will hide you. He will lift you upon a rock.

If you have fear of the Lord, you will be strong and have confidence in Him, and you will have refuge in His wings. The eternal God is your dwelling place, and underneath are your everlasting arms. He drove out the enemy before you and said to it, "Be destroyed." The Lord is your rock, your fortress, and your deliverer. God is your rock in whom you take refuge. He is your shield and the horn of your salvation.

MY DAUGHTER ELIZABETH'S STORY

ISAIAH 44:24

"This is what the LORD says—Your Redeemer, who formed you in the womb: I am the LORD, the Maker of all things, who stretches out the heavens, who spreads out the earth by myself,

ISAIAH 43:1

But now, this is what the LORD says—He who created you, Jacob, He who formed you, Israel: "Do not fear, for I have redeemed you; I have summoned you by name; you are mine.

I was so glad that God intervened for me to keep the baby after her dad wanted me to get an abortion even though I was five months pregnant. God spoke to me and made a promise to me that He would provide and protect all of us. I believed God's Word, and I trusted His leadership over our lives. God perform miracles for me to keep my unborn baby.

In October 10, 2002, I had a C-section for my baby Elizabeth. I was excited to hear that my daughter was now here on earth with me. She was born beautiful, alert, healthy, and alive. My daughter gave me joy and laughter; my heart was full of love toward her. When the nurse put her on my chest so I could see her beautiful face, I was filled with passion, love, and joy as a mother. At that moment, I felt like she completed me because just by looking at her face, I felt like I was healed and restored from all the pain, hardship, and brokenness that I experienced before she was born. I called my baby a miracle from God because He gave her a chance to live. While I was in the room with my baby, the nurse separated us and brought each of us into a room. After she brought me to my room, I started to experience pain. I was about to faint and was having difficulty breathing, I was giving the nurse a sign that I was having a hard time breathing and that I was also in so much pain. The nurse saw me and put ventilation on my face so I could easily breathe. After putting the ventilation on my face, but I still had a hard time breathing. I thought I was going to die that day. The nurse didn't know what to do with me; she decided to leave me in the room to ask for help.

When I saw her leave the room, I started to panicked. I was losing hope until I remembered my dad telling me that I needed to pray. I was hoping that God would answer my prayer. I close my eyes, and after I did that, I don't remember anything what happened to me. I had fallen asleep. When I woke up, I thanked God because He answered my prayer. I didn't feel any pain anymore. I was so glad that I was still alive.

I came back to my house and tried to rest, and I prayed for the Lord to heal me from the surgery. I tried to be content with what I had and what I didn't have. Because I had not worked for two months and was a single mother of two, I lacked money, so I was experiencing hardships in my life—financially, emotionally, mentally, and physically. I thought my friends would be there to help me; but they were the first ones to mock, criticize, and insult me. One person even said that my life was over. But I knew that person was wrong because I knew that my life was just beginning.

GOD RAISES MY DAUGHTER'S HANDS UP IN MY WOMB

One day, my daughter and I went to an orphanage event; she had been chosen to share her powerful testimony about God using her mightily for His glory. Her testimony was about God performing miracles for her while she was still in my womb. When she was an unborn baby three months in my womb, the miracle of God had just been revealed with her hand being raised up from inside my womb. That made the nurse jump for joy because she had never seen anything like that before. That miracle led her to have life. As the years went by, I saw the glory, miracles, and blessings of God being poured out in her life. God gave my daughter her life abundantly.

People were amazed as to how I managed to raise my two children and also had more abundant blessings in my life. I shared with them that the hands of the Lord were with me, and they all believed me because they saw with their own eyes the evidence of the abundance of blessings in our life. Not only am I blessed, but I am also a blessing to other people.

To God be the glory!

EZEKIEL 16:6

"Then I passed by and saw you kicking about in your blood, and as you lay there in your blood I said to you, "Live!"

JOB 33:4

The Spirit of God has made me, and the breath of the Almighty gives me life.

JOB 10:12

You gave me life and showed me kindness, and in your providence watched over my spirit.

God's love is powerful. He created all things, and He created you. Before you came into this world, your life has been ordained for His glory. Every breath that you take is every love, passion, and resurrection from your God. You are the one who can make God move with power.

The power of your love and faith in God brings you to the next level of your knowledge and wisdom in Him. The favors and blessings of God bring wonders of His love within you. God is your refuge and reliable shelter; He is your reason to live. He is the radiance of your countenance. He is your resurrection power, refiner, and refining fire burning inside you. God is the one who renewed your strength. He is your solid rock, your rescuer, and your revelation. God is your support, shield, safety, and security. He is your righteousness of love, and healing within you.

CHAPTER 2

WHERE IS GOD?

ISAIAH 53:7

He was oppressed and afflicted, yet He did not open His mouth; He was led like a lamb to the slaughter, and as a sheep before her shearers is silent, so He did not open His mouth.

One day, at the very young age of six, my cousins, my neighbor's children, and I decided to play hide-and-seek. We were six children trying to have some fun. One child was it, and He was counting all the way up from one to ten. While the other children were trying to find a place to hide, I remember hiding far away from them because wherever I went to hide, there was always some child hiding there also. So I went farther than the rest of them. I went around behind the tall and thick bushes, hoping that the child who was it would not find me.

While I was hiding, I saw a skinny man in His late thirties; he was a Filipino man, and he was also my neighbor friend's uncle. He was watching me hiding behind the bushes. I saw him coming toward me, and when I saw him coming toward me, I started to become concerned because I thought that he would tell somebody that I was hiding there, and I didn't want my friends to find me. As I was looking at the man, I felt fear come over me because he looked very scary. When the man got closer to me, he grabbed me, pushed me down to the ground, and torn my clothes. Then the man raped me. I tried to scream, but he put his hand over my mouth. I remember crying because I was hurt, and at the back of my mind, I was thinking about where my dad was so he could help me. I was terrified and scared of the man.

Later on, while the man was on top of me, I heard the children talking as if they were very close to us. But I was wrong because they were actually far away from us, and I could not see them, and they could not see us. Then the sound of their voices faded away from me. The man saw that I was very scared. After he finished raping me, he decided to leave and left me there alone. I was crying. I was very hurt, and I was bleeding everywhere. I started putting my torn clothes back on to me one by one, with tears pouring down my face, I was very hurt.

My dad was looking for me, and when I saw my dad, I immediately felt safe. When he noticed the way I walked and saw my torn clothes and blood from me, he asked me what happened to me. I was so scared to tell my dad, so I decided not to. At that time, I didn't know what the man did to me; all I knew was that the man hurt me. I didn't know that it was called rape. Also, my parents were poor, and they didn't have any money to take me to the hospital. They were just glad that I was alive. When we were at the dinner table, I started to get very scared, and I was shaking, I thought I was going to pass out. My dad and my mom asked me why I was shaking. I told them that I didn't know. I was having anxiety, and I was very confused.

I always had nightmares when I was sleeping, and I thought the man was always chasing me and was always there beside me and trying to hurt me again. I would get up in the middle of the night, afraid of that man. Sometimes I put the bed linen to cover my face, hoping the man would go away.

One day, I found out that the man left the city and returned to where he came from. I felt so glad because I knew that he would never hurt me again. And after that, I tried to move on with my life. I tried to be normal, acting as if nothing happened, and I even tried to forget what happened. Years later, the man came back; and this time, I was already older with a better understanding of what occurred. I saw him one day, and I looked at him, and he looked at me. We were face-to-face with each other, and this time, I didn't feel scared of him anymore. I let him know that I knew what he did to me. I saw the look of fear on his face, as if he thought I was going to tell my parents; instead, I let him know that I forgave him by showing him that I would not tell my parents. When he realized that I forgave him, he found peace in his heart. When I saw his eyes, I felt like he was saying sorry to me; he left me alone and never touched me again.

One day, I asked God several questions: Where was He when the man was hurting me? Did God see what happened to me? Was God going to do something about it? Was God going to protect me? I thought, *If God is real, why did He let bad things happen to me?*

And God did answer me. He said that He saw and knew everything and that He was there in my moment of being shattered and broken, and that is why I am not dead; the man could have killed me, but He did not kill me. I was still alive. God sent angels to fight for me. God was there, and that whole time, He was protecting me. I felt blessed and restored. God whispered in my ears, saying that He loved me. When I heard His voice comforting me, I found peace in my soul.

As the years went by, I learned to forgive the man. It was a good feeling, and it was the best thing that happened to me. What I am saying is that I forgave him to release me from my agony and pain so I could find peace and joy within my soul. In the form of darkness, I have found God, and God gave me a powerful testimony to share to everyone.

Whatever situation you are in, God is always in control.

In my situation, I learned to forgive, and I learned to love. And I just left the rest to God because He is the *beginning* and the *end* of my life. He is in control over me.

MATTHEW 6:14–15

For if ye forgive men their trespasses, your heavenly Father will also forgive you. But if ye forgive not men their trespasses, neither will your Father forgive your trespasses.

PSALM 22:1–31

My God, my God, why have You forsaken me? Why are You so far from saving me, so far from the words of my groaning? O my God, I cry out by day, but you do not answer, by night, and am not silent. Yet You are enthroned as the Holy One; You are the praise of Israel. In You our Father put their trust; they trusted and You delivered them. They cried out to you and were saved; in You they trusted and were not disappointed.

But I am a worm and not a man, scorned by men and despised by the people. All who see me mock me; they hurl insults, shaking their heads: He trust in the Lord; let the Lord rescue Him. Let Him deliver Him, since He delights in Him. Yet you brought me out of the womb; you made me trust in You even at my mother's breast. From birth I was cast upon You; from my mother's womb You have been my God. Do not be far from me, for trouble is near and there is no one to help. Many bulls surround me; strong bulls of Bashan encircle me. Roaring lions tearing their prey open their mouths wide against me. I am poured out like water, and all my bones are out of joint. My heart has turned to wax; it has melted away within me. My strength is dried up like a potsherd, and my tongue sticks to the roof of my mouth; you lay me in the dust of death. Dogs have surrounded me; a band of evil men has encircled me, they have pierced my hands and my feet. I can count all my bones; people stare and gloat over me. They devide my garments among them and cast lots for my clothing. But You, O lord, be not far off; O my Strength, come quickly to help me. Deliver my life from the sword, my precious life from the power of the dogs. Rescue me from the mouth of the lions; save me from the horns of the wild oxen. I will declare your name to my brothers; in the congregation I will praise You. You who fear the Lord, praise Him! All you descendants of Jacob, honor Him! Revere Him, all you descendants of Israel! For He has not despised or disdained the suffering of the afflicted One; He has not hidden His face from Him but has listened to His cry for help. From you comes the theme of my praise in the great assembly; before those who fear you will I fulfill my vows. The poor will and be satisfied; they who seek the Lord will praise Him—may your hearts live forever! All the ends of the earth will remember and turn to the Lord, and all the families of the nations will bow down before Him, for dominion belongs to the Lord and He rules over the nations. All the rich of the earth will feast and worship; all who go down to the dust will kneel before Him—those who cannot keep themselves alive. Posterity will serve Him; future generations will be told about the Lord. They will proclaim His righteousness to a people yet unborn for He has done it.

DEUTERONOMY 33:27

The Eternal God is your refuge, and underneath are the everlasting arms. He will drive out your enemy before you, saying, "Destroy!"

PSALM 71:18

Even when I am old and gray, do not forsake me, my God, till I declare your power to the next generation, your mighty acts to all who are to come.

LUKE 1:49–51

For the Mighty One has done great things for me—holy is His name. His mercy extends to those who fear Him, from generation to generation. He has performed mighty deeds with His arm; He has scattered those who are proud in their inmost thoughts.

YOUR IDENTITY WITH GOD

Your personality, nature, role, qualities, character, mind, emotions, your ways, and actions create the passions of God's love for who you are in Him. Be grateful and thankful for what you are, who you are, what you do, what you have, and who you are going to be. You are created worthy into His image; you and God are one, and no one will ever take that away from you. Your past does not define you. You are created for Him and by Him for a very special purpose. You are loved by God, and you are precious and beautiful to His eyes. Always remember you are matter to God. No matter how you feel, think, and act, right now, you are called the child of God; and you are important to Him. He desires you and delights in you. His eyes are not sleeping. He is watching over you.

Keep your head up and have hope, faith, and joy that your day is going to be fresh, beautiful, revived, and renewed and that everything you do or need is coming your way because you deserve the best life that God created. You will overcome your enemies by the words of your testimonies and by the blood of Jesus Christ. Your testimonies are God's trophy for His victory. God has a purpose and plan for your life. You are not too old or too young or unworthy to step into your special destiny and purpose in Him. God wants to show you, lead you, and guide you by His Spirit into all that He has for you.

No matter what comes your way, stay truthful and have faith in Him. No matter who turns against you and no matter how long you wait and whatever it takes, stay in faith in the Lord Jesus Christ, for every test and trial you go through is an opportunity and hidden treasure in the eyes of God. God's Word is power; there is power in the name of Jesus. Whatever you ask for will be given to you in His perfect love and will in your life. God has a perfect time and a perfect plan for you. God has brought you from your tests and trials to bring you to victory.

You are the victor and not the victim in any circumstances and challenges in your life. You have been transformed by your Creator, and He sustains you. All glory to Him, for God continues showing you what true and not-true living really is.

Even though you may feel like you're at your darkest or lowest point (e.g., tragedy, pain, and hurt), if you pray and persevere in trusting God, He will put you in the realm of victory in His kingdom and in His own way and time.

God chooses you to put your trust in Him. He knows you. And remember, God will fight your battles. The question is, "Do you trust Him?"

PSALM 23:1–6

The LORD is my shepherd; I shall not want. He maketh me to lie down in green pastures: He leadeth me beside the still waters. He restoreth my soul: He leadeth me in the paths of righteousness for His name's sake. Yea, though I walk through the valley of the shadow of death, I will fear no evil: for thou art with me; thy rod and thy staff they comfort me. Thou preparest a table before me in the presence of mine enemies: thou anointest my head with oil; my cup runneth over. Surely goodness and mercy shall follow me all the days of my life: and I will dwell in the house of the LORD forever.

To win every battle, you will have to stand on the Word of God to fight for you and only to speak what is written in His word. The Word of God has power and has life over you.

Today, you need to claim authority over your surroundings by declaring the Word of God over your life. Your faith in God will not be shaken and will not be move. You will always believe and have faith that all things are possible for every situation and challenges in your life.

God will protect you, provide for you, heal you, restore you, and redeem you. Today, your faith is stronger than ever, and the peace you find in Him surpasses understanding. You are not a quitter—you are a fighter. And from this day forward, God will fight His way for your life, and He will win every time for you.

God planted a good seed of strong faith in your heart, so all you have to do is activate it with prayers. The Word of God brings power, and through His actions, you will see His heart full of love and the manifestation of His glory over you.

PSALM 121:1–2

I lift up my eyes to the mountains—where does my help come from? My help comes from the LORD, the Maker of heaven and earth.

PRAYER

As your child, Abba, Father, thank you that I am covered with your blood. I am washed, cleansed with your blood, and thank you for molding me with the scars of your hands. Thank you, Jesus. You are my Savior, my redeemer, my rescuer. You are all things that give me hope. Thank you that I am released from my sins and the sins of my ancestors. The cross and the resurrection of Jesus stand between me and them.

Thank you, God, for giving me the power to overcome fear. I receive your love, and I choose to stand strong in you. I trust in you, Lord, to guide me, to strengthen me, to bless me, and to protect me. Lord Jesus, thank you for knowing my heart. Thank you, Lord, for making me, creating me, saving me, and being my Savior. Lord, thank you for giving me faith with hope, joy, and peace as I trust in you.

In Jesus, Mighty name, Amen.

CHAPTER 3

THE RESURRECTION AND
THE VOICE OF GOD

JOHN 11:25-26

Jesus said to her, "I am the resurrection and the life. The one who believes in me will live, even though they die; and whoever lives by believing in me will never die. Do you believe this?"

As an innocent young child at the age of five, I remember going to my neighbor's house to play with my friends. My friends were not home, but my friend's mother was, and she wanted to give me some fruits and vegetables instead. I picked up the edge of my skirt and put the food inside of it. I walked on the right side of their house. As I was walking toward the side of the house, I saw this fascinating wheelbarrow, which was just standing on the side of the house. As I was looking at the wheelbarrow, I thought about that I should maybe bring it with me, so I can play with it. I thought it would be cool to have it. When I got closer to the wheelbarrow, I picked it up with my right hand, and I started pushing it; the wheelbarrow is not stable while I was trying to push it. My left hand was holding my skirt with food in it. While I was pushing the wheelbarrow, I saw my cousin from afar. I started calling her name; as I was calling her name, I noticed that she did not hear me. As I was pushing the wheelbarrow and calling my cousin at the same time, I found myself being distracted that I lost control, the wheels turned toward the edge of the cliff of the creek, and I also noticed that the wheelbarrow was going to fall down.

I also noticed that I kept dropping the food from my skirt; at the same time, I was trying to bring the wheelbarrow back up, hoping that it would not fall. I was very scared at that moment. I knew how far and deep the creek was, and while I was pulling the wheelbarrow back up, I was looking to see if my cousin could see me and help me. But again, I wasn't sure if she saw me. The wheelbarrow was very heavy for me, and I was so scared that I knew I was going to fall down the creek. I tried my best to hold on to the wheelbarrow. I remember holding it very tight with all my strength, but I still could not bring the wheelbarrow back up. And suddenly the wheelbarrow fall all the way down on the creek. I could not stop myself and fell down with it. And when I fell down, I landed on a huge rock from the creek. And while I was lying down on top of the rock, *I lost my breath, and I died immediately.* I remember my spirit leaving my body, and I saw my body lying on top of the rock.

JOHN 12:27–28

"Now my soul is troubled, and what shall I say? 'Father save me from this hour? No, it was for this very reason I came to this hour. Father, glorify your name!" Then a voice came from heaven, "I have glorified it, and will glorify it again."

LUKE 23:46

Jesus called out with a loud voice, Father, into Your hands I commit my spirit, when He had said this He breathed His last.

I have never questioned God as to why my body was lying lifeless on top of the rock and why I was just standing and staring at my body. I just didn't know what was happening to me. I was very confused at the same time. I was at the bottom of the creek, and there was nobody around to help me. Suddenly, before I could even blink my eyes, I saw two angels come from out of nowhere standing beside my body, and they looked like people and were covered in a beautiful bright light. When I saw them, I felt peace and I realized that I was not alone. I actually had company. I was just standing there, looking at my body and the two angels.

LUKE 4:10–11

For it is written: He will command His angels concerning you to guard you carefully. They will lift you up in their hands so that you will not strike your foot against a stone.

While I was looking at myself and to the two angels from on top of the rock, I suddenly heard a voice calling my name and the voice it was saying, "Esther." And it was coming from heaven. I looked up to see who was calling my name, but I did not see anybody. I heard the voice from heaven calling my name a second time and I looked up but I did not see anybody.

ACTS 9:7

The men traveling with Saul stood there speechless; they heard the sound but did not see anyone.

The third time I heard the voice of God coming from heaven, I looked up; and this time, I saw a light brighter than the sun. It was a beautiful radiance, and it was very inviting to approach. I felt like I was receiving peace and love. It was a beautiful feeling that came over me. It was heaven, and nothing here on earth could compare it. It was a place that I should go and the place that I belonged that I would call my home. I realized that I had just encountered God face-to-face. And at that moment, in the blink of my eyes, I felt like I would be going up with Lord.

JOHN 12:28

Father, glorify Your name! Then a voice came from heaven, I have glorified it, and will glorify it again.

I saw the beauty of God, with His beautiful lights, magnificent radiance, and powerful glory. At the same time, I was waiting for the voice of God to speak to me again. And while I was watching God's glory;

At the same time my father and five men were carrying my body from the creek, and my dad is praying for my body to come back to life.

MATTHEW 17:2–8

There He was transfigured before them. His face shone like the sun, and His clothes became as white as the light. When they looked up, they saw no one except Jesus.

HEBREWS 1:3–4

The Son is the radiance of God's glory and the exact representation of His being, sustaining all things by His powerful word. After He had provided purification for His sins, He sat down at the right hand of the majesty in heaven. So He became as much superior to the angels as the name He has inherited is superior to theirs.

I was about to take one step forward to the bright lights to come home with the Lord; but suddenly, *I heard my dad's voice praying for me, asking for my spirit to return to my body and for me to come back to life. My dad was calling God to perform a miracle for Him, for me, and for everybody.* When I opened my eyes, I saw my father was kneeling down; he was pleading and praying to God for bringing me back to life, Because of my dad's faith in the Lord. God answered his prayers. God did bring me back to life. When my dad saw me come back to life, he was full of awe of God. I saw my dad smiling at me with tears of joy pouring down his cheeks. God just gave my dad peace beyond his understanding. God answered my dad's prayer for me to come back to life.

MARK 5:22–24

Then one of the synagogue leaders, named Jairus, came, and when He saw Jesus, He fell at His feet. He pleaded earnestly with Him, "My little daughter is dying. Please come and put your hands on her so that she will be healed and live." So Jesus went with Him.

MARK 5:41–42

He took her by the hand and said to her, "Talitha Koum!" (Which means "little girl, I say to you, get up!"). Immediately the girl stood up and began to walk around (She was twelve years old). At this they were completely astonished.

Other people were looking at me as if they saw a ghost; they were amazed and astonished, and they rejoiced the goodness of God. My father prayed and believed that God would perform miracles for me, and God did—He brought me back to life. To God be the glory!

Many years later, as I was sharing my story about God bringing me back to life to some people, one person asked me if I was at the tunnel of light. I told him that at that time I'm not sure, but I knew that I was in the presence of God with bright lights in front of me. The man shared with me that he saw a vision of me; and he told me that "at the time I was lying on the huge rock at the creek with water all around me, he saw that God was baptizing me with water, the Holy Spirit, and His fire. Then the bright lights came and dwelled inside me." When the man told me that, I embraced the word because I knew that it was from the Lord.

1 SAMUEL 1:27

I prayed for this child, and the Lord has granted me what I asked of Him.

PSALM 21:4

He asked you for life, and you gave it to Him—length of days, forever and ever.

JOHN 15:7

If you remain in me and my words remain in you, ask whatever you wish, and it will be done for you.

A person that was dear to my heart saw everything—she told me everything at that time I fall at the creek and died and came back to life. She also saw that I was very thirsty. She saw that my father rushed to the kitchen to get me a full glass of water. And I drank it. My dad gave me not just one full glass of water, but at least seven full glasses of water, and I drank them all. I felt like I was dehydrated and needed the water.

JOHN 5:24–25

"Very truly I tell you, whoever hears my word and believes Him who sent me has eternal life and will not be judged but has crossed over from death to life. Very truly I tell you, a time is coming and has now come and the dead will hear the voice of the Son of God and those who hear will live.

After drinking all the water that my father gave me, I started to get sick in my stomach. I was so sick that I was feeling nausea, and my body started to shake as if there was a fire inside of me that was trying to burn everything that was not of God. I was shocked, and so was everybody when I vomit three times. I felt like I expelled all the food I ate that whole day; as I was vomiting, I felt like there was something in my throat that needed to come out. When something finally came out, I was very scared of what I saw, and the people that were watching me were very scared also—there were two huge worms, about ten inches each long, that came out of my mouth. I thought they would never stop coming out of my mouth, and the worms were dead. My dad and the rest were shocked because they had never seen anything like that before; my dad picked up the two dead worms and threw them away. My father thanked God for His faithfulness in our lives and for giving me back my life.

I looked around, and I saw a lot of people who were amazed and in awe of God. I felt love, bless, confidence, courage, and assurance with the Lord. The people thanked God for the miracles in my life, and they all believed Him.

My father did not take me to the hospital; He believed that God already healed my body completely. I believed in my heavenly Father and my dad. I fell down from the edge of the cliff and landed at the bottom of the creek on top of a huge rock. But none of my bones were broken, my head was not cracked open, and no blood came out of my body. I only had bruises on my body. And I owe all my life to God. God is good. He is real, and He is alive. I love Him, and He gave me a reason to live.

God is my healer and restorer, and God resurrected me from death to life.

JOHN 11:25

Jesus said to her, "I AM the resurrection and the life. He who believes in Me will live, even though He dies; and whoever lives and believes in Me will never die." Do you believe this?

JOB 5:9

He performs wonders that cannot be fathomed, miracles that cannot be counted.

THE VOICE OF THE SON OF MAN

JOHN 5:24–28

I tell you the truth, whoever hears my word and believe Him who sent Me has eternal life and will not be condemned; He has crossed over from death to life. I tell you the truth, a time is coming and has now come when the dead will hear the voice of the Son of God and those who hears will live. For as the Father has life in Himself, so He has granted the Son to have life in Himself. And He has given Him authority to judge because He is the Son of Man. do not be amazed at this, for a time is coming when all who are in their graves will hear His voice.

MATTHEW 27:50–52

And when Jesus had cried out again in a loud voice, He gave up His Sprit. At that moment the curtain of the temple was torn in two from top to bottom. The earth shook and the rocks split. The tombs broke open and the bodies of many holy people who had died were raised to life.

1 CORINTHIANS 15:54–55

When the perishable has been clothed with imperishable, and the mortal with immortality, then the saying that is written will come true: "Death has been swallowed up in Victory."

"Where, O death, is your victory? Where, O death, is your sting?"

IDENTITY WITH GOD

Trust in Him, and everything is added unto you even in every bad situation and challenges in your life (e.g., doubt, fear, anxiety, poverty, sickness, disease, even death). Jesus Christ of Nazareth will give you the strength and courage so that you can be alive in Him. God wants to release His power and might so that you can overcome fear and transform it to love, slavery to freedom, poverty to wealth, and mourning to dancing.

God will intervene for you to remove every act of the enemy in your life. He gave you His life so that you can be alive in Him. God has a purpose in your life; you have been predestined to be here on earth for His glory so that His glory will be revealed throughout the nations. You are His creation and masterpiece of love and power. You are everything to God, and with Him, you will find the inner core of your destiny and future in life. You are created wonderfully by the Almighty God. God will rescue you. He will even send His angels to guide you and put you upon the rock and cover you with His feathers. God will be with you and will give you unforgettable miracles. Only God is the one who can protect you. God is the one who will get you out of trouble. God will stretch out His hand to answer all your prayers and perform signs, wonders, and miracles for you. Jesus is the resurrection and a life over in every situation of your life. God wants to manifest Himself in you beyond your understanding. His beauty will be revealed to you because of your faithfulness in Him. God's Mighty acts of power will overshadow you.

You will feel God's glory by receiving the victory that has already been ordained for you to have. You will find comfort in His love and power in your life. God will resurrect, heal, restore, and save you; for you are worthy in His sight.

1 PETER 1:3

Praise be to the God and Father of our Lord Jesus Christ! In His great mercy He has given us new birth into a living hope through the resurrection of Jesus Christ from the dead,

The will of your heavenly Father is that when you seek the Son of God and believe in Him, you should have eternal life, and He will raise Him from the dead on the last day. If the Spirit of Him who raised Jesus from the dead dwells in you, He who raised Christ Jesus from the dead will also give life to your mortal bodies through His Spirit who dwells in you. God raised the Lord and will also raise you up by His power.

You were buried with Him by baptism into death in order that, just as Christ was raised from the dead by the glory of the Father, you too might walk in the newness of life.

Jesus said, "Yet a little while and the world will see me no more, but you will see me, because I live, you also will live. And you will be blessed, because they cannot repay you. For you will be repaid at the resurrection of the just. Your dead shall live, your body shall rise. You who dwell in the dust, awake and sing for joy, for your dew, is a dew of light, and the earth will give birth to the dead. Jesus said whoever feeds on my flesh and drinks my blood has eternal life, and I will raise Him up on the last day."

"Truly, truly I say unto you, He who hears my word and believes Him who sent Me has eternal life. He does not come into judgment but has passed from death to life."

"But you were washed, you were sanctified, you justified in the name of the Lord Jesus Christ and by the Spirit of our God. That the God of our Lord Jesus Christ, the Father of glory, may give you a spirit of wisdom and of revelation in the knowledge of Him, having the eyes of your hearts enlightened, that you may know what is the hope to which He has called you, what are riches of His glorious inheritance in the saints, and what is the immeasurable greatness of His power towards you who believe, according to the working of His great might that He worked in Christ when He raised Him from the dead and seated Him at His right hand in the heavenly places, far above all rule and authority and power and dominion, and above every name that is named, not only in this age but also in the one to come."

EZEKIEL 37:1–14

The hand of the LORD was on me, and He brought me out by the Spirit of the LORD and set me in the middle of a valley; it was full of bones. He led me back and forth among them, and I saw a great many bones on the floor of the valley, bones that were very dry. He asked me, "Son of man, can these bones live?" I said, "Sovereign LORD, you alone know." Then He said to me, "Prophesy to these bones and say to them, 'Dry bones, hear the word of the LORD! This is what the Sovereign LORD says to these bones: I will make breath enter you, and you will come to life. I will attach tendons to you and make flesh come upon you and cover you with skin; I will put breath in you, and you will come to life. Then you will know that I am the LORD." So I prophesied as I was commanded. And as I was prophesying, there was a noise, a rattling sound, and the bones came together, bone to bone. I looked, and tendons and flesh appeared on them and skin covered them, but there was no breath in them. Then He said to me, "Prophesy to the breath; prophesy, son of man, and say to it, 'this is what the Sovereign LORD says: Come, breath, from the four winds and breathe into these slain, that they may live.'" So I prophesied as He commanded me, and breath entered them; they came to life and stood up on their feet—a vast army. Then He said to me: "Son of man, these bones are the people of Israel. They say, 'Our bones are dried up and our hope is gone; we are cut off.' Therefore prophesy and say to them: 'This is what the Sovereign LORD says: My people, I am going to open your graves and bring you up from them; I will bring you back to the land of Israel. Then you, my people, will know that I am the LORD, when I open your graves and bring you up from them. I will put my Spirit in you and you will live, and I will settle you in your own land. Then you will know that I the LORD have spoken, and I have done it, declares the LORD."'

REVELATION 1:17–20

When I saw Him, I fell at His feet as though dead. Then He placed His right hand on me and said: "Do not be afraid. I am the First and the Last. I am the Living One; I was dead, and now look, I am alive forever and ever! And I hold the keys of death and Hades. "Write, therefore, what you have seen, what is now and what will take place later. The mystery of the seven stars that you saw in my right hand and of the seven golden lamp stands is this: The seven stars are the angels of the seven churches, and the seven lamp stands are the seven churches.

CHAPTER 4

SACRIFICE LAND FOR LIFE

ISAIAH 53:8–9

By oppression and judgment He was taken away. Yet who of His generation protested? For He was cut off from the land of the living; for the transgression of my people He was punished. He was assigned a grave with the wicked and with the rich in His death, though He had done no violence, nor was any deceit in His mouth.

At the age of seven years old, I remember sitting on a chair. My dad was standing in front of me. I saw a lot of gun men forcing themselves into the house, and they were carrying a lot of guns. The leader came toward my dad, grabbed him, and put his gun to my dad's head, threatening to kill him. The man demanded for my dad to hand over our land to them, or they would kill him and his family. My dad looked right at me, and I looked right back at him. I saw fear in his eyes fear that the bad men would kill us all; he knew that they would hurt me and the rest of the family. When my dad was looking right at me with the gun to his head, I saw that he was already defeated and hopeless; he knew that he could not protect us because we were in the hands of the enemies. My dad was so scared of the bad men, and he didn't want them to hurt us. He was forced to hand over our land to the bad men, hoping they would not kill us.

My dad prayed and believed that God would make a way to free us from the hands of the enemies. When my dad agreed that he was handling the land over to them, the bad men let all of us go. They gave my dad two weeks to leave the property, threatening him not to tell anyone, or they would kill us all. After they said that, they all left the house. My dad did not tell anybody, even to his brother or the authorities. He was afraid that the bad men would come back to hunt, hurt, and kill all of us if he said anything to anyone.

JOURNEY WITHOUT A HOME

The following day, my dad decided to make a huge four-wheeler wagon where all of us could fit and also easy to push. After my dad made it, it was the time for us to get out of our home. We put all our belongings that would fit in the wagon, and we left our land. We started our journey on the street, walking and pushing the wagon toward the city. As I was walking, I started to limp and cried as I was having a hard time walking because one of the slippers that I was wearing was broken. My dad and my mom were confused and scared; they didn't know how, when, and where to go. All I knew was I would go wherever my parents went.

I noticed my parents were quiet while they were pushing the cart; no word came out from their mouths. I saw my parents' eyes full of tears; my mom kept wiping her tears with her dress. They were scared, shocked, unbelief, and hurt, for what just happen to all of us. My parents was confused not knowing where to go, where they were going to bring their two children, how they were going to raise us, where to start, and where we were going to sleep—all these were going through their mind. No words could explain what just happened to us. They were shocked and could not believe what just took place in our lives.

As my parents pushed the wagon, they thought about where to park it so we could have something to eat and get some rest. They decided to go toward the market, and when we got there, my parents bought some food. After we ate, we left and went to the park close to the market; my parents just parked the wagon there beside the school. There were also houses around it.

And when it got dark, my dad decided to just stay in the park. I remember my younger brother and I slept under the wagon, and my parents slept on top. While we were trying to go to sleep, there was a huge storm that came our way, and the rain was pouring so hard inside the wagon. We could not escape the water inside, and the rushing winds were blowing very strongly on the plastic that was used to cover the rooftop and the cart. The plastic rooftop kept falling, and every time it did, we would all get wet; my parents kept trying to fix the plastic rooftop until they give up. They were not able to fix it because we did not have enough tools, and the rain was very heavy also. My parents decided to just not fix the roof. Because they were tired, weary, and sleepy, we slept with the rain on us. As the night kept getting darker and darker, our eyes just gave up, and we slept deep in the middle of the storm.

The following morning, I noticed the neighbors who were just passing us by; they were just watching us. I felt pain from my stomach; my stomach told me that I was hungry. I was so glad to see my mom cooking food from the small portable stove; my mom served us the food, and it looked and smelled so good. We all ate, and I was very happy that we had food to eat because I was very hungry.

Again, I noticed other people passing by, looking at us like they wanted to ask us where we came from; but they never asked us a question. They just left us alone, and they did not call the police on us. I was so glad. It was so hard not having a place to live. I experienced being sick all the time—also being tired, weak, hopeless, alone, and being different from other children. I saw children playing, and they were so happy; they were wearing beautiful clothes, and their parents were with them. In my mind, I desperately wanted to play with them. But then, I looked at myself; my clothes were torn, and I looked very dirty. I thought that maybe the children would not want to play with me, so I decided to be by myself and watch them play instead.

My dad had an idea to stay in the park for a while. After seeing a lot of people walking, tricycle drivers, and jeepney drivers, my dad saw an opportunity to start a new business—selling street food. My dad and my mom would cook dessert foods, seafood, and other kinds of food. When the people saw that we were selling food, they came and bought food. They would bring friends, who also bought food. The business was growing, and it was good.

After school, my brother and I would be at the market selling grocery bags (*supot*) to the customers. Also, if the bags were too heavy for them, we would help them carry the bags. We made a lot of money, and we give the money to our parents for us to survive. I did not have time to have fun; all I knew was how to survive.

One day, I was walking in the city. This place had many bars and clubs, stores, and the market; and it was close to a location foreigners frequented. At a young age, I learned to sell dessert food to foreigners and also to those who wanted to buy food. The first time I encountered a male foreigner, I saw that he had a white complexion and spoke a different language (English). He was surrounded by a lot of homeless children, and the children were talking to him in English. One of the children came to me, and she told me to talk to him, but I told her that I didn't know how to speak English; the girl told me to just say "why" to the foreigner man and the foreigner would understand me. So I also followed the foreigner along with the other children, and I did what the girl told me to ask him. When the man was looking at me, I asked the man, "Why?" That was the only English word that I knew how to communicate with him; the man responded to me, but I could not understand him. I just looked at him, and he just looked at me, and we were just looking at each other. Then the other children were talking to him and asking him questions.

Later on, the foreigner gave all the children some money, and the man gave me some money too. I was very happy because it was my first time holding a foreigner's money. I gave my money to my dad. I'm not sure if my dad ever touched foreign money before; all I know was that my dad was very happy. I will never forget that foreigner man. I will always remember him and how he was kind to all of us.

OUR NEW HOME

Years later, my sister, who worked for a wealthy family as a housekeeper, decided to buy a piece of land from our old neighborhood for all of us to live on. So we moved from the park to our new land, and there, my dad built our new home.

ISAIAH 53:10

Yet it was the Lord's will to crush Him and cause Him to suffer, and though the Lord makes His life a guilt offering, He will see His offspring and prolong His days, and the will of the Lord will prosper in His hand.

PSALM 33:18–22

But the eyes of the Lord are on those who fear Him, on those whose hope is in His unfailing love, to deliver them from death and keep them alive in famine. We wait in hope for the Lord; He is our help and our shield. In Him our hearts rejoice, for we trust in His holy name. May your unfailing love be with us, Lord, even as we put our hope in You.

PSALM 34:17

The righteous cry out, and the Lord hears them; He delivers them from all their troubles.

ISAIAH 64:1–4

Oh, that you would rend the heavens and come down, that the mountains would tremble before you! As when fire sets twigs ablaze and causes water to boil, come down to make your name known to your enemies and cause the nations to quake before you! For when you did awesome things that we did not expect, you came down, and the mountains trembled before you. Since ancient times no one has heard, no ears has perceived, no eye has seen any God beside you, who acts on behalf of those who wait for Him.

God's love and goodness can be seen from His mighty acts through signs, wonders, and miracles. His passion for His people brings closeness and comfort in His heart. God wants to manifest Himself by coming down to you for His glory. Are you ready for God to come down for you today? God wants to depart the Red Sea for you. He wants to close the mouth of the lions. He wants to make the sun still and break down the walls of Jericho for you. He wants to split the rock. He wants to walk on water. He wants to calm the storm. He wants to bring the fire from heaven. He wants to heal every sickness and disease for you. He wants to perform miracles for you, and nothing will be impossible for Him.

None of your challenges are too hard for the Lord. He wants to take care of you. He wants to protect you. He wants to rescue you. He wants to provide for you. He wants to heal you, and He wants to give you rest and peace, In Jesus' name, amen.

JEREMIAH 17:7–8

"But blessed is the one who trusts in the LORD, whose confidence is in Him. They will be like a tree planted by the water that sends out its roots by the stream. It does not fear when heat comes; its leaves are always green. It has no worries in a year of drought and never fails to bear fruit."

God is a God of wisdom and knowledge, for He knows His plans for you—plans to make you prosper and not to harm you, plans to give you hope and a future. And He will meet all your needs according to the riches of His glory in Christ Jesus. And as you worship the Lord your God, His blessings will be food and water for you. God will take away sickness from you. He will let you taste and see that the Lord is good. God says blessed is the one who takes refuge in Him. For God command you today to love the Lord your God, to walk in obedience with Him, and to keep His commands, decrees, and laws. Then you will live and increase, and the Lord your God will bless you in the land you are entering to possess. God is saying do not repay evil with evil or insult with insult. On the contrary, repay evil with blessings because to this you were called so that you may inherit blessings. God wants you to bring the whole tithe into the storehouse, that there may be food in my house. Test me in this, says the Lord Almighty, and see if I will not throw open the floodgates of heaven and pour out so much blessings that there will not be room enough to store it. Blessed are you who hunger and thirst for righteousness, for you will be filled. And if you obey the Lord your God and carefully follow all His commands I give you today, the Lord your God will show you high above all the nations on earth. Blessed are you the peacemakers, for you will be called children of God, blessed are you who keep His statues and seek Him with all their heart. When you rest in the Lord, and wait patiently for Him. Fret not thyself because of the man who bringeth wicked devices to pass.

CHAPTER 5

A BROKEN ARM

One day, when I was in second grade, I went to school early so I could play with my friends before going to class. I had three friends, and we loved to play before we went to class. My friends and I decided to play a game called "elastic garter." The game is played when two people hold each end of the elastic garter so that the other person can jump from the bottom all the way up. When it was my turn to play, my friends held the ends of the elastic garter, and I jumped from the bottom all the way to the top. When I got to the top, it was time for me to land on the ground, but the ground had a lot of tiny rocks. So I landed on a lot of little rocks, and I fell down to the ground. I used my right arm to protect my body so I would not get hurt. Instead, I hurt my right arm when I landed on the ground. I felt like my arm was broken. I cried so loud because I was very hurt. A lot of children just watched me cry.

When it was time for me to go to class, I did not tell my teacher that I was very hurt. I also didn't tell my parents. I was so scared to tell them because they might get mad at me. And every time I saw my parents, I hid my arm. I didn't want them to know what happened to me. Sometimes I slept crying because the pain from my arm was bothering. It was getting worse. My arm started to look black-and-blue. It didn't look good at all.

Two weeks later, I was riding a jeepney, and I saw my older cousin's wife. She noticed my arm was black-and-blue, and she immediately took me to my uncle, who was my father's brother. My uncle told her to rush me to the hospital. When we got to the hospital, the doctor checked my arm, and he told my cousin that he was going to amputate my arm because it was infected with bacteria that had spread all throughout my arm. I was having a hard time moving my arm; the doctor said that it was too late for him to fix my arm, and they could not do anything about it. I was very scared because I liked my arm, and I didn't want the doctor to cut my arm. I remember crying, wishing for my arm to be healed.

My cousin sent somebody to let my parents know about what happened to me, and right before my father got to the hospital, my cousin gave the doctor a heads-up to amputate my arm. So the doctor was preparing my arm for surgery. There was a lot of waiting. When the doctor was going to operate on my arm, my parents finally came, and my dad stopped the doctor. My father told the doctor that he believed that Jesus was the healer and that God would heal me. So my father prayed for me, and the doctor did not amputate my arm. Instead, he put a cast and bandages on it and gave my dad the antibiotic and other medicines for me to take. There was nothing that the doctor could do because of my father's decision, so he just sent me home.

My parents did not have any money to pay for the doctor, so my dad decided to remove the cast from my arm. After doing so, I saw that my arm had completely healed. I was so glad that I still had my arm. Glory to God in the highest! God is my healer.

IDENTITY WITH GOD

JOHN 5:5–9

One who was there had been an invalid for thirty-eight years. When Jesus saw Him lying there and learned that He had been in this condition for a long time, He asked Him, "Do you want to get well?" "Sir," the invalid replied, "I have no one to help me into the pool when the water is stirred. While I am trying to get in, someone else goes down ahead of me." Then Jesus said to Him, "Get up! Pick up your mat and walk." At once the man was cured; He picked up His mat and walked.

MARK 11:22–25

"Have faith in God," Jesus answered I tell you the truth, If anyone says to this mountain, Go throw yourself into the sea, and does not doubt in His heart but believes that what He says will happen, it will be done for Him. Therefore I tell you, whatever you ask for in prayer, believe that you receive it, and it will be yours. And when you stand praying, If you hold anything against anyone, forgive Him, so that your father in heaven may forgive you your sins.

1 JOHN 5:14–15

This is the confidence we have in approaching God: that if we ask anything according to His will, He hears us. And if we know that He hears us—whatever we ask—we know that we have what we asked of Him.

TRUSTING GOD IS THE KEY FOR YOUR HEALING

God says for you to pay attention to what He is saying and to listen closely to His words. He does not want you to let them out of your sight. Keep them within your heart, for they are life for you and health to your body. Above all else, guard your heart, for it is the wellspring of your life.

He says if you listen carefully to the voice of the Lord your God and do what is right in His eyes and if you pay attention to His commands and keep all His decrees, He will not bring on you any of the diseases He brought on the Egyptians, for He is the Lord who heals you.

Because He loves you, He will rescue you. He will protect you, for you acknowledge His name. You will call Him, and He will answer you. He will be with you in trouble. He will deliver you and honor you. He will satisfy you and show you His salvation.

CHAPTER 6

KIDNAPPED

When I was eight years old working at a restaurant as a dishwasher, I remember sitting on a chair, and there was a woman staring at me. She approached me and told me that I was a beautiful little girl; she asked me if I wanted new clothes and new shoes. She also told me that she could make me look like a princess and that she would buy me new clothes and new shoes. When she said these to me, I said, "Wow!" I wanted to look like a princess too, so I agreed to have her buy me some clothes and shoes. The woman did not have any children, and she thought that I could be her child.

It happened so fast that I left work and did not even ask my boss if I could leave. The woman took me to a nice clothing store and bought some clothes and shoes for me. I was the happiest child ever. I thought that I was a princess. After we finished shopping, she took me to a nice restaurant and fed me. I thought to myself that I was blessed because this woman that I didn't know was giving me so much stuff even without me doing anything for her. But little did I know that the woman just kidnapped me.

Then later on, we rode a jeepney, and she brought me to a hotel. She told me that I needed to call her Mom and not to call her by her name (can't remember her name). From then on, she said that I was her child and she was my mother. I did not know then what she was doing, and as a child who was alone with her, I did everything she told me to do. It was already late at night, and I did not go home to my parents.

The woman was very kind and nice to me. She lived in the hotel. I will never forget the night she brought a foreigner man to the hotel with her. This was the second time I saw a foreigner. The foreigner man had a white complexion, blond hair, and blue eyes. I was so concerned. I thought that the foreigner was from another planet. Even though this was the second time I saw a foreigner, I had never seen anybody like him before. I asked myself where the man came from.

The woman told me to steal the man's wallet while he was in the room with her. I was so scared of that man. I thought He had some power. I did not even touch the man's wallet, so I did not do what she told me to do. I thought that the man had authority. I thought He came from another planet or something. I felt like he was like Superman. So I did not touch his wallet. When she found out that I did not steal his wallet, she did not get mad at me, so I was glad. Instead, she was the one who stole the wallet from him. I found out later on that the woman was a prostitute, and that was how she supported herself.

One day, we left the city, and she brought me to her birthplace, where I met her family. She introduced me as her child to them, and her family loved me. The woman was very nice to me; she took good care of me, and she showed her love for me. We stayed in her hometown for two months.

After, we came back to my home town, and she took me to a restaurant. While we were eating dessert, I saw my parents coming toward us with the police. The police took the woman and put her in jail. My parents told me that they were looking for me the whole time. I saw my parents' fear of not having me around. I was so glad to see my mom and dad and to come back home to them. I knew that my parents loved me; they did not give up looking for me. I love my parents.

I thanked God for protecting me that whole time and for not letting bad things happen to me while I was with the woman who kidnapped me.

As the years went by, she would suddenly come to my mind while I was praying in church. I would wonder if she was still alive. I was hoping that she was still alive because I wanted to see her again to let her know that I was praying for her. I wanted God to forgive her, and I wanted to forgive her, and I wanted the best for her.

Wow, sometimes I think that I'm not normal because the woman kidnapped me, yet I wanted God to forgive her. I also wanted to forgive her, and I wanted to see her again, and I wanted the best for her. Who thinks like that?

In God's perspective, He is not normal either. Even though people sin against Him, He still forgives them and gives them His only Son, Jesus Christ.

JOHN 3:16

For God so loved the world that He gave His One and only Son, that whoever believes in Him shall not perish but have eternal life.

Moses pleaded to God for divine forgiveness for His people . . .

EXODUS 34:9

O' Lord, If I have found favor in Your eyes, He said, then let the Lord go with us. Although this is a stiff-neck people, forgive our wickedness and our sin, and take us as Your inheritance.

God's kingdom, though you and I are the worst people on the earth, (kidnappers, prostitutes, murderers, thieves). God the Father will forgive our sins if we accept Jesus Christ as our Savior. God still love us. He forgives us, and He gave His only begotten Son for us. He wants us to sit in the heavenly realms with Him. We have a mercy seat set aside just for us in heaven. Wow, God is a forgiving god and is full of love and compassion for us.

IDENTITY WITH GOD

PSALM 12:5–7

Because of the oppression of the weak and groaning of the needy, I will Arise, says the Lord. I will protect them from those who malign them. And the words of the Lord are flawless, purified seven times. O Lord You will keep us safe and protect us from such people forever.

THE LOVE OF GOD

God is your refuge and strength, an ever-present help in times of trouble. He gives you eternal life, and you shall never perish; no one will snatch you out from His hand. He will not leave you as orphans. He will come to you. Jesus says, "Peace I leave with you. My peace I give to you. Not as the world gives do I give to you. Let not your heart be troubled. Neither let it be afraid." For God has not given you a spirit of fear, but of power, love, and a sound mind. For He himself has said, "I will never leave you nor forsake you." So you may boldly say, "The Lord is my helper. I will not fear. What can man do to me?" Though you walk in the midst of trouble, God preserves your life. He stretches out His hand against the wrath of your enemies, and your right hand delivers you. The Lord will rescue you from evil deeds and bring you safely into His heavenly kingdom. To Him be the glory forever and ever. Amen.

CHAPTER 7

HOW TO GO BACK HOME

One day, when I was fourteen years old, my neighbor came to my house and asked me if I wanted to work for her big sister as a live-in housekeeper. She said that they lived in the other city. I told her that I would let her know after I talked to my mother about it. I asked my mom if I could go with her and work for her sister, and my mom said yes. So I told my friend that it was okay for me to work for her sister.

One week later, I packed my clothes I would bring with me to work. After I finished packing, my friend and I traveled to her sister's city. When we got to her sister's house, she introduced me to her big sister; her sister liked me and hired me on the spot. I worked for them for two months without pay. Her family and her uncle had just come from the province and he was staying in her house. Three months later, her uncle, who was probably thirty years old, he saw me being beautiful girl and he liked me, he tried to touch me. I didn't want Him to touch me. But He told everyone that I was his wife, and everybody believed him. I was young. At the age of fourteen, I didn't know any better. Everybody was happy for us even though it was against my will. He started trying to have relationship with me.

At that time, I was very frustrated because I wanted to go home, but I didn't know how to get back home or even how to contact with my parents. Her sister did not help me go back home. The man and I did not get married. I didn't want to marry him, but I was forced to stay with him.

One day, the sister and her husband had to move to another country. So her father, mother, and uncle had to move to another city; and they forced me to come with them. I didn't have any choice but to go with them. Because I didn't know how to get back home and I was not familiar with the place, I decided to go with them. We lived with his other sister. I thought that I was farther away from home. I thought to myself that I would definitely not be able to go back home. I was so scared, homesick, miserable, and unhappy. I missed my parents.

One day, three months later, I remember leaving the house at one o'clock in the morning. It was very dark; it was hard for me to see the road, but as I was walking, I was so glad that the moon was bright enough to help me see in the darkness. I thanked God that I was able to see my path to get to wherever I needed to go.

I was thinking of leaving him and never coming back. As I was walking on the street, I saw a huge church. When I saw it, for some reason, I felt peace. I remember coming toward the door, and surprisingly, the door was open. There was nobody in there except me. I felt like God left the door open for me. I went to the corner, and I curled myself up like an unborn baby from my mother's womb on the floor. I was praying and asking God to help me. I was so scared. I didn't know where to go. I didn't really want to go back to that man again. I prayed to the Lord that He would send me back to my parents. I didn't know how to get back home. I didn't have any money to buy a ticket for the bus, and I didn't even know where the bus was located. I felt so desperate, lost, confused, and alone.

After I prayed, I decided to come back to their house because it was dark, and I didn't know where to find the bus station anyway. But when I came back, his dad was waiting for me; he called me to come toward him. When I got closer to him, he immediately hit my face for leaving the house; his dad didn't want me to leave the house. I had bruises all over my face, and I was in so much pain that day. Since then, I never tried to go anywhere because I was so scared of them.

One month later, they decided that I should do something. They wanted me to go to work. They decided that I should sell street food, and I did. I sold a lot of desserts to the neighborhood, and people started to get to know me. When his parents saw that I was doing well and making a lot of money, I earned their trust, and I was allowed to go beyond the neighborhood so I could make more money—and I did make more money. I went outside the neighborhood and made more money than before, and I was so glad to be able to see different people. There were not many women in the neighborhood, and if there was one, there were inside the house.

One day, as I was selling food outside the neighborhood, I met this man who was probably around thirty-five years old. I asked him if he knew the bus to get to my hometown, and he said yes. He said that he could also take me there if I wanted. I was very happy, and I asked him if He could take me there, and he said yes. But he wanted me to come the night before so we could leave first thing in the morning because he had to go to work very early the next day. It was also on the way to the bus where I was going, so I said okay.

That night, there was a moment that I changed my mind because I didn't know the man. I was desperate yet afraid that I might not be able to go back home, so I thought that this was my chance to do so. I decided to go with him. So that night, I snuck out of the house, and I brought some of my clothes. Then I went to this man's house. The man let me stay at his house before we left in the morning. But that night, the man raped me. I was very confused as to why the man would do that. I was very upset, but there was nothing I could do.

The following morning, the man took me to the bus station where the bus goes to my city; he paid for my bus ticket and gave me some money and food for my travel. While I was sitting in the bus, I started to cry. I noticed my tears coming down from my cheeks, and suddenly, I was having a flashback of what had happened to me while I was with the family. I felt like I was hurt, abandoned, and snatched away from my family. I thought about everything that had happened to me and what I left behind—the man, His father, and His mother. The whole time, I felt lost and confused, and I had anxiety. I was trying to find life in my situation.

The bus passed by places with all the trees and the mountains; my heart was full of pain, as I watched the trees and the mountains that was passing by I starting to get sad, I asked God is to why those things had to happened to me. I remember going to church that early morning and prayed. I asked God why He did not protect me from that man who raped me. I asked God why He did not intervene in what was happening to me. I asked God why He allowed those things to happen to me. I asked God where He was all those times while bad things were happening to me.

As the bus continued its journey, I saw all those trees and mountains. I thought I saw the trees and mountains moving around as if they were talking to me, saying that God was there for me and was comforting me. After seeing those trees and mountains and hearing the voice of God, peace and comfort came to my soul. So I just wiped my tears away. I was anxious to get back home. I felt joy.

When I saw that I was almost in my hometown, I was very happy, and I jumped for joy of being home. Then I saw my city, and it looked familiar to me. I was overwhelmed with excitement, and hope came over me. I felt protected knowing that I was going to be close with my parents again. I knew my dad would protect me from that moment on.

When I saw my house, I felt like kissing the ground. I thanked God that He brought me back home. Even though bad things happened to me, God used them for my own good and to know that God loved me. When I got home, my parents gave me a hug and asked what happened to me. I did not tell my parents what happened to me. I was so embarrassed and just kept it to myself. I was so glad that God bring me back home.

Two months later, the man came to my house, but I was not home. He talked to my dad, telling him that I was his wife and that he wanted me to come back home with him. My dad was confused as to what the man was saying to him. I never told my dad about him. My dad was not mad or upset at the man; he just told him that I was home now and that it was my decision if I wanted to come back with him or not. Since I was not with him, my dad told Him that I was not going with Him, and He asked the man to leave.

Later, my dad confronted me about the man, and I told him what happened to me in the city. After I told my dad everything, I looked at him, thinking that he would get mad at me. Instead, I saw my dad's eyes full of tears, and he prayed for me.

And that was the last time I heard from the man.

I asked God to forgive him, and I learned to forgive the man, and I move on with my life. Forgiveness set me free from all the fears I was experiencing.

DANIEL 9:17-19

Now, our God, hear the prayers and petitions of Your servant. For Your sake O, Lord, look with favor on Your desolate sanctuary. Give ear, O God, and hear; open Your eyes and see the desolation of the City that bears Your Name. we do not make a requests of You because we are righteous, but because of Your great Mercy. O Lord, Listen! O Lord, forgive! O Lord hear and act! For Your sake, O My God, do not delay, because Your City and Your people bear Your Name.

PSALM 57:1

Have mercy on me, my God, have mercy on me, for in you I take refuge. I will take refuge in the shadow of your wings until the disaster has passed.

YOU AND GOD

PSALM 139:1–18

You have searched me, LORD, and you know me. You know when I sit and when I rise; you perceive my thoughts from afar. You discern my going out and my lying down; you are familiar with all my ways. Before a word is on my tongue you, LORD, know it completely. You hem me in behind and before, and you lay your hand upon me. Such knowledge is too wonderful for me, too lofty for me to attain. Where can I go from your Spirit? Where can I flee from your presence? If I go up to the heavens, you are there; if I make my bed in the depths, you are there. If I rise on the wings of the dawn, if I settle on the far side of the sea, even there your hand will guide me, your right hand will hold me fast. If I say, "Surely the darkness will hide me and the light become night around me," even the darkness will not be dark to you; the night will shine like the day, for darkness is as light to you. For you created my inmost being; you knit me together in my mother's womb. I praise you because I am fearfully and wonderfully made; your works are wonderful, I know that full well. My frame was not hidden from you when I was made in the secret place, when I was woven together in the depths of the earth. Your eyes saw my unformed body; all the days ordained for me were written in your book before one of them came to be. How precious to me are your thoughts, God! How vast is the sum of them! Were I to count them they would outnumber the grains of sand—when I awake, I am still with you.

How good and precious to know that God is thinking about you . . .

GOD AND YOU

My beloved child, I knew you before the universe form and began. I knew very well, when and where are your grandparents and your father and your mother fell in love with each other. I knew every move, every activity, every attitude, every character, and every detail about you. When I thought of you, I put together My love and My power to make, create, and mold you in your mother's womb. It is I who created you, made you, and formed you. I created you into My Image. I know the number of your hairs. I AM the one who blesses you and loves to see you grow. You are beautiful in My sight, and your beauty and love radiate in the core of My eyes. When I see you, I immediately jump with joy and love because I see your destiny and your future in My will, my purpose, and they are all good in My throne.

I even give you the huge blessings of joy, faith, gift, and talent to fulfill them; and no one can take them away from you. I will do it, and I will perform it immediately in your favor. I always want you to be ready and prepared for new and good things that I will give and make for you. My heart and my word concerning you, it was settled in my heart and in my kingdom, and in my throne in heaven and on earth. You are my beautiful and precious child. I desire you, I AM pleased with you, I AM so proud of you for being Mine, My commitment to you is to show you everything about Me—who I AM, what I AM, and when I AM. I have given you My heart and My kingdom.

When your world is upside down, you can trust Me and lean on Me to be there for you. You can learn so much about Me. I will be your Father, your healer, your restorer, your provider, your deliverer, your redeemer, your husband, and your King. Delight yourself with my Word, for it is the path and direction for your destiny and your future. Be like a tree growing by a river and you will be fruitful and prosper in all that you do.

I love you, My child.

Your Heavenly ABBA, FATHER

CHAPTER 8

I AM SOLD

I worked for this family of five as a live-in housekeeper in a city of the Philippines. I worked Mondays through Sundays from nine to five. I worked for them for six months.

One day, I decided to go to High school for the night classes. My boss let me go to school and decided to pay for my full tuition and also my books, but not the uniforms. The school wanted the students to wear uniforms. On my first day of school, my teacher threw an eraser at me because I was not wearing a uniform. After my boss paid for my tuition and books, my boss didn't have enough money to buy my uniform. So I did not go to school for two weeks because I didn't have the uniform. So I tried to save some money.

I thought going to school was going to be fun. I realized it was not easy; the good thing about it, though, is that I got to learn a lot of stuff, things that I didn't know before. I also got to meet a lot of students. One in particular was this girl who was beautiful, active, and vibrant. She wanted me to be her friend. One day, she took me to the city where the soldiers had a party and went to the clubs and bars. I came with her to work for this one club. She introduced me to the manager, and the manager hired me on the spot because he thought that I was a beautiful woman. So I start working that same night. The whole night, I was just sitting on a chair watching a lot of women and soldiers dancing on the dance floor.

Then my friend came toward me and introduced me to this one American soldier; the soldier asked me to dance with him. I was so scared because I had never been in a club before, and I didn't know how to dance and even how to speak English. And I also didn't know how to talk to the soldier. I was very shy and humble. I remember talking to the soldier at the club, and all I could say was "yes." I also moved my head and hands to communicate with him. I thought working at the club was not for me because I did not know how to speak English very well. I told my friend that I could not work there anymore, and she told me that it was okay and that it would get better later. She tried to give me some comfort, so I tried working at the club once more.

One evening, the manager of the club sold me to a soldier for ₱600 (Philippine pesos). I did not know what all the things happening to me meant. I did not even know that the manager just sold me to go with the man—all I knew was that I had to go with the man wherever he would take me. I remember he brought me to other clubs and bars, and we drank alcohol all night long. At the end of the night, the man took me to a hotel. He already paid for the hotel, but I did not want to go with him; he kept telling me to come with him, but I did not. Instead, I started walking toward the club where I worked. I was terrified and also drunk that night because I never drank alcohol before in my life.

The man followed me all the way to the club. There, I saw him talking to my manager. I thought that my manager would get mad at me and fired me. Instead, the manager sold me again for ₱600, and he told me that I needed to go with the man again. I did what my manager told me. I went with him again, and we came back to the hotel. I told the man that I was a virgin, hoping the man would not touch me. The man showed respect for me because he did not touch me that night. I thanked God for His goodness and kindness over me. That night, I went home with peace.

One day, I met a woman who shared with me that she saw me coming to America. I was amazed that she could see my future. Many years later, God did fulfill His glory. I came to America. And my story was just beginning.

PSALM 28:7

The Lord is my strength and my shield; my heart trusts in Him, and He helps me. My heart leaps for joy, and with my song I praise Him.

PSALM 9:9-10

The Lord is a refuge for the oppressed, a stronghold in times of trouble. Those who Your name will trust in You, for You, Lord, have never forsaken those who seek You.

PSALM 138:8

The Lord will vindicate me; your love, Lord, endures forever—do not abandon the works of your hands.

God knows you destiny and your future; and God has a dream, a plan, and a purpose for your life.

PRAYER

Dear heavenly Father,

Your love, compassion, Your authority, and Your power have been revealed to us like never before. The deity of your wisdom and the knowledge from Your heart have been given to us, and for that, we are faithful to Your will in our life.

Heavenly Father, I thank You for loving, protecting, and healing us. Thank You because the works of the enemy failed through Your nailed hands. Thank You for guarding us with the blood of Your words and actions. Thank You for teaching and leading us, and with your scepter, we have found Your power poured out over us. Thank You for giving us your wisdom and purpose to let us know that we are worthy in Your sight. We love you Jesus, In Jesus' name. Amen.

CHAPTER 9

COMING TO AMERICA

I was telling my friend again that I didn't want to work in the club anymore after the incidents, but she insisted that I should continue going to the club with her.

Three weeks later, my friend introduced me to this soldier; he was very handsome and very easy to get along with. Every woman wanted him, but he asked for me. So we got to know each other. Three months later, we fell in love. I was very happy being in love with him. But he had to go back where he was stationed, but that did not stop us from loving each other; we decided to start writing each other. Three months later, he surprised me by coming back to the Philippines to visit me.

He stayed in my house. One day, he asked my father if he could marry me, and my dad told him to ask me if I wanted to marry him. So he came to me, he went down on his knees, and asked me to marry him. But I said no because I was so scared to come to America. I was so afraid that I might get lost again and not be able to come back home and see my family again. He was very sad going back to where he was station.

Three months later, he came back to the Philippines again; he stayed with us in our house so he didn't have to stay in a hotel. This time, he gathered all my family, including my aunt and cousins, my parents and my sister and my brothers. He bent down on one knee again and asked me to marry him in front of everybody. Everybody was shouting for me to say "yes" to him. I felt so much joy and comfort toward him, so I finally said yes! I was the happiest woman in the world at that moment of my life.

He was so excited when we got engaged. He immediately wanted me to get my passport and to take care of my papers for me to come to America. But his job gave him only fifteen days to stay in the Philippines. He was helping me process my papers before he went back to where he was stationed. He didn't want to leave with my papers are not being finished yet. He tried to help me, but he had to go back to his job.

In 1985, after I finished processing all my papers, he decided to pay for my plane tickets. Then I finally went to the Philippine airport. I was so scared about riding the airplane, but at the same time, I was happy knowing that I would be with him. It was my first time riding an airplane; it was a good experience for me.

After the airplane landed in America, I remember seeing so many people that I couldn't find him. I decided to sit on a bench and wait for him to pick me up because I thought he was running late. I tried to be brave without my parents. While I was waiting for Andrew at the airport, I realized that he was actually at the airport watching me the whole time. I had no idea what he was thinking when he was watching me. He approached me when there were only fewer people in the place and introduced himself to me. I was so glad when I saw him. I barely recognize him. I thought that he gained a little weight, but he looked more handsome than ever before. I felt safe with him.

As we passed by the city, I saw these beautiful buildings. I felt blessed to have a chance to see such beautiful buildings and beautiful landscapes. I was amazed because I had never seen those kinds of buildings and landscapes before. When my fiancé and I got to our destination, I saw this beautiful home; it was white, and it was our new home. I was very happy and filled with joy because I never had a beautiful home like that before in my whole life. Back home, our house had rocks on the side; so every time it rained, the whole house was flooded. Coming to America was a blessing for me. I was amazed by all the good things I saw.

Three months later, we got married, and it was a beautiful wedding. I was a very happy bride. I could not have asked for more; it was a perfect wedding for me. We got married at the church. Only his family came to the wedding because we got married right away.

Later on, I started learning how to use appliances like the microwave, stove, washer, and dryer. We didn't have them in our house in the Philippines, and I also had never seen them before. I remember my hair being wet one day, and I didn't know that there was a blow-dryer that I could use to dry my hair with. At that time, it was winter, and it was very cold for me to go outside with my hair wet. I felt l like a little three- or four-year-old child that didn't know anything and like I had to start all over again. It was like a new beginning for me being in America.

SNOWSTORM

One day, there was a snowstorm. When I saw snow for the first time in my life, I was fascinated by how beautiful the snow was. But as many days went by, the snow did not stop falling. It kept falling down from the heavens for many weeks. When it did not stop falling, I thought that it was going to be the end of the world. I started to panic. I was very scared of the snow. I thought that we were going to get buried in it because there was so much snow. I had never seen any snow in my whole life.

One day, we lost the power. Andrew decided to go to his parents' house in the snowstorm, but his car would not start at all; his car broke down. But that didn't stop him from wanting to go to his parents'. So he decided to hitchhike on the street. Somebody stopped to give us a ride; the man had a truck. I was sitting inside the truck, and Andrew was sitting outside because there was not enough space inside for him; He was very cold being outside the truck. The man dropped us off on a street a little farther up his parents' house. I couldn't wait to get inside his parents' house because it was freezing outside. Because I didn't want Andrew to get upset with me, I was being obedient to him. So we walked on the snow. There was ice, which was very slippery for me to walk on, but I still needed to walk. I was already wearing two layers of clothes and four heavy jackets, but I was still cold. I was crying as we were walking down the street. I noticed my tears were turning into ice. I was very sad because I was very cold. I felt like I was going to get sick. I asked him if I could go back home, but he said no. We walked for a long time. I don't know how long.

By the time we got to his parents' house, I felt like my whole body was very stiff. I could not move my lips, and they were turning blue. His parents removed my clothes right away, put a heavy blanket on me, and brought me near to the fireplace. I thought I was going to die because I was feeling very sick and my whole body was hurting. I could hardly even talk. Being in a snowstorm was a very bad experience for me at the time. But now, I'm okay. I can handle bad snowstorms. I love and enjoy snow now.

One day, I was feeling sad and lonely. I was missing my family in the Philippines. I wished they were in America having fun with me, especially on my birthday and Christmas. It was the worst days of my life, not having my family around. I felt all alone. But at the same time, I loved being here in America, especially when I got to meet other people. One day, I met this wonderful lady; she volunteered to pick me up and take me places and then drop me off at my house because I could not drive and didn't have a driver's license or a car. So I was so glad that the lady wanted to pick me up and take me home after.

One day, at around six o'clock in the morning, the woman stopped at a fast-food place to get something to eat. I was amazed that she could order food from the drive-through. I did not know that people could actually order food outside the fast-food establishment because I have never seen anything like it before. At the time I was growing up, we didn't have fast-food restaurants like that in my country. I asked her if she could order any food at the drive thru, and she said yes. I was amazed by it. After experiencing that, since then, I've always wanted to go to that place. I was fascinated by it. All I could say was, "Wow." I had never experienced that before. I started to like America even greater.

America is a good place to live in, and I wish my whole family is with me to experience what I'm experiencing and see all the good things about America. I like being in America, and *I love America*.

GENESIS 12:1–9

The Lord had said to Abram, "Go from your country, your people and your father's household to the land I will show you. "I will make you into a great nation, and I will bless you; I will make your name great, and you will be a blessing. I will bless those who bless you, and whoever curses you I will curse; and all peoples on earth will be blessed through you." So Abram went, as the LORD had told Him; and Lot went with Him. Abram was seventy-five years old when He set out from Harran. He took His wife Sarai, His nephew Lot, all the possessions they had accumulated and the people they had acquired in Harran, and they set out for the land of Canaan, and they arrived there. Abram traveled through the land as far as the site of the great tree of Moreh at Shechem. At that time the Canaanites were in the land. The LORD appeared to Abram and said, "To your offspring I will give this land." So He built an altar there to the LORD, who had appeared to Him. From there He went on toward the hills east of Bethel and pitched His tent, with Bethel on the west and Ai on the east. There He built an altar to the LORD and called on the name of the LORD. Then Abram set out and continued toward the Negev.

DEUTERONOMY 28:8

The Lord will send a blessing on your barns and on everything you put your hand to. The Lord your God will bless you in the land He is giving.

When God speaks, you must follow because God knows everything about you, and He is in control over your life. You have been chosen to carry His glory. God will take you to the place you have never been before in your life, and there, He will show you His mighty act of power over your life.

God wants you to anticipate for His love, kindness, and blessings. Through the inner core of His compassion, there is joy for you. Hope with God is the reason for you to have life.

ROMANS 15:13

May the God of hope fill you with all joy and peace as you trust in Him, so that you may overflow with hope by the power of the Holy Spirit.

PROVERBS 16:20

Whoever gives heed to instruction prospers, and blessed is the one who trusts in the LORD.

CHAPTER 10

TILL' DEATH DO US PART

In 1986, I remember Andrew cooked food in the Crock-Pot one night; and that whole night, the meat was slowly cooking. The smell of the food was making me hungry. When I woke up that morning, I decided to bring some food with me to eat. When I came back home in the late afternoon, Andrew was very mad at me because I ate a little bit of the food he cooked; He said that it was for dinner. I was trying my best with the little English I knew how to explain to him that I accidently forgot to tell him that I ate some of the food and I did not know that he would get mad at me for eating the food. I thought that it would be okay with him. I assumed everything was okay with him because I thought it was only a food. But I was wrong. I was in a hurry, and he was also sleeping that morning. It did not occur to me how he would feel about me eating the food he cooked. With my poor English, I managed to explain to him what I thought and begged him to forgive me, but it was too late.

Because of that, the demons came over him. He snapped and attacked me. He started screaming at me, which brought fear into my soul. He was very angry, hostile, and violent toward me that day; and he had a hard time controlling himself.

A FISH WITHOUT WATER

I remember late that afternoon, standing beside him in the bedroom, shocked came to me when he suddenly in the blink of my eyes, picked me up from the floor, he threw me on the bed, and jumped on top of me. I remember all those things, and I will never forget how I was struggling with him. We were fighting on the bed, I was screaming. He was very strong for me. I was getting tired and weak until I could not fight anymore. He took advantages of my weaknesses; He put my legs between his legs, and he grabbed one pillow from the right side of the bed and he put it over my face. I knew then that he was trying to suffocate me. While he was on top of me, he pushed his hands over the pillow with all of his might and power. Having his hands on my face with the pillow, it made my soul being broken and destroyed. He stayed on that position for a long time. I was having a hard time breathing I tried to wiggle my whole body around, but as if like I cannot move them. I even tried to hit his chest and other parts of his body. I tried to move my hands and legs, hoping that he would let me go. And the more I struggled with him, the harder he pressed the pillow onto my face.

I tried to scream as loudly as I could, but with the pillow on my face, I could not, I did not have a chance. I could scream only under the pillow, and I could hear my own shattered voice. I felt like I screamed so much under the pillow that I was losing my voice little by little. I was so scared, broken, shattered, confused, and hopeless while my face was under the pillow. My voice was fading away; his hands and the pillow muted me all the way to death. I felt like a fish without the water. I felt like I was drowning, going deeper into the sea. I was dying little by little. I felt like I was dying quietly. I was desperate for help, but I knew that no one will help me, I knew at that moment that my life was over.

While the pillow was on my face, darkness was all around me. The fear, pain, shock, and confusion brought back memories of my dad. I saw myself talking to my dad. I remember all the promises I made to him—that I would come back home for him and for everybody and that we all would be together again. I also promised my dad that I would bring them to America. I told him that I wanted to make a difference for them and that I wanted to help them. I told my dad that I loved him. But with the pillow on my face, I thought that all the promises I made to my dad would be broken. I knew that I was going to die that day. I knew that I was not strong enough to fight for my life. I felt like my body was fading away from the face of this earth at that moment.

I was very weak and could not fight anymore. I knew right away that I was going to be with the Lord and that I would die without a voice.

While Andrew's hands with the pillow still on my face, I suddenly heard the faint sound of someone knocking at the door. For me, it was a faint sound because the pillow was on my face, but that person was knocking at the door very loudly. When I heard that, my heart was revived. I felt hope that someone was going to rescue me after all. But I was wrong—the more the person knocked, the harder Andrew pushed the pillow on my face. I felt like he had a mission at that moment, and that mission was to kill me. Because he knew someone was knocking on the door and he didn't want that person to know that he was going to kill me, he was in a hurry to complete his mission. I was terrified of him. He knew that somebody was knocking. He kept pushing the pillow harder and harder into my face. At the same time, the person kept knocking many times at the door. I was fading in and out because Andrew was a very strong man, and I knew that there was absolutely no hope for me. I felt like the person at the door was too late in rescuing me. I thought God was too late in rescuing me.

That horrifying experience in my life was like what Jesus experienced while He was hanging on the cross, waiting for God the Father to rescue Him. But God the Father did not intervene. When Jesus was on the cross calling on God, saying, "Eloi, Eloi, lama sabachthani?" (Which means "My God, My God, why have You forsaken Me?), Jesus felt like God the Father abandoned Him. He felt like that He was alone on the cross, as if God was not going to help Him. That was exactly what I was feeling—that God had abandoned me. I felt like God was not going to rescue me and that He was not going to feel pity for me. I felt deserted from Him. I felt like God the Father had forsaken me.

I DIED

So in that horrifying moment of my life, because Andrew wouldn't stop pushing the pillow on my face, I was getting weak and weaker until finally I stopped moving and breathing. I actually finally died—I died silently. When Andrew realize and saw me being breathless and lifeless lying on the bed, without any sounds, no movement, and no life, that was when he finally removed the pillow from my face. He knew right away that I was dead. Andrew did not call somebody or ambulance to see if I was okay or was concerned about my body since he knew that I was dead within twenty three seconds. Instead, he just walked away, satisfied.

My spirit lifted up from my body; I saw my body lying on the bed. I was just looking at my body. I was very confused, not knowing what to think. I saw Andrew coming down from the bed, and he decided to go to the door to see who was knocking at the door. When he opened the door, there stood a man from the church who was assigned to visit us that day. And it just happened that he was at our house at the right time and at the right place. I was amazed with God. I thought God was too late to protect me, but I was wrong, God was always on time to rescue me. God sent the man and His angel to rescue me before I died. God was on time to rescue me.

FLAMES OF FIRE

When Andrew opened the door, I immediately saw the "flames of fire of God" coming towards me. At that moment, I knew right away that I was face-to-face with God, that God Himself breathed on me so that I could live. Through His holy fire, my spirit immediately returned to my body. God brought me back to life, and my whole body was healed and restored. When God showed up in that moment I knew that there is nothing that the enemies of darkness can do to me. God is my protector. God was fighting for me I saw His love over me. God brings me back to life and that is how I can be able to breathe and that is how I was not dead, but alive in Him. When I saw the "fire of God," I realized that God did not abandon me or deserted me after all. God was with me the whole time. He was roaring and fighting for me against the hands of my enemy. I thanked God for rescuing and fighting for me from the hand of my enemy. I love God.

I was so glad that God sent the man to knock the door and it gives Andrew the time to leave my dead body alone on the bed, so that God can bring my body back to life. I was thinking that if Andrew still in our bedroom and God brings me back to life again while he still in our bedroom, I knew that Andrew will still kill me again. God is so smart, He is in control.

The man who was knocking at the door was my angel. He just waited for Andrew to open the door for him. It was through the "Flames of Fire of God" coming from the door that I came back to life. God revive me from death to life. God brought me back to life for His glory.

ANGELS PROTECTION

The promises of the Lord concerning angel to protect me, is been revealed to me at that hour. God is so good.

God command His angels concerning you to guard you in all His ways.

God save You from the fowler's snare and from the deadly pestilence.

He covered you with His feathers, and under His wings that you have found refuge in Him.

Because of His faithfulness you felt His shield and rampart over you.

You conquered death and you win life of victory over you.

God is supernaturally manifesting Himself to let you know that He had a power to perform miracles.

When Andrew opened the door, he immediately closed it. He didn't want the man to know that he had just left me lifeless on the bed, that he had just killed me. Andrew went outside to talk to the man. And while he was talking to the man outside, in the meantime I was so glad that I am alive. I was trying to get myself back to normal. I was so glad that I was able to breathe again. I was coughing a lot as I was trying to swallow my saliva, but I felt like there was no saliva for me to swallow; it was so painful for me to swallow my saliva. My mouth was very dry, and I was very weak. My whole body was shaking intensely. I tried my best to be strong and get myself together. When I felt like I had enough strength, I slowly tried to crawl myself down from the bed.

I went toward the window to see what was happening outside the house. I was concerned for the person who was knocking at the door because Andrew was very angry at that time. I was afraid that he might hurt the man also. When I peeked outside the window I saw Andrew's hands moving as he was talking to the man, but I could not hear what he was saying. I was thinking that I should go outside and talk to the man, but I was afraid that Andrew would hurt me again and that he might also hurt the man. So I decided not to go outside.

After Andrew talked to the man, the man left and went toward to his car. I watched the man leave until he faded away from my sight. I started to cry when I did not see his car anymore. I was very sad and afraid. I was hoping that the man would come back to save me from Andrew's hands. I was very terrified, and I was losing hope. I thought for sure that Andrew was going to try to kill me again when he came back in the house.

Ever since the man left, I didn't know what to do. I thought about running away, but I didn't know where to go. I thought about hiding, but where and how? I was very scared for my life. I didn't know anybody I could ask help from. I felt like I was in a dead-end situation; there was no place to hide or escape to, and there was no hope. I felt like I didn't have any energy.

I didn't know anybody in America except Andrew. He was the only person I knew in America that I thought I could depend on to protect me. I thought he was the perfect man for me and that he was the only person I knew who could help, love, comfort, direct, and guide me. I thought that he was the person I could depend on to be there for me, to teach me, and to show me the way. I thought he was the husband that I could trust and show my love and affection for. I thought that he was the person I wanted to do those things for me. I was wrong. Instead, he was the one who was hurting, betraying, deserting, rejecting, abandoning, mocking, and insulting me. He was the one who didn't care about me and didn't love me and the one who wanted to kill me—and the one who actually killed me.

I felt like I was a worthless wife in his hands. I was lost and confused that day. I realized then that I married the wrong man. I realized that I didn't know him. I remember he told me that he loved me, yet he was the one who hurt me and even desired to kill me. I was very confused. I did not know what to do. At that time, I did not know that getting help was just a phone call away, but I didn't know whom to call. I felt like a three-year-old child with fear in my heart who doesn't know anything. Instead of me running away, I found myself sitting on a chair, waiting for him to come in to see what he was going to do to me next.

EYE TO EYE WITH THE ENEMY

When I saw Andrew opening the front door to come back inside the house, I was shaking while he was coming toward me; he saw me sitting on the chair from our bedroom. I remember looking at him, and my eyes weren't blinking as I was staring at him the whole time. I was waiting to see what he was going to do to me. I was scared and terrified of him; my whole body was shaking, and my heart was pounding very hard. I thought I was going to faint. The whole time I was staring at him, I was thinking that he would for sure is going to kill me again. I was not sure what I was going to do.

I was just sitting on the chair, waiting for him to hurt me again. At that time, I was hoping that he would not touch, hurt, or try to kill me again. I was thinking of running away, but I didn't know where to go. And I knew that with my little English. I definitely will not be able to go far. I wished that I had a friend who could help me at that time, and I wished that my parents were with me so that they could help me. I felt so helpless and hopeless.

As I continued staring at him while sitting on the chair, he was also staring back at me. As he passed by me going to towards the kitchen, I didn't know what he was thinking. I tried not to do anything that would make him angry. He did not stop to speak to me or to comfort me to see if I was okay or if I needed to go to the hospital to see a doctor. He did not know that he had killed me and that God revive me back to life; all he knew was that I was alive. He passed by me as if he just saw a tree, as if he did not see me sitting on the chair, as if I did not exist. But then at the same time, I think that he was shocked seeing me sitting on the chair alive, it's something that he did not expect.

I finally looked at him intensely as if I saw his soul looking right at me. I felt like he just saw the Holy Spirit through me. I felt like I was looking at his soul. As I was looking at him, I felt like he was a totally different person; he was not like he was before who looked like an angry tiger, getting ready to eat me alive. He saw me, and he did not hurt me. It was as if God did something good to him. After calming himself down for three hours in the kitchen, he immediately realized what he did to me; the Holy Spirit talked to him. He came crying to me and begging me to forgive him. Fear and love drew him to wanting me back in his life. He tried to ask me to stay with him and not to leave him. He was broken inside his heart; he felt really bad for what he did to me. He was glad that I was not dead, but he did not know that I actually died. I was so glad for the man who knocked at the door; he was my angel. In the blink of my eye, I saw Andrew being changed. I felt like God removed the demons from him. I cried with joy, and tears flowed down like a river on my face.

I was so glad that Andrew was changed and that the demons were out of his body at that moment. I was so glad that I was still alive because of God's love and kindness toward me and that He performed a supernatural miracle for me. Jesus said the following to his disciples:

MARK 9:1

And He said to them, "Truly I tell you, some who are standing here will not taste death before they see that the kingdom of God has come with power."

GOD WINS THE VICTORY

God is never late for me. He heard my cries. He came to me, and He rescued me. God wins the victory over the enemy. God's love for me brings life, strength, and hope into my soul.

Because I did not know where to go and what to do in that situation, I decided to forgive Andrew and stay with him even though I still feared him. I was so scared that if I tried to leave him, he would hurt or kill me again, and I also did not have a place to go. I did not tell anyone, even his parents and mine, what had happened to us. I did not share it with the woman I knew at that time. I learned to be silent, being a broken and battered woman. After what happened to me, sometimes I had bad dreams about a man trying to kill me but never succeeding.

After seeing the man (my angel) fading away from my sight, I thanked God that the man came and knocked on the door to get our attention. I call the man my angel sent by God for me. The man was ordained to be there to protect me. The angel brought me back to life. Somebody was supposed to come with the man to visit us because his church always had two people visiting people and never just one person. But in my situation, God spoke to only one man concerning me. God spoke only to him to come to my house to protect me.

I was thinking about the man is to how and when God spoke to him concerning me at the right time and at the right place to come in my house, and how miraculously managed from where he is and drive to come to my house on time to protect me. All I can say is God loves me. He is in control of my life. I was so glad that he was being obedient to the Lord to visit us that day. I thanked God for him.

I thought about it in a deeper way of all those things that was happening to me. I thought that if God did not bring me back to life that day, I asked myself, what would have happened to my dead body? What would Andrew have done with it? I thought that maybe he would have buried me somewhere in the woods, under the ground or under the water. Thinking about those things that could've happened to my body without God rescuing me made me shake tremendously. I felt like my whole body started to melt down and melt away, and I felt the tears of God's love for me. It brought my knees to the ground, and I said to Him, "THANK YOU LORD FOR SAVING MY LIFE. I OWE MY LIFE TO YOU, MY CREATOR MY SAVIOR JESUS CHRIST OF NAZARETH." I defeated death, and I won the victory over my life. God has a purpose for me. I did not choose God. But God chose me to be alive for His glory.

I found out the name of the man (my angel), and I tried to look for him so I could thank him for saving my life. But I have not found him yet until to this day. But I know that God will make away and I will meet him again.

It was the worst moment of my life. I was horrified and sad. Since then, I've been having anxiety and feared to all men. I was very confused. I thought that Andrew loved me and that we loved each other. At that moment, I realized that he did not love me and it hurts me. I felt so low, worse than the first time it happened to me while I was still in the Philippines. I felt like I was nobody, and nobody wanted to care for me. I cried every day and night thinking about my dad. I felt like I let him down. I was embarrassed and ashamed to myself, and I asked myself why I let this happen to myself again. Why did I leave my parents again? There was so much blame and regret in my heart. I loved my dad. I always wanted my dad to be proud of me. But at that moment, I felt like my dad was disappointed in me. But at the same time, I knew that my dad loved me and was praying for me.

I didn't have any money to buy a plane ticket, and I didn't know anyone who could help me. Also, I didn't know how to get back to my country. I didn't know how to get to the airport. At that moment, I felt like coming home to the Philippines right away so I could tell my dad that I was sorry. I felt like I could not move forward. I felt like if I left Andrew, I would not have shelter. I was so concerned about myself, not knowing what was going to happen to me from that moment on. I felt like I didn't have a choice but to stay with Andrew. I was just hoping that he would not hurt me again. I needed a miracle from God. I stayed with Andrew in that house because of the fear and love I had for him.

One day, I met Christy, and she came to my house. She went to the same church I go, and she gave me her telephone number. I was so happy to meet her, and I kept her number in my heart.

One week later, the landlord told us to move out of our apartment.

COUNTING THE COST

Later on, we moved to Andrew's parents' house. While we were staying there, I tried to help by cleaning the house. I tried my best to clean the house in the mornings and also in the evenings before I went to bed. This went on every day for months. One night, I did not clean the dishes. I was very tired that night, so I decided to go to bed early. So I went to bed without washing the dishes, not knowing what would happen early that morning after I woke up. What happened to me next, it terrified me.

The following morning, I decided to cook breakfast for everybody. Andrew was still sleeping; his brother came to me and, with a harsh voice, demanded for me to wash the dishes immediately. I said no to him. I told him not until I finished cooking. I told him that I could not cook and wash dishes at the same time; his brother was so angry with me because I cannot wash the dishes right away. But he really wanted me to wash the dishes that morning. I asked him to wait for me to wash dishes until I was finished cooking. I was not very happy with him. I was thinking of standing up for myself to let him know that he could not treat me like a slave. Because he couldn't wait for me to wash the dishes, he suddenly acted unkindly toward me. He was so angry with me that he went to his room, grabbed a big long gun, and put it beside him for me to see. I was so scared and terrified of him, so I rushed to our bedroom. Andrew was sleeping at that time. I tried to wake him up to tell him about his brother threatening me with a long gun. He woke up and went to the kitchen, and he talked to his brother. When his brother told him about the dishes, Andrew took his side. He did not defend me or protect me from his brother; instead, he came toward me, and he was very angry with me. He asked me is to why I did not wash the dishes when his brother commanded me to do so. I explained to him that I was cooking food for everybody and that I couldn't cook and wash the dishes at the same time. I told him that I was going to wash the dishes after I cooked. I saw from his eyes and action that he was very mad at me. I was shocked; my body started to shake. Fear came over me. I thought Andrew would help me, but instead, he did not protect me from his brother; he was the one who wanted to fight me. I felt lost and confused, and I felt deserted by him. I felt all alone, trying to fight for my life so I could stay alive again.

I thought Andrew did not want me to talk back to him and explain anything to him or even say anything. I felt like I made him even angrier by explaining to him what I was going to do. If I knew that it would cost so much trouble not following his brother's command, I would have done it right away. I wished that I just washed the dishes so that we would not have any problem. I had so much regret; my poor mind could not comprehend what was happening to me. I was in another country, always trying to fight for my life. I didn't know when all this was going to end. I told them that I was going to wash the dishes immediately so that I could please them.

When I was about to start washing the dishes, I started to feel sad. I noticed tears were pouring down on my cheeks, and I was blaming myself. I thought that I was the problem and that it was my fault all the time. I didn't know that I would bring many problems to everybody because I was not able to wash the dishes right away. I didn't know that it was going to be this hard. I started to have anxiety. I was feeling weak, and I didn't have any words to say. I was giving up. I felt like I wanted everything in my life to end.

After washing all the dishes, I went to the living room, where Andrew was sitting on the couch. I felt like talking to him and I decided to sit with him and even tried to cuddle up with him while I was sitting on the couch resting with him. I found out that he was still felt angry with me. Because of so much anger in his heart he could not control himself and he starting to hurt me again. For whatever reason, I heard him start talking to himself, and suddenly he picked me up while I was sitting on the couch. Then he pushed me on the wall, and I crumbled down on the carpet. He grabbed me again from the floor, and he hit me on my face and threw me on the couch. And while I was on the couch, I saw his right hand, and he was getting ready to hit me with it on my face again. I looked at his brother to see if he was going to help me, but I did not see him moving or at least tried to help me, but he was just watching us.

When I saw Andrew coming towards me and ready to hit me, I acted right away, and I positioned myself to fight back. This time, I was ready to fight back; at that moment, I had strength to fight back. I felt like I was not scared of him anymore, I thought, *enough is enough. I have been hurt so many times.* I felt like I had energy to fight. I felt like it was my time to *rise up.* When I saw him getting closer and closer to me, I act quickly to raise my two legs up and kicked him as hard as I could in his privates; and I saw him kneeling down on the floor, touching his private part. He was in so much pain, and his brother was just watching us, and he did not try to hurt me or to stop me. I got up from the couch, and I went toward the living room, and I picked up my little purse hanging from the chair.

I took the opportunity while Andrew was still on the floor to get out of the house. I went to the door and I slammed the door and walked away. I run and I run and run as fast as I could. I did not look back, and there was no turning back for me. I was so scared of Andrew and to his brother that they might come after me. While I was fleeing from them, I decided to turn around to see if they were following me. I was so glad to see that they were not. That whole time I was running, I was thinking that they might both hunt and kill me. I had so much fear while I was fleeing from them. My whole body was intense and was shaking. I was very weak; my heart was pounding really hard. I felt like my whole body was like a grenade that it was about to explode with fear. I didn't have energy to fight anymore. I felt like I could not go on. I felt like the road was not going to end. I was running as fast as I can for my life.

I told myself if I could just reach the railroad track, that I would be saved. I ran for one mile until I reached the railroad. While I was in front of the railroad track, I had to make an executive decision, and I needed to do it fast. I was thinking about that I should turn to either the left or the right of the track to escape from the enemy. But I decided to go straight because I knew there was a store that had a telephone booth where I could make a phone call to the woman from the church to ask for help.

I was running so fast that I felt like I was losing my breath; my heart was pounding really hard, and my body was shaking again and again. As I was fleeing from them, I felt like I had fear and joy at the same time because I knew that I would have freedom from them. I thought about my clothes and family pictures I left behind; there would be another time, I thought, that I could come back and get them. I needed my clothes and especially my family pictures, but I knew that I could not come back to get them. I ran as fast as I could. I was running away for my life. I was running away for my freedom. I was running away for my hope until I saw the gas station with telephone booth at the end of the road.

As I was running for my freedom, I remember meeting Christy for the first time; she gave me her phone number. When I thought of her, my heart was revived, and she gave me hope. I was thinking of calling her, but something stopped me—I was concerned that she might call

Andrew to get me instead. Because I was desperate and needed help, I tried to take a chance to call Christy anyway. When I did, I was so glad that she answered the telephone because I was so concerned that Andrew might follow me and hurt me again. When I heard her voice, I jumped for joy. I knew I was safe at that moment. I told her what happened to me and Andrew; she was very concerned for me that she decided to called the pastor, who told her to pick me up. So Christy came and picked me up at the gas station, and then she took me to church so I could talk to the pastor. After I talked to the pastor, they helped me stay with one of the families at the church who had three children. I stayed with them and took care of their children. The family was pleased with me staying with them.

I had not heard from Andrew since then. And later on, we got a divorce. My battle with him was over.

For the first time in my life, I thought that I had found peace and that the battle was over. But I was wrong. I found out that the husband of the family I lived with had the wrong motives toward me; the man raped me while I lived with them. I could not tell anyone because I felt like I was nobody. I felt like I was worthless, and I also didn't know whom to tell. I was going to tell Christy, but I was too ashamed of myself. I felt like my whole life was shattered. I felt like I didn't want to know what was going to happen in my future. At that moment, I felt like I didn't have a future and that God didn't love me. I was feeling broken while deciding to look for another place to live.

As the years went by, I did not have the chance to stay connected to the church due to my poor English, I wanted to thank them from the bottom of my heart. I knew that without them, I would not be who I am right now. I knew that the angel was with them, and God was using them mightily concerning me.

Later on, I met a family with one baby; they let me take care of the baby, and I lived with them. I stayed with them for two years, taking care of their baby. God blessed me and gave me peace. The family loved me. I thanked God for keeping me alive and for His comfort, help, and cared toward me. I have found God's love, and His love has been with me the whole time.

God gave me the victory from death to life. Jesus has overcome the world, and I over come death.

I thank God for supernatural miracles that took place in my life. By bringing me back to life.

1 CORINTHIANS 15:55

O death, where is thy sting? O grave, where is thy victory?

PSALM 18:1–50

I love You, O Lord, my Strength. The Lord is my Rock, my Fortress and my Deliverer; my God is my Rock, in whom I take Refuge, He is my Shield and the Horn of my Salvation, my Stronghold. I call to the Lord, who is worthy of praise, and I am saved from my enemies. The cords of death entangled me; the torrents of destruction overwhelmed me. The cords of the grave coiled around me; the snares of death confronted me. In my distress I called to the Lord. I cried to the Lord; I cried to my God for help. From His temple He heard my voice; my cry came before Him, Into His ears.

The earth trembled and quaked, and the foundations of the mountain shook; they trembled because He was angry. Smoke rose from His nostrils; consuming fire came from His mouth, burning coals blazed out of it. He parted the heavens and come down; dark clouds were under His feet. He mounted the cherubim and flew; He soared on the wings of the wind. He made darkness His covering, His canopy around Him—the dark rain clouds of the sky. Out of the brightness of His presence clouds advanced, with hailstones and bolts of lightning. The Lord thundered from heaven; the voice of the Most High resounded. He shot His arrows and scattered the enemies, great bolts of lightning and routed them. The valleys of the sea were exposed and the foundations of the earth laid bare at Your rebuke, O Lord, at the blast of breath from nostrils. He reached down from on high and took hold of me; He drew me out of deep waters. He rescue me from my powerful enemy, from my foes, who were too strong for me. They confronted me in the day of my disaster, but the Lord was my support. He brought me out into a spacious place; He rescue me because He delighted in me. The Lord has dealt with me according to my righteousness; according to the cleanness of my hands He has rewarded me. For I have kept the ways of the Lord; I have not done evil by turning from my God. All His laws are before me; I have turned away from His decrees. I have been blameless before Him and have kept myself from sin. The Lord has rewarded me according to my righteousness, according to the cleanness of my hands in His sight. To the faithful you show yourself faithful, to the blameless you show yourself blameless, to the pure you show yourself pure, but to the crooked you show yourself shrewd. You save the humble but bring low those whose eyes are haughty. You, O Lord, keep my lamp burning; my God turns my darkness into light. With your help I can advance against a troop; with my God I can scale a wall. As for God, His way is perfect; the word of the Lord is flawless. He is a shield for all who take refuge in Him. For who is God besides the Lord? And who is the Rock except our God? It is God who arms me with strength and makes my way perfect. He makes my feet like the feet of a deer; He enables me to stand on the heights. He trains my hands for battle; my arms can bend a bow of bronze. You give me Your shield of victory, and your right hand sustains me; You stoop down to make me great. You broaden the path beneath me, so that my ankles do not turn. I pursued my enemies and overtook them; I did not turn back till they were destroyed. I crushed them so that they could not rise; they fell beneath my feet. You armed me with strength for battle; you made my adversaries bow at my feet. You made my enemies turn their backs in flight, and I destroyed my foes. They cried for help, but there was no one to save them—to the Lord, but He did not answer. I beat them as fine as dust borne on the wind; I poured them out like mud in the streets. You have delivered me from the attacks of the people; you have made me the head of nations; people I did not know are subject to me. As soon as they hear me, they obey me; foreigners cringe before me. They all lose heart; they come trembling from their strongholds. The Lord lives! Praise be to my Rock! Exalted be God my Savior! He is the God who avenges me, who subdues nations under me, who saves me from my enemies. You exalted me above my foes; from violent men You rescued me. Therefore I will praise you among the nations, O lord; I will sing praises to Your name. He gives His king great victories; He shows unfailing kindness to His anointed, to David and His descendants forever.

JOHN 16:33

"I have told you these things, so that in me you may have peace. In this world you will have trouble. But take heart! I have overcome the world."

REPENTANCE AND FORGIVENESS

From 1986 through 2017, Andrew kept that dark moment of his life from everybody. He never found peace for trying to murder me from all those years. He must've felt pain, regret, and guilt and had lifeless memories that drew him to try to find God and me so that he could at least ask for forgiveness so that he can find peace in his soul and so that God could set him free. But He never found God and me all those years. He thought that whole time that God was not with him and that demons were trying to creep into his life to bring destruction to him. He thought that I went back to my country after that; he knew that he could not ask for forgiveness from me. So he felt loss, broken, hopeless, helpless, and lifeless when he found out that I was gone for good, not knowing what was to come. He carried that guilt and shame for many years, and his soul cried out for deep things and purpose in his life. He tried to find a source to cover the shame, but nothing worked—the darkness was the same. He was still in the dark, without light. In his mind, death was his only solution. He was trying to end his life. But God intervened instead.

On December 14, 2017, after thirty three years of us not having any contact with each other. He came to my path by finding me on facebook. I saw his picture on my Facebook page. When I saw his picture, fear came over me right away. I was asking God is to why he showed up in my life again meant. I tried to avoid him. But on December 18, 2017, he left me a message on Facebook Messenger, asking me if I was the person he once knew. My heart was pounding very hard while I was reading his message; my whole body was shaking. I felt like my mind was frozen, darkness crippled me and it brings back the memories about him from all those years again in my life. I didn't know what to think of it. I asked myself, is to *why is it that this man trying to reach me again after all those years?* I thought for sure that he would try to kill me again, but I knew that he would not win this time because God was on my side. I came to God, and I prayed and ask Him what He wanted me to do in that situation—Andrew was the one who left me lying on the bed without life, the one who killed me, the one who had no fear of God, and now he suddenly showed up in my life again. God spoke to me within those two days, and He said to me that if God is for me, who can be against me? No one, God told me to talk to him. I was shocked. I asked God again to make sure that I was hearing Him right. Because I want to make sure, I wanted to be obedient to God, and I did respond to God and I thought that God wanted me to have another chapters of my life again.

So I reached out to Andrew. He wanted to say hello to me. The minute I heard his voice, I trembled before God; the first words that came out of my mouth were "Andrew, I forgive you." It was a beautiful moment of my life saying that I forgave him. As I was talking to him, I felt like the mountain of darkness in my life was coming down before my eyes. I was so glad that I knew God and that I had a relationship with Him. I was so glad that I was able to find in my heart to forgive Andrew. I was so glad that God taught me about forgiveness, grace and mercy. The scripture says in the following:

MATTHEW 18:15

"If your brother or sister sins go and point out their fault, just between the two of you. If they listen to you, you have won them over.

LUKE 23:34

Jesus said, "Father, forgive them, for they do not know what they are doing."

MICAH 7:18–1 9

Who is God like You, who pardon sin and forgives the transgression of the remnant of His inheritance? You do not stay angry forever but delight to show mercy. You will again have compassion on us; you will tread our sins underfoot and hurl all our iniquities into the depths of the sea.

JOHN 13:3

Jesus knew that the Father had put all things under His power, and that He had come from God and was returning to God.

MATTHEW 9:6

But I want you to know that the Son of Man has authority on earth to forgive sins." So He said to the paralyzed man, "Get up, take your mat and go home."

I was so glad that God gave me the power to forgive Andrew because God is a forgiving God. He gave me the power to overcome obstacles, challenges, and even death. I felt the love of God overshadow me. My God, my Almighty God picked me up from the deep waters and set me upon the rock. I cannot be shaken, I cannot be moved, I cannot be changed, and I am the unstoppable one. God is on my side, and He is my hero.

After Andrew receive my forgiveness from me, I felt like the pain of death that was crippled him was gone, and he felt love instead. He knew right away that God already forgave him. As we were sharing old the memories of our life, the Spirit of God came upon me, and I start sharing with him about Jesus. When Andrew showed himself to me again, this time, it was with love, hope, peace, healing, forgiveness, repentance, restoration, reconciliation, and for him to have freedom. He wanted God to set him free from the captivity. And God set him free. God revived, renewed, and refreshed him. He had found another chapter of his life to let go of the past and move on to the greater things. He broke down and bowed down to God. He asked God to forgive him, and he also asked for my forgiveness with tears in his eyes. God washed and cleansed him so that he can be whiter than snow, and he found that God forgave his sins. Andrew found God, and he gave himself to the Lord. God won over him. To God be the glory!

FORGIVENESS

Why do you want to forgive the person who did you wrong? Is it because you want your heart to be right, submissive, and obedient to the will of God over your life?

Forgiveness is for you to have the knowledge, wisdom, and revelation that Jesus Christ died for your sins.

You forgive the person who did you wrong because of your love for God Almighty.

Forgiveness is to have the dedication, passion and care for the heart of God.

Forgiveness is the key to have faith, peace and freedom into your soul.

Forgiveness is knowing, what you are and who you are in the heart of God.

Forgiveness is to pray and to love the person who offended and mistreated you.

Forgiveness is about renewing your mind to be a better person to the person who hurt you and offended you.

Forgiveness is being face-to-face with the person who did you wrong, to let go of the past and to look toward to a good future together.

Forgiveness is having love and peace for each other.

Forgiveness is freeing the person from the guilt he committed.

Forgiveness is a new beginning from being shattered and broken into being healed.

Forgiveness is to love yourself and loving the person who afflicted you.

Forgiveness activates God's mercy for you and the other person.

LUKE 17:3–4

So watch yourselves. "If your brother or sister sins against you, rebuke them; and if they repent, forgive them. Even if they sin against you seven times in a day and seven times come back to you saying 'I repent,' you must forgive them."

MATTHEW 6:14

For if you forgive other people when they sin against you, your heavenly Father will also forgive you.

1 JOHN 2:1-2

My dear children, I write this to you so that you will not sin. But if anybody does sin, we have an advocate with the Father—Jesus Christ, the Righteous One. He is the atoning sacrifice for our sins, and not only for ours but also for the sins of the whole world.

ISAIAH 1:18

"Come now, let us settle the matter," says the Lord*. "Though your sins are like scarlet, they shall be as white as snow; though they are red as crimson, they shall be like wool.*

ROMANS 8:1

There is therefore now no condemnation for those who are in Christ Jesus.

FACE-TO-FACE

In February 2017, I invited Andrew to come to my church, and he did come. And for the first time in thirty-three years in his life, Andrew and I were actually face-to-face to each other. He came and hugged me, and he broke down with tears pouring down on my shoulders; he said to me with his voice broken down voice that he was sorry to God and to me. Andrew humbled himself before God. I was so glad that he understood the mercy seat of God in his life.

We decided to go to a restaurant to catch up some more. He shared with me the details about his life, and also I shared mine. We both thanked God for sparing our lives, for picking us up from the deep waters of darkness and sitting us upon the rock with lights. For the first time in his life, Andrew found and experience God from darkness to light.

BAPTISM

He was so excited that he decided to be baptized in my church. He got baptized on Easter Day, 2018. The day before he got baptized, he came to me and asked me again with sincerity in his heart to forgive him; tears poured down from his face again. Because he didn't want anything in his heart that was not of God, he wanted to get baptized, with full of love and passion for the Lord. I felt like his heart was very sincere with the Lord. He didn't want to have a rebellious spirit and even to carry the sins in his heart for the rest of his life. When I saw that, I felt the love of God come over me and that all I had in my heart was to love Andrew and to have compassion for him.

My heart was pounding really hard as I listened to him. I remember with the tears in my eyes that my God, who died for me on the cross, said the same thing to the soldier who killed Him:

"Father, forgive them for they do not know what they are doing."

After I remember the words of God, I held Andrew's hands and genuinely told him that I forgave him. I felt the overwhelming love of God in my life. I felt like all the pain and brokenness in my life from all those years were lifted up and I have found peace into my soul. I was so glad. I thanked God that He gave me the freedom and released me from captivity, and I was healed completely.

I found love and strength in my soul as I was talking to him. It shocked me that I was actually talking to him at that moment. I was so glad that God was with me, and He gave me the boldness and strength to do what He asked me to do concerning Andrew and that I was able to talk to him without fear in my heart but had love and compassion for him instead.

We continued to see each other, and we both shared the defeats and victories of our past. I was so glad to be able to hear his side of the story. With shaking lips, he told me that he was glad that I came back in his life as his friend; he thanked God for me that through my prayers, God got him out from the gates of hell. Andrew had won the victory over death, and he is now walking in the righteousness before God; He now has a purpose and has hope. To God be the glory!

TESTIMONY

Andrew was excited for God's mercy toward him that he decided to share his testimony with everyone in the church. He told them how much agony of pain that he experienced in his heart by killing me. He had so much regret for the things he had done; by the grace of God, he found God in his desperate moment. By sharing his testimony, he was hoping that somebody would have the same breakthrough—to know the righteousness of God and to be able to stand up knowing that God is about love and not death. Everyone was listening and amazed by his testimony. And everyone was blessed. To God be the glory!

THE RESURRECTION HOUSE

After thirty-three years, on April, 5, 2018, Andrew and I decided to return to our old house—the place where I died and came back to life. We were thrilled and fascinated by the move of God over our lives, just being able to come back and see the power of God perform miracles in that very room. When we got to the house, we talked to the owner, and we shared with the owner that we used to live there on 1985. We asked the owner of the house if we could come in and see the inside of the house. To our amazement and awe, the owner of the house said yes. I was so excited; my heart was pounding. I felt like I wasn't breathing. My mind was racing, trying to bring back the memories of the past and this time is for God's manifestation of His power over me. I was very excited I was trying to put myself together.

GOD'S FLAMES OF FIRE

When the owner of the house opened the door, my heart jumped for joy. Then we came inside, and for the first time in thirty-three years, I could look back at what happened in the past—that I saw God in the form of "holy flames of fire" in that very room. There, I felt the peace and love of God in my life. As I was walking and looking around in the living room, I felt the goodness of God over me, knowing He was with me the whole time. He loved, protected, and healed me in that place. When I walked in the bedroom and looked around, I could feel the power of God in that very room. I could feel God flames of fire in that very room. I felt the eyes and finger of God fighting on my behalf in that very room. God was on my side in that very room.

The whole time that I was standing in the bedroom, I thanked God for all the signs, wonders, and miracles that He performed for me in that very room. I thanked God for bringing me back to life. I thanked God for bringing me joy and strength, and I thanked God for showing His glory over me. I was so glad that I came back to the old house with Andrew without fear.

The owner of the house was pleased with us. Later on, I asked the owner of the house if I could pray for him, and he said yes for me to pray for him, while I was praying for him, I noticed about his tears pouring down his face as if like a river it never stop. At that moment the owner of the house felt the presence of the Lord, Glory to God. I was so glad that I won the victory over the enemy. God is faithful. He will do what He says He will do.

RAILROAD TRACK

In June 7, 2018, we decided to come back to the railroad track, the place I ran for my life to. When I saw the railroad track for the first time after all those years, tears poured down my cheeks, remembering all the love and wisdom that the Lord bestowed upon me in that moment. I remember how God protected me from that place. I thanked God for protecting me while I was fleeing from Andrew. God is my hero. He won my battles. He gave me my victory.

FRIENDS

Later on, Andrew and I visited our old friend from thirty-three years. I was so glad to see her and her husband. I remember her sharing with me all the things that happened to me while we were together going to different places; she shared with me that the places we went shopping at were racist, and they were trying to hurt me. She protected me from the people who were hurting me. I thanked God for her for being brave and protecting me from them.

I was born with brown skin. By the grace and mercy of God, He allowed me to experience having "white" skin for ten years of my life. And in 2017, God brought my color back. So in this moment and season of my life, I can testify and share with you with boldness and confidence that the testimony of Jesus Christ is real through me. God does not look at a person through the color of their skin; instead, God looks at them through their hearts.

Every nation, tribe, tongues, people, and languages—God looks at all of us as "one light," in heaven and on the earth. People of all colors are loved by God, and we are one with the one who sits on the heavenly throne, Jesus Christ of Nazareth!

I pray that you will know God in such an intimate way that your eyes will be enlightened to see God face-to-face. I pray that you will have freedom, peace, healing, love, restoration, blessings, and deliverance, In Jesus' name. Amen.

I was so glad to be able to show my genuine forgiveness and love toward Andrew and to have the love from the Lord. For the first time in my life, I actually experienced the heart of our heavenly Father as I forgave and invited Andrew into my little circle of my life. In the same way that our heavenly Father forgives those people that sin against Him, God also gives them His kingdom from heaven.

Only through forgiveness and the love of Jesus Christ was I able to face the person who hurt me. The person who killed me and the one I was fleeing from for thirty-three years ago was the same person who brought me to the old house where God's power is been revealed and also to the railroad track. While I was with him, he was showing me the railroad track and taking pictures of me, I didn't feel any fear toward him. Instead, I felt full of love, compassion, and peace for him.

God transformed the tragedy in my life into triumph and victory.

I GIVE UP MY LIFE AND GIVE HIS BACK

On June 2, 2018, I shared with Andrew about Jesus praying while He was dying on the cross. Jesus gave His life so that God will forgive their sin and people would have life.

LUKE 23:34

Then Jesus said, "Father, forgive them, for they do not know what they are doing."

I told him that our story was the same as Jesus' story, that Andrew was the one who took my life away. And God brings me back to life. At the same time, with my forgiveness and the love of God over me. I gave Andrew's life back by forgiving him and shares Jesus to him. For thirty-three years, he always wanted to kill himself because of the shame and guilt that haunted him. It reminded me of the story of Judas. Judas betrayed Jesus; because of his guilt and shame, he decided to kill himself.

And one day, I showed up in his life. I forgave him and showed kindness toward him, and I shared with him about Jesus. The love I had with Jesus compelled me to forgive and do the right thing toward him. Because of it, Andrew found life. God revived him, and God gave him another chance to live. God brought me back to life, and God and I gave Andrew's life back.

Jesus Christ is the one who brings the life back, and He is the one who is life itself.

ROMANS 4:25

He was delivered over to death for our sins and was raised to life for our justification.

JOHN 11:25–26

Jesus said unto her, I AM the resurrection, and the life: He that believeth in Me, though He were dead, yet shall He live: and whosoever liveth and believeth in Me shall never die. Believesth thou this?

LUKE 23:34–35

Jesus said, "Father, forgive them, for they do not know what they are doing." And they divided up His clothes by casting lots. The people stood watching, and the rulers even sneered at Him. They said, "He saved others; let Him save Himself if He is the Christ of God, the Chosen One."

LUKE 23:46

Jesus called out with a loud voice, "Father, into your hands I commit my spirit." When He had said this, He breathed His last.

HEBREWS 1:7+

In speaking of the angels He says, He makes His angels Spirits, His servants FLAMES OF FIRE.

EXODUS 3:2

There the angel of the Lord appeared to Him in FLAMES OF FIRE from within a bush.

REVELATION 19:11–16

I saw heaven standing open and there before me was a white horse, who's Rider is called Faithful and True. With justice He judges and makes war. His eyes are Flames of Fire and on His head are many crowns. He has a name written on Him that no one knows but He Himself. He is dressed in a robe dipped in blood, and His name is the word of God the armies of heaven were following Him, riding on white horses and dressed in fine linen, white and clean. Out of His mouth comes a sharp sword with which to strike down the nations. He will rule them with an iron scepter. He treads the winepress of the fury of the wrath of God Almighty. On His robe and on His thigh He has this name written: King of kings and Lord of lords.

GALATIANS 3:26–27

You are all sons of God through faith in Christ Jesus, for all of you who were baptized into Christ have clothed yourselves with Christ.

2 CORINTHIANS 6:18

"And I will be a Father to you, and you shall be My sons and daughters to Me," Says the Lord Almighty.

PROTECTION

PSALM 91:1–16

Whoever dwells in the shelter of the Most High will rest in the shadow of the Almighty. I will say of the LORD, "He is my refuge and my fortress, my God, in whom I trust." Surely He will save you from the fowler's snare and from the deadly pestilence. He will cover you with His feathers, and under His wings you will find refuge; His faithfulness will be your shield and rampart. You will not fear the terror of night, nor the arrow that flies by day, nor the pestilence that stalks in the darkness, nor the plague that destroys at midday. A thousand may fall at your side, ten thousand at your right hand but it will not come near you. You will only observe with your eyes and see the punishment of the wicked. If you say, "The LORD is my refuge," and you make the Most High your dwelling, no harm will overtake you no disaster will come near your tent. For He will command His angels concerning you to guard you in all your ways; they will lift you up in their hands, so that you will not strike your foot against a stone. You will tread on the lion and the cobra; you will trample the great lion and the serpent. "Because He[b] loves me," says the LORD, "I will rescue Him; I will protect Him, for He acknowledges my name. He will call on me, and I will answer Him; I will be with Him in trouble, I will deliver Him and honor Him. With long life I will satisfy Him and show Him my salvation.

PSALM 23:1-6

The LORD is my shepherd, I lack nothing. He makes me lie down in green pastures He leads me beside quiet waters, He refreshes my soul. He guides me along the right paths for His name's sake. Even though I walk through the darkest valley, I will fear no evil, for you are with me; your rod and your staff, they comfort me. You prepare a table before in the presence of my enemies. You anoint my head with oil; my cup overflows. Surely your goodness and love will follow me all the days of my life, and I will dwell in the house of the LORD forever.

You can count on God to protect you because He wants to fight every battle you have with the enemy; you need only to be still. God will keep you safe, and you can take refuge in Him. The Lord is always with you. You cannot be afraid of the enemy. What can a mortal person do to you when God releases His angel to protect you! You can do all things through Christ, who gave you strength. Always keep your eyes on the Lord, and with Him, you will not be shaken. The Lord will be your shield, and He will lift your head high. Trust God because He is the only way that can protect you. No matter what you are going through, believe that God has already done it for you. He wants to take you to the other side of the tunnel of light. His promise is to cover you with His blood for you to able to have life.

DEUTERO NOMY 31:6

Be strong and courageous. Do not be afraid or terrified because of them, for the Lord your God goes with You; He will never you nor forsake you.

2 THESSALONIANS 3:3

But the Lord is faithful, and He will strengthen you and protect you from the evil one.

PSALM 138:7

Though I walk in the midst of trouble, you preserve my life. You stretch out Your hand against the anger of my foes; with Your right hand You save me.

PSALM 57:1

Have mercy on me, my God, have mercy on me, for in You I take refuge. I will take refuge in the shadow of Your wings until the disaster has passed.

THE LOVE OF THE FATHER

ROMANS 8:37–39

No, in all these things you are more than conquerors through Him who love you. For I am convinced that neither death nor life, nor angels nor demons neither the present nor the future, nor any powers, neither height nor depth, nor anything else in all creation, will be able to separate you from the love of God that is in Christ Jesus our Lord.

But God—because He is rich in mercy and because of the great love with which He loved you, even when you were dead in your trespasses—made you alive together with Christ. The Lord your God is in your heart, a Mighty One who will save you. He will rejoice over you with gladness. He will quiet you by His love. He will exalt over you with loud singing.

PRAYER

Lord Jesus, Your fruits are full of love and compassion toward Your people. Your blood and blessings bring peace into our lives. Lord Jesus, thank You for Your love and compassion toward us. Thank You for helping us and being there for us. Thank You for comforting us and protecting us. You are truly the God who knows Your children. Thank You for teaching, directing, and leading us to the place where You want us to be. Lord Jesus, we love You with all of our heart, mind, and soul. Thank You Lord that we are alive in You.

Lord Jesus, thank You for allowing Your people to feel Your presence and love toward them. Thank You for giving them a purpose and hope in their walk with You. Thank You for giving them strength to stand tall in your love and presence over them. Thank You that they are not backing down or put aside and pushed away by the works of the enemy. Thank You that You listen and send them to Your angels to protect them. Thank You for not abandoning them when they thought all their hope was lost. Thank You for sending them a mentor that will teach them about You so that they can grow and have the knowledge of You.

Thank You, Lord, for the quiet moment that You breathed upon them to give them their life back. Thank You, Lord, for touching them, changing them completely, and using them as your instrument for Your people. Thank You, Lord, for loving them and taking care of them, In Jesus name. Amen.

CHAPTER 11

A BLIND MAN IN MY DREAM

In 1987, I met a family that loved me and wanted to bless me; they wanted me to live with them. They were nice and wonderful people. I loved taking care of their beautiful baby. I fell in love with the family. They treated me like I was also part of their family. I felt peace and love just being with them.

One day, someone invited me to go to a young adult dance party at the church. I met a lot of people, and I was having a good time meeting people who loved to talk about God. Later that evening, I met Angela, and she became a really good friend to me. She invited me to come to her house and visit her, and I did. I drove many hours to get to her place, and when I got there, she introduced me to her brother and sister. As I got to know her brother James, I saw His gentleness and pure heart; He was a very funny and courageous man. James started to fall in love with me. But I was concerned about his mom and his sister. Because Angela was my friend, I didn't want to ruin our friendship because of James.

As the months went by, I started falling in love with James too; we decided to be there for each other. We had a long-distance relationship; he lived very far away from me, but we managed to see each other. We were very happy every time we were together; one day, He wrote me a letter in Filipino. In his letter, he talked about his feelings toward me, how much he loved me and how much he wanted us to be married one day. He said in his letter that He couldn't live without me and that he would rather die if he could not be with me. I felt goose bump all over my body when I read that. I tried to brush it off, and I moved on.

Tears were coming down my cheeks, knowing that he loved me. His letter really touched my soul little did I know that his letter would be the last I would receive from him because he died after He wrote the letter.

DREAM

One day, one of my friend and I were going to visit her mom's house; it was a three-hour drive. On our way there, I was feeling concerned about something, but I didn't know what it was about it yet, until four nights later. While I was sleeping, I had a dream about a man standing under a tree. As I looked at him very closely, I noticed that the man did not have any eyes. I saw his hands moving as if he was talking to me; his hands and lips were also moving as if he was saying something to me. As I was staring the man standing under the tree, I felt like the man was in so much pain, hurt, and disappointment; but then at the same time, I saw him glowing radiantly from heaven as he was trying to let me know who he was. But I was having a hard time understanding him. I didn't know what he was saying to me, and I didn't recognize him. But I felt like I knew him from my heart, and then I woke up.

I thought I was having a nightmare. When my friend and I came back home that Sunday afternoon, Angela called me from their home phone; at that time, there were no cell phones. Angela asked me if I was sitting down, and I said yes; she told me that James got into an accident on the way home. He fell asleep while he was driving his car. They rushed him to the hospital, but there was nothing the doctor could do for him. She tried to call me, but no one answered the phone. She didn't know that I was four hours away from home, and only James knew where I was. And at that time, there was no place for them to contact me. When I found out that he was dead, I felt like I was hit with a huge rock on my head. I was hurting so much. I was having a hard time eating and sleeping. I was always thinking about him. Angela had asked me to come to their house to visit, and I said yes.

When I got to their house, they told me what happened to James; everybody was shocked with what happened to him. I was so sad the whole time. While I was there, I decided to spend the night with them. I remember lying on the bed, trying to go to sleep. I heard the dog, as if it was talking to somebody. I saw the dog running as if someone was playing with it. The following morning, I told Angela about the dog; she told me that James loved his dog and that he always played with his dog. Then I understood why the dog was so playful that whole night— because the dog was James's best friend. I also shared my dream about the man without any eyes with her. When Angela heard that, she looked at her mom to see if it was okay for her to tell me about what happened to James, and her mom said yes.

So Angela started telling me about what happened to James while they were in the hospital. They told me that they could barely recognize James because his body was swollen all over. The only way they can communicate with him was for him to move his little toe. Every time they mentioned my name, James would move his toe, meaning that he wanted to see me. They also donated James's eyes to someone, so he did not have any eyes. I was so sad to hear that he didn't have any eyes, but I was glad for the person that had his eyes. I wished that I would someday be able to see the person he gave his eyes to. They told me that James really wanted to see me before he died, but I was too late. I was very sad, and I mourned for him. I prepared myself to be married to him for the rest of my life. But the Lord took him away from me. I was crushed inside my heart. But I knew that one day I would see him again in heaven.

So without a doubt, the man in my dream was James. I was so glad that God gave me an opportunity to see him in my dream. God's love for me brings assurance and confidence into my soul.

DANIEL 4:5

I had a dream that made me afraid; as I was lying in bed, the images and visions that passed through my mind terrified me.

LOVE ONE ANOTHER

God's command is this: "Love one another as I have loved you. Greater love has no one than the one that lays down His life for His friends."

Jesus replied, "Love the Lord your God with all your heart and with all your soul and with all your mind."

This is the first and greatest commandment. And the second is like this: love your neighbor as yourself.

Above all, love one another deeply because love covers over a multitude of sins.

God is saying, "Let love and faithfulness never leave you. Bind them around your neck. Write them on the tablet of your heart. Then you will win favor, victory and a good name in the sight of God and man. Now these three remain in your heart: faith, hope, and love. But the greatest of these is *love*."

CHAPTER 12

FROM DARKNESS TO LIGHT

I MET JOE ON 1988, WHEN I WAS TWENTY-TWO YEARS OLD AT THE TIME, AND I LOVED THE WAY OF THIS WORLD. I MET HIM AT THE PARK WITH MY FRIEND. I SAW JOE COMING OUT FROM THE WATER ON THE LAKE. AS MY FRIEND AND I WERE WALKING BY, THE FIRST WORDS THAT CAME OUT FROM JOE'S MOUTH WERE "YOU SHOULD JUMP IN THE LAKE AND SWIM WITH ME." WHEN HE SAID THAT, MY FRIEND AND I LOOKED AT EACH OTHER, AND WE STARTED TO GIGGLE AND LAUGH. WE LOOKED AT HIM AND SAID NO. WHEN MY FRIEND AND I WERE INSIDE THE CAR STARTING TO LEAVE, MY FRIEND DECIDED FOR US TO COME BACK TO WHERE JOE WAS. WE SAW JOE PLAYING FRISBEE WITH HIS FRIEND. I REMEMBER STANDING UNDER THE TREE WHEN JOE SUDDENLY THREW THE FRISBEE CLOSER TO ME ON PURPOSE SO I WOULD PICK IT UP AND THROW IT BACK TO HIM. BUT HIS FRIEND IMMEDIATELY TRIED TO WALK CLOSE TO ME SO THAT HE COULD MEET ME, BUT JOE DECIDED TO COME CLOSER TO ME ALSO. HE INTRODUCED HIMSELF TO ME. SO JOE AND I FINALLY MET. HE AND I GOT TO KNOW EACH OTHER VERY WELL, AND WE STARTED TO DATE. A FEW MONTHS LATER, WE FELL IN LOVE WITH EACH ANOTHER. AS THE YEARS GO BY, JOE ASKED ME TO MARRY HIM; AND OF COURSE, I

SAID YES. WE GOT MARRIED ON AUGUST 25, 1990, AND IT
WAS A GOOD MOMENT IN MY LIFE. WE HAD A BEAUTIFUL
WEDDING; ALL OF HIS FAMILY COOKED AND MADE A
BEAUTIFUL WEDDING CAKE FOR US. A LOT OF PEOPLE
CAME, INCLUDING HIS FAMILY AND FRIENDS. I DID NOT
HAVE FRIENDS WITH ME BECAUSE MY FEW FRIENDS
FROM MY HOMETOWN COULD NOT COME. WE HAD A
BEAUTIFUL HONEYMOON, FULL OF LOVE AND PASSION.

I was very happy with Joe; He was a nice man, and I felt loved by
him. He was very funny and also kind, and everything about him was
good. We were a very young couple. Later on, I got pregnant. We had
a baby girl; she was full of love and joy, and I loved our baby. I was so
glad she came into our life. She brings love and joy to me. But one day,
something changed, as the years went by, we started experiencing a
hard life, as if the world was upside down. We felt like we didn't know
how we were going to make it in life. We saw ourselves in the form of
darkness. We realized being married was not easy. Our schedules and
lifestyle changed completely. At the same time, we had a hard time to
meet things meet.

Joe decided not to get a job; He decided to build his own business.
He thought that he would get rich one day. He used all our resources
to build the business, but later on, the business did not succeed. He
realized that it was not easy putting up a business. He refused to get a
job and found himself in a dark moment, which left us in poverty in
the end.

I started to get sad and unhappy, and I shared that with him, hoping
that he would challenge himself to get a job. I was there supporting him
for many years. Five years into our marriage, his situation still did not
change, He refused to get a job and I noticed that our marriage was
falling apart. I decided to remove my ring from my finger, and I told
him that I would put the ring back on once I knew for sure that I could
take care of him until the day I died without him working. I managed
to take care of everything in our household. I tried to bring my daughter
to my job so I didn't have to pay for day care.

I wanted to help my mom and my dad in the Philippines, but I ended up taking care of Joe instead. When my dad died, I blamed myself. I should have been there for him. I was very hurt. I did not see my dad when they buried him. I could not afford a plane ticket to see my dad. I thought about all the things that my dad loved to do when he was still alive. I thought about apples—my dad loved to eat apples. I wished I was there for my dad. My body and my mind were getting weak and tired. My heart was mourning for my dad. The guilt was creeping in. I felt like I needed help. I felt like I was at the end of my rope. I was broken, shattered, and helpless in my soul.

I was having a hard time getting back up. I tried to find peace, but I could not find; the whole time, I was asking myself if God was there, if He was real or was even with me. I was sure there was God, but I just didn't know where He was at that moment in my life. As the years went by, I could not find rest and peace in my life. My world was not what I thought it would be. I could not find the rainbow with many colors in my heart. I knew I could use it at that time for me to have peace. I tried to find peace from Joe, but it did not work.

MICROWAVE IS ON FIRE

Years later, I brought my mom to America to help me with my daughter. At that time, my daughter was three years old. I was so glad to see my mom. She was taking care of my daughter. But one day something happened, I came home early from work, and I saw my mom o utside talking on the phone. When I went inside the house, I saw my daughter put something inside the microwave, and she turned on the microwave right away right when she saw me. I was shocked when I saw the microwave was on fire. My daughter put my metals earrings in the microwave. I was so scared. I knew that the microwave could explode any minute and the house could catch on fire. I started to panic, and I didn't know what to do. I tried to turn off the microwave, but it wouldn't turn off. I didn't think that opening the microwave door would be a good idea, but I tried it anyway. When I opened it, the fire was gone, and I took the earrings out. I was so scared. The microwave could have exploded; and we could have been hurt or, worse, died. But I thanked God that He was watching over us and protecting us the whole time.

GIVING UP

During that dark time in my life, I noticed that I felt that life was unfair, and that feeling continued to follow me. I started to feel depressed, weak, taken advantage of, and lost. I had so many issues that I was getting overwhelmed with fear and anxiety. I was having a hard time as to how to handle all the problems by myself, and I share with Joe about my dark moments, hoping that he would come and rescue me. But one day, I lost hope; our relationship turned sour. I had so much pressure on me and too much anxiety in my life, and these drove me to give up. Our problems kept piling up, and the pressure on our lives continued to get worse. We found ourselves in a dead-end situation. I felt like the whole world was collapsing on me. I didn't know what was happening to me. I felt like I had a postpartum moment or something. There were so many challenges, obstacles, and problems in our lives; and I didn't know how to face them. My world was getting darker and darker, and I didn't know how to solve it. In our marriage, I was hoping that he would care for us and help remove all my stress. I was at the point of giving up in life. With him not having a job brings me down to the core, our problem weaken my soul.

THE FORM OF DARKNESS TO LIGHT

One day, my mom was staying at her friend's. Joe and our daughter went to the mall. I remember this very moment; it was Saturday at three o'clock in the afternoon. I was all by myself that day; there was a form of darkness that stood in front of me. It led me to depression, and I resolved to take my own life. I thought ending my life would be the best thing for me to do I thought killing myself would be the best answer to all my problems. I thought killing myself would finally give me rest. I thought killing myself would give me freedom from all the darkness that surrounded me. I thought for killing myself would be the right things for me to do. I thought walking away from all the issues and the problem would be a good things for me to do. Until I convinced myself that it was so.

In the darkness of my mind, I decided to go to the kitchen, where I saw a sharp knife. I picked it up. I thought that the knife would do a good job and kill me right away. After I picked up the knife, I went upstairs to my room. I locked the door and jumped on the bed, and while I was holding the knife. My mind was surrounded with darkness. I have felt the pain, and the confusion. At that time, I knew I was ready to go all the way to end myself, and I knew that nothing could stop me.

GOD CALLS ME

But right when I was about to slice myself to my wrist so that I would die, something unexpected happened. I did not realize at that moment that God was interfering in what I was trying to do. Somebody started calling me on the phone. But I tried to ignore the call so I could go ahead and kill myself, but the telephone kept ringing. Because I didn't want the telephone to keep ringing while I was busy trying to kill myself, I decided to stop what I was doing and check the caller ID to see who it was. I saw that it was my friend that I liked and respected, so I decided to answer it. I was thinking to tell her quickly that I would call her back later after I was finished with what I was doing.

But my friend did not want me to hang up the phone; she just wanted to chat with me. I told her that I was busy, but she just kept ignoring me as if she did not hear me. She just kept talking and talking to me, and I kept telling her that I was very busy. I told her that I would call her back later; for some reason, I was having a hard time hanging up the phone on her. Something told me that I needed to hear what she had to say. So I listened to my friend. She was trying to share with me about her husband; she said that her husband did not want her to go to work, and she was very angry with him because she wanted to go to work so she could get out of the house instead of staying home all day long. But her husband loved her so much that he didn't want her to work; He wanted to treat her like a queen. He didn't want her to worry about things of this life. He wanted to support her, take care of her, and treat her like a princess; but she was not very happy with that. They found themselves struggling with their relationship.

As I was listening to her story and trying to understand her situation, I felt like my story was the opposite. I felt like sharing with her what it was like being married to Joe. In my mind, I wished I was in her position, for Joe to love me, to take care of me, and to treat me like a queen or princess—that he would serve me breakfast in bed or just show that he cared for me. I started sharing my story with her.

I tried to give her advice to the best of my knowledge. I told her to thank God that she was blessed and that she should appreciate her husband even more and thank him that he was a good provider for her. I told her to appreciate everything she had. I told her that her husband loved her and wanted to take care of her and treat her like a princess because he believed when they got married that the wife should be taken care of. I had never experienced that before with my own husband. I told her to love her husband the same way she loved God because he was sent to her by God. I told her that God was using him to bring love, peace, blessings, and shelter for her. I told her to love and be submissive to him and to put God first and make God the center of their marriage.

I was being honest when I shared to the woman that I wanted to be in her position because her husband loved her and cared for her and showed it. She was blessed having him in her life. We had a long conversation, and I convinced her that her husband was a good man and that his wish for her not to get a job was for her own good. Much love and compassion and many tears followed. When she realize what I was saying to her was true, she said thank you to me, and I said, "Good." Then we hung up.

GOD RESCUES ME

After we hung up the phone, I was shocked because I don't know where all those word of knowledge coming from, because at that time I was not saved yet but God gave me a word for her.

I noticed the knife I held in my hand. I was shocked, and I asked myself, *why is there a knife in my hand?* For a moment, I forgot what I was supposed to do. When I realized I was supposed to end myself, I started to become afraid. In my own fearful mind, I said, *I don't want to end myself.* I put the knife down, and I said to myself, *nothing like that will happen to me again because I love my life.*

The mystery of God has just been revealed in my life by giving me a second chance. God made a way for me to forget the darkness in my life and put the light in my soul and heal me at that moment. I thank God for my friend who called me. God was using her to protect me. I am so glad that I am still alive. To God be the glory!

Being in the darkness is not from God; instead, it is from the devil. The revelation of God has been revealed to me when I gave my life to God in 2007, and as I focus on God, prayer is the key to fight the battles for me. But the battles do not belong to me; instead, they belong to God. God is in control in my life.

BONDAGE

Six months later, my mom decided to go back to the Philippines. I was having a hard time as far as who was going to take care of my daughter while I was at work. Not having someone to take care of my daughter really slowed me down. I really needed help.

The difficulties continued every day of my life with him. I did not know when my everyday situation of feeling abandoned and not knowing how to make ends meet was going to end. I felt like the whole world was just crumbling down on my head. I was so busy in my everyday life for us to survive that I forgot for a moment that I had a husband. Because my husband at that the time refused to get a job to feed the family.

One day at work, my coworker came to me and asked me what I did during the day (the old man had wisdom). I told him that I felt like I had never experienced rest. I worked all the time to support the family. He was shocked when I told him that; He asked me if I was married, and I said yes. He asked me if my husband was handicapped, and I said no. Then he asked me is to why I was working so hard to support him. I was shocked when he made that comment to me—because he was right. But I did not answer him.

That night, I was having a hard time going to sleep. I kept thinking about what the man said to me. In that moment, I felt like Joe did not love us or care for us. I felt like we were abandoned by him. I was so confused during our entire marriage. Because our relationship lacked love and care as time wore on, we decided to get a divorce. Our marriage ended in 1998, and I moved on, raising our daughter by myself.

After we got divorced, Joe fulfilled his promises to our daughter. Joe did the best he could for being a father to our daughter, and I appreciated that about him. He loved and cared for our daughter, and he was always there for her. He helped our daughter whenever she needed him; He loved her and always had a good relationship with her. And that was the most important for me. For the first time in my life, I felt like I had freedom. I was so glad that the battle was over for me. I felt like the enemy could not hold me down. Joe and I forgave each other, and we moved on in our new journeys in life.

MAKE THE WRONG THINGS RIGHT

On 2016, the years went by, my life changed. I found the form of darkness in the lowest point of my life. I hit rock bottom. I experienced tests, trials, and hardships in my life. I experienced pain, brokenness, and being alone. In my moment of brokenness, Joe come and rescued me. I wanted to thank him for being a hero for me and my children. He is always there for us, helping us and showing love and kindness toward us. It was a long road for him, but I was so glad that He found the way. We became better friends to each other than ever before. We are both healed blessed, and restored. To God be the glory!

Right now, at this point in my life, I call Joe my hero because after I was diagnosed with cancer, the fighting for my life began; and he was the one who was always there to rescue us and help us in everything we needed. I want to thank God for him. To this day, Joe and I are good friends. He found it in himself to make the wrong things right into our lives.

COMFORT

Whatever struggles and storms you have and no matter how big they are, God still sits on the throne, taking charge of your life. When you feel afraid, lost, and overwhelmed, you can count on God to perform miracles for you because He is a big God. Nothing is impossible for Him. You have purpose in God; and your purpose is to have intimacy with Him, worship Him, and find joy by knowing Him.

The following message is from my heart for all the readers: Married couples should put God first before anything else in your life. God must always be at the center of your hearts. God is in control, and He will make a way. There is nothing that God can't fix. He wants to protect you, to heal you, to provide for you, to bless you, and to deliver you. You are very important to Him. Your marriage is a covenant of God's love over you. Love and forgiveness is the key to be closer to God. I encourage you to pray and ask God; "for God to be in CONTROL in your marriage". God wants to perform miracles for your marriage.

Jesus Christ loves you!

THE MAJESTY

Your heavenly Father loves you and cares for you. He has the authority and power to give you the very best for your destiny and your future. He desires for you to be victorious and successful and to anticipate His powerful glory. So stay focused on His actions to achieve the excellence of His faithfulness. God wants to show the floodgates of heaven with His riches and wealth for you. Your majestic God has promised to you the abundance of life without limits. He is on your side.

God wants to protect you and bless you because He desires you, He delights in you, He is pleased with you, and you are important to Him. God wants to speak to you with His powerful words; you will be transformed into His image and likeness.

God doesn't want you to have fear, for He is with you. He doesn't want you to be dismayed, for He is your God. He will strengthen you and help you. He will uphold you with His righteous right hand. God's direction will protect you, and His understanding will guard you. May the Lord answer you when you are in distress, may the name of God protect you, may you have many troubles, but the Lord will deliver you from them all, God is your refuge and strength, an ever-present help in times of trouble. God has mercy on you, for you have to take refuge in Him. You take refuge in the shadow of His wings until the disaster has passed. You are victorious. You are His bride, and He loves you.

CHAPTER 13

GOD COMMANDS HIS ANGEL CONCERNING ME

One day, I was at a building with my younger daughter, who was four at the time. I remember carrying her and sitting her on the chair beside the door. I was going towards the door, and while I was trying to open the door, I did not know that there was a man hiding on the left side of the door. When I open the door he immediately grabbed me, and forced himself in. The man did not have any pants or underwear on. He was only wearing a T-shirt; when the man grabbed me and pushed me all the way back inside the building, my whole body shakes and fear jump into me. We passed by my daughter sitting on the chair, and she was just looking at us. As I was looking at my daughter while the man was dragging me toward the back, fear keeps getting bigger all over me. I felt like we might die at that moment. That whole time, I thought at the back of my mind that maybe it would be the last time I was going to see my daughter because I was at the hands of the enemy. I felt helpless, s cared, and confused; my heart was pounding very hard, not knowing what would happen to us next.

The whole time, I was thinking that maybe the man might rape me first and then kill me and then my daughter; there was so much things was going through my mind while the man was very violent toward me. He was like a crazy dog. He never let me out of his sight. I felt like I needed to act immediately to protect myself and my daughter. I thought that if

I did not fight the man, He might kill us both. I felt like trying to fight him. All I knew was that I needed to fight him for my daughter's sake, so I started feeling strong and hopeful. I tried not to be scared anymore. That whole time, I was thinking about my daughter and that I didn't want anything bad to happen her.

So I tried to fight the man. I grabbed everything from the table and hit him with them. The man was like a leech; He would not let me go, and he was grabbing me so tight. I fought and fought the man, trying to kick and hit him. I fought until I couldn't fight anymore. I finally gave up because he was very strong; he kept dragging me down, pushing me to the ground, and he was smashing my head to the ground over and over. I was very hurt and weak, and the whole time, I was thinking about my daughter and how I could not help her. My tears started pouring down on my cheeks because I knew that the man would take control of us. I felt like I could not protect my daughter anymore. I was feeling helpless and defeated. I felt like I didn't have any control of the situation. I needed a miracle from God at that moment.

The man felt superior over me in that moment, and he was taking control of the whole situation; when he knew that I was too weak and could not fight him anymore, that's when he forced himself on top of me. He tried to rip off my shirt, but by the grace of God, he could not. My shirt was still intact in my body. The man started to get upset as to why he could not rip off my shirt. He knew that he was running out of time. He tried to rip off my shirt so many times again until he finally gave up.

He looked very confused so he tried to look at me instead and for the first time, we actually got a chance to look at each other; the enemy and I were face-to-face. We were looking at each other intensely. I was looking into his eyes, and he was looking into mine. I felt like something supernatural was taking place. I felt the heat all over my body as if I was about to explode. The presence of God has been revealed to me and to him at that moment.

I saw the fear appear in the man's eyes; he was so afraid that his eyes started to get bigger and bigger, as if he saw a ghost. He was staring at me; and at the same time, I was staring at him. Then the power of God came to me like a bolt of lightning.

I was waiting to see what he was going to do next, and I was sure he was also waiting to see what I was going to do, but he realized that there was one that was greater than he was; the man just saw the Almighty God, my protector. (Because of his fear of God, he cannot rape or hurt me or hurt my daughter). While his eyes were on me, he was slowly trying to get off me; he takes off his hands from me and lifted his body up until he could stand up. Then he realized that God was with me; the man was so scared that he ran as fast as he could toward the door. He passed by my daughter and left the building, and he never looked back.

Meanwhile, I was still on the ground, wondering what the man saw that scared him to death. He was so scared, like he saw a ghost. I thought the reason why he was so scared was because somebody was behind me. The minute I got up from the floor, I immediately looked around to see if there was anybody around me, but I did not see anybody. I was so scared for him. When I saw the fear that he had, I felt like I needed to help him. But little did I know that God was just trying to intervene to protect me from the bad thing that was about to take place in my life and my daughter. So I got up and ran toward my daughter as fast as I could. I thought that maybe the man might take my daughter, but I thanked God when I saw her still sitting on the same chair unharmed the whole time.

I called 911 immediately, and I told them everything what happened to us. The police came and investigated everything. After their investigation, they sent us home. On the way home, I looked back at what just happened to us. I was so glad that my daughter and I were safe. I had tears of joy because I knew that our angels were protecting us, and I was thanked God. We could have been badly hurt or even died, but by the grace of God, He opened the heavens to protect us.

Two days later, the police called me to ask me if they could come to my house because they wanted to show me the pictures of all the men that were rapists in the neighborhood and the community. I said yes. Two days after that, the police came to my house and showed me those pictures. They asked me if I recognized any of those men as the one who tried to hurt us, but I did not recognize any of them. But I just chose two pictures of men that I thought it might look like him. Two days later, the police came back to my house; they told me that they found the rapist and that he was in their custody. The police told me that they were looking for him for a long time because he raped and hurt so many women all over the states. They said that I was so lucky that the man did not rape or hurt me and my daughter. The man was in jail for many years.

I was amazed with God for showing up at the time I needed Him. I saw God's glory upon my life and my daughter. When I was looking at the man, I saw fear on his face, and I knew then that what He saw was the face of God. With God's wrath, there was no place for him to escape or to hide. God is so good.

My older daughter also shared with me that we experienced the same thing twenty-three years ago, but I forgot all about it. She told me that she saw a man grab me and take me all the way to the back. She was hiding under the table across the chair she was sitting on before. She was scared and terrified when she saw the man. I was so glad that she was brave. God was so good. He was with us, and He was protecting us. I was so glad that my daughter did not follow us and did not leave the building; she was waiting for me to take care of her. God wins victories for us.

FORGIVENESS

Eighteen years later, in 2015, I met a woman who wanted to be friends with me. One day, she said that she wanted me to meet her brother. The woman and I became friends; three months later, she introduced me to her brother. As I shook his hand and looked at him in the face, I immediately recognized him. I felt like he was the one who attacked me. As I was shaking his hand and smiling at him, everything that happened to me before flashed back to my mind while I was talking to him. To my surprise, I had feelings of love and compassion toward the man, and I realized that in my heart, I forgave him. God healed the wounds in my heart. I was completely healed the minute I shook his hand, and I had been given freedom that day. Later on, the woman told me that her brother went to jail, but I did not ask any questions as to why he went to jail. I kept everything to myself. All I knew was that God gave me the power of forgiveness, mercy, and grace.

THE LOVE OF GOD

PSALM 91:11

For He will command His angels concerning you, to guard you in all thy ways.

God is the protector of all. He sends His angels to protect you because you are precious to Him. Put on the armor of God so that you can take your stand against the devil's scheme. The Lord will fight for you; you need only to be still.

God is a shield all around you, and His glory lifts up your head high. Always keep your eyes on the Lord. He is in your right hand. With Him, you will not be shaken. He will keep you safe. In Him, you take refuge. He is your shield; you have put your hope in His Word. You will be strong and courageous. You will not be afraid or terrified, for the Lord your God goes with you. He will never leave you nor forsake you.

God is your hiding place. He will protect you from trouble and surround you with songs of deliverance. God is your refuge and strength, an ever-present help in times of trouble. The Lord is your helper; you will not be afraid. What can mere mortals do to you? He makes your saving help your shield, and His right hand sustains you. He provides a broad path for your feet so that your ankles do not give way. You can do all things through Him who gives you strength.

God is watching over you and keeps you safe, and you are protected from all harm now and forevermore.

PRAYER

I decree and declare the powerful Word of God over you that whatever you ask in His name will be given to you.

In your distress, you called to the Lord, and He answered you. From the depths of the grave, you called for help, and He listened to your cry. He hurled you into the deep and into the very heart of the seas.

CHAPTER 14

THE VALLEY OF THE SHADOW OF DEATH

After being single for two years, I was alone and in despair, I thought that maybe it was time for me to do something for myself. I felt like I had been single for a long time. I thought that maybe after two years, it was time for me to meet other people. I tried not to think that all men are the same. So I decided to start dating.

One day, I met Scott through a friend. We started dating and fell in love for three years. But that love and comfort turned into distraction; there were so many years that I felt like our relationship was already over. But I was so scared that if I let him know that, I knew that he would hurt me. I felt like that if he could not have me for himself, no one else could. But I could not find a solution as to how to get out of that relationship. It was a battle of which there was no escape.

One day, my friend asked me if I could babysit her children, which required for me to sleep at their house because they were going to be out of the country. I said yes because I was very happy that they were going spend some alone time together in another country. They had been my friends for so many years.

One day, when the children went to school, I came back to my house to get some clothes. Scott was there. I remember the first thing he asked me was that if I still loved him, but I did not answer him right away because I knew that I didn't love him anymore and didn't want to have relationship with him anymore. If anything, I was so scared of him. I saw a vision of him trying to kill me one day. I was so scared that I tried to separate myself from him little by little. I felt like I couldn't break up with him right away because he might try to hurt me.

SLAVE TO FEAR

One day, we were in my living room, when he asked me a question and I did not answer right away, he picked up a ball and threw it at my head. I asked him why he threw the ball at me; he said it was because he felt like it. Then He started to grab me while I was sitting on the couch, picked me up, and threw me all the way to the ground; he picked me up again and slammed me against the wall. Then he pulled my hair and dragged me like a doll all over the carpet. Then he dropped me on the ground and smashed my head. I could feel my whole body was in so much pain. While I was on the ground, I was very confused; my heart was pounding, and I was struggling with fear. I knew right away that I was facing death. I thought about my daughter, wondering how she would live without me in this world.

While I was on the ground, Scott got on top of me and started to wrap his hands very tightly around my neck. I immediately had hard time breathing; I tried to remove his hands from my neck but I did not succeed. I did not have a chance to breathe even a little bit I tried to say something to him, hoping that he would let me go. But it did not work at all; his hands were still very tight around my neck. It was then that I started to lose hope. In my helpless state, while his hands were around my neck, I felt like my eyes started to roll back. As I tried looking at the ceiling, I noticed that it was changing colors, and I saw the ceiling was turning black and gray—it was not white anymore.

I felt like the grave was calling my name while the intensity of his anger was crumbling down on me. I didn't know when this battle was going to end. I was losing energy to move around, and I was very weak and felt so much pain all over my body. I was getting weak and I cannot move anymore, he was chocking me to death. When he saw this, he let me go. I felt like my angel was fighting for me and was protecting me from him. After he let me go, I was able to move again. Scott was afraid of what he did to me. So as I was getting up, he decided to talk to me and was being nice to me. He came to his senses and realized what he did was wrong.

After I positioned myself to sit down on the couch, I felt my throat is hurting me really bad. I tried to speak, but I lost my voice. But later on, I was able to speak a little bit again. When I knew that I could speak, I asked him to give me a glass of water, and he did. I tried to drink the water, but for some reason, my throat was hurting so bad that I could not drink the water even from a cup or a straw. My throat was in so much pain. Scott told me that I could not call the police on him because he said that nothing was wrong with me. He was trying to threaten me. He looked at my neck, and he said that there was nothing wrong and there was no sign on my neck or body that I was hurt. He thought that he will be able to be free for what he did to me. I was terrified of him, and I told him that I was not going to call the police on him, hoping that he would take it easy on me and not hurt me anymore. When I got the chance, I asked him if I could go outside to get some fresh air, but he did not want me to.

I felt like I was a hostage in my own home. I was having anxiety, thinking that I would never get to escape from my own home. I was emotionally, mentally, and physically broken. I wanted to come out from that nightmare. In my desperation, instead of being angry toward him, I decided to be nice to him, hoping that he would let me go. I told him sweet things I never told him before. I was trying to bring out good things about me so that he could find it in his heart to show kindness to me and let me go. I was praying to God for him to let me go. My heart jumped with joy when he started being nice to me for the first time in the years that I was with him. I knew right away that God answer my prayers.

When I noticed that I won him over, I asked him if I could go to the market. And he said yes. After he said that, I felt like I had freedom from him. While I was getting the key and my purse, my whole body was shaking, and my heart was beating really fast. But I did not show him that I was very scared of him. When I was sitting in my car, I saw him coming toward me. I started to panic. I could feel my body shaking tremendously with fear. But I managed to calm myself down. When he approached my car, he asked me to roll down the window. I remember my hand was shaking intensely as I rolled down the window. I was very scared at that moment. I thought that he was going to ask me to come back inside the house again. But instead, he just checked to make sure that there was no mark on my neck or body for the police to see. After checking me, he let me go. I felt like I could breathe with the triumph of victory over my life. I was shaking, and I was weak while I was driving. I didn't know where to go. I thought about everything he did to me while I was in the house. I started to cry, and tears just gushed down my face. I was feeling hope, victory, and fear all at the same time.

After I put myself together, I called my friends. I started to have the courage to expose what happened to. In my weak voice, I told them what was happening to me. They immediately wanted to help me. We all met at my other friend's house, and they told me to call the authorities on him. I was terrified when they told me that because he specifically told me not to call the police on him.

But I listened to my friends instead. I let them take me to the authorities, where I disclosed everything that happened to me. They checked my neck and body, and they found bruises around my neck and on my body. The authorities issued a search warrant for him. I did not see him because he was hiding. Three days later, they found him at his job, and they brought him to jail, where he stayed for a while. When I came back home, my friend found a blade on top of the entertainment cabinet. I did not have any blade in the house before, but I knew it belong to him. I believe that he was planning to kill me. I was so glad that God was with me and was protecting me from Scott.

ISAIAH 35:4

Say to those with fearful hearts. Be strong, do not fear; your God will come, He will come with vengeance; with divine retribution He will come to save you.

PSALM 23:4

Even though I walk through the darkest valley, I will fear no evil, for you are with me; Your rod and Your staff, they comfort me.

EAR TO EAR WITH THE ENEMY

The years went by; it was 2012 when he found me on Facebook page. He wanted to connect with me. When I saw his name, I immediately felt my whole body shake with fear. I was terrified when I saw him. I was overwhelmed thinking that maybe he was following me all those years. There were so many things I thought that he might do to me. So I asked my younger daughter to remove him from my Facebook, and she did. So I found peace for a little while. Then two months later, I saw him on Facebook again, asking me again if he could connect with me. Fear came over me again, but later on, I started to pray and ask God to direct me concerning him. Suddenly, peace came over me, and I heard the voice of God saying that it was okay for me to contact him. After I heard that from the Lord, I did not hesitate to connect with him.

While I was dialing his number, my heart told me not to fear him. When I heard God's voice, I felt peace, and I knew I did the right thing by connecting with him. When he answered the phone, he heard my voice for the first time in years when I said hello to him. He was shocked; there was silence. When he started talking, I heard him speak in a broken voice. Repentance came from his lips as we started talking. I felt like everything that he did to me is disappeared, the only thing that is in my heart is full of forgiveness towards him. When he receives forgiveness from me, he felt like he had been release from the captivity of the devil. We starting to feel safe and to feel love, we talked about a lot of stuff.

At the end of our conversation, I asked him if he knew God, and he said, "Not really." I asked him if he knew Jesus Christ, and he said no. That opened the door for me to share about the salvation and the goodness of Jesus Christ in his life. While I was sharing with him about Jesus, he was very quiet. I thought that he was not on the phone, so I asked him again. And he said yes; he was just listening to me because he never heard about Jesus dying and rose again to be his Savior before and that Jesus could forgive him. Jesus was the only one who would remove every sin he committed; everything about Jesus was new to him. So I continued sharing with him about the goodness of Jesus in his life. After sharing everything I knew about Jesus, including that Jesus was his Savior for eternity, He started saying something; and his voice sounded like there was something in his throat. He spoke with a soft and broken voice, and he said that he liked Jesus. He didn't know that God could forgive him for all his sins he committed. After sharing his feelings toward God, I asked him if he wanted to give his life to Jesus, and he said yes. We prayed and he gave his life to Jesus Christ, and his whole family was saved.

Even though he hurt me and almost killed me, I had a heart with love, peace, and compassion toward him; in my loving moment, I found to forgive him. And it was only through God's grace and mercy that I was able to forgive. It was good to know that the love of Jesus Christ always wins against the works of the enemy in this world. God always has purpose. Scott and I no longer have any contact, but he will always remain hidden in my heart. Forgiving him was the only key to have my life back, and the same was true for him; repentance was the key for him to have the mercy seat of the throne of God.

God is about Love, Peace, Faith and life.

2 TIMOTHY 1:7

For the Spirit God gave us does not make us timid, but gives us power, love and self-discipline.

When fear overcomes your life, it will take hold of your strength, mind, body, and emotions. It will paralyze your every activity and the movement of your soul, and it will suffocate your future, destiny and your life. Fear is a form of darkness that will prevent you from following your ordained dreams and plans and the ordained message from heaven. Fear will threaten your mind, freedom, stability, and it will weaken you to go forward to what God has planned for you.

But the Son of God has shed His blood for you and has given you the power and tools to overcome fear and other obstacles that are trying to get in your way. God has given you the power and strength to destroy the works of the enemy over your life. God has given you the power to face and conquer fear by His Word. In God's way, you cannot be defeated. In Christ, you are victorious.

THE LOVE OF JESUS

PSALM 23:1–6

The Lord is my Shepherd; I shall not want. He maketh me to lie down in green pastures: He leadeth me beside the still waters. He restoreth my soul: He leadeth me in the paths of righteousness for His name's sake. Yea, though I walk through the valley of the shadow of death, I will fear no evil: thou art with me; thy rod and thy staff they comfort me. Thou prepares a table before me in the presence of mine enemies: thou anointest my head with oil; my cup runneth over. Surely goodness and mercy shall follow me all the days of my life: and I will dwell in the house of the Lord forever.

Your heavenly Father paid the ultimate price to adopt you. He paid for your adoption with the blood and life of His Son Jesus Christ. Jesus gave His life so that He could have you as His child.

ROMANS 8:15

The Spirit you received does not make you slaves, so that you live in fear again, rather, the Spirit you received brought about your adoption to son ship. And by Him we cry, Abba, Father.

The reason people have fear is because of lack of love. But it is not so much with you because you know God, and His love with you is eternal. You may not experience the love of our heavenly Father because of what you experience with your earthly father. But God's love for you is more than you could ever think of—it's an everlasting love.

JEREMIAH 29:11–14

For I know the plans I have for you, declares the Lord, the plans to prosper you and no to harm you, plans to give you hope and a future. Then you will call upon me and come and pray to me, and I will listen to you. You will seek me and find me when you seek me with all your heart. I will be found by you, declares the Lord, and will bring you back from captivity. I will gather you from all the nations and places when I have banished you, declares the Lord, and will bring you back to the place from which I carried you into exile.

COURAGE BY GOD

You will have courage knowing your Creator knows everything about you. God knows your future, destiny, and plan for your life. You can have hope and rest in God. God will never forget about you even though you forget about Him sometimes or all the times.

God sees your situation, affliction, hardship, pain, and suffering. God will always be there for you. He will never leave you nor forsake you. He will bring you out from captivity and sit you upon the rock so that you will not be moved by the winds of darkness but experience His love and peace in your life.

His heart toward you is a heart of unconditional love, and He wants to lavish you with His love. His love for you is unending, perpetual, everlasting, and eternal. You are in the palm of His hand.

Your heavenly Father chose you since the foundation of this world. He is watching over you. He knows your thoughts, and He knows you completely. You are His cherished treasure from heaven, and He rejoices over you. You can call Him Abba, Father.

God says to you, "I *AM* your healer, restorer, and deliverer, I *AM* your provider. And I have the love and the power to perform it." *I love you.*

CHAPTER 15

GOD SAVE MY BABY FROM MY WOMB

I moved on with my life. I stayed active and went out to my only friends. I tried not to date for those three years to any man anymore, but one of my friends tried to encourage me to date again.

For the past three years, I tried my best to be content being by myself. I decided not to be close to any man who wanted to have a relationship with me. All those years, I found myself hiding and not being found. But later on, I found myself lonely and alone. I tried to find happiness again. But because of my lack of understanding about God and not having a relationship with Him, fear always haunted me. One day, I tried to put my fear aside. I decided to fly away to see what was out there. I made myself available to meet someone again, hoping I would find what I was looking for—peace and love with someone I loved and cared for, but I realized that the whole world have so much to offer me and I have follow and suck in to that whole without knowing God in my life.

One day, I met this man, and we started dating. We dated for six months until we decided to go further in our relationship as boyfriend and girlfriend, and we decided to be together as a couple, hoping that we would be married one day. One day, the man got very sick. I had to take him to the doctor, and I stayed with him so I could take care of him. Our relationship became very strong. I was very happy and we were fall in love to each other. We were getting comfortable, and I thought that he would be the one for me and that I was going to be married to him one day in the future. But I was wrong!

One day, I found out that I was one month pregnant. I told him about my pregnancy, and he was not very happy about it. I thought that he would be very happy, but instead, he wanted me to get an abortion. He even offered to pay for me to have an abortion. I was shocked to hear that from him, I thought that he would be very happy, because he is going to be a father for the baby. But instead he was very upset and wanted the baby to die. I was hurt and confused in our relationship and I felt like I was alone, knowing that he got me pregnant.

I thought about what I was going to do. I thought that my whole world was collapsing and tumbling down before my eyes. I needed to make a decision: either I was going to keep the baby, or I had to do what he wanted me to do, which is trying to get an abortion.

I felt like my whole body was paralyzed. I was very confused, and I didn't know what to do. In my mind, I was already defeated. I already had one child, and I didn't know how I was going to support another one. I made less money than my bills every month, and I thought, *how can I support another baby?* I had so much fear come over me. I felt like I was all alone. I thought to myself, is to *how can I make it in this cruel world?* My belief in God at that time was not strong enough, and I knew I was very weak. I cried every night for God to answer me about what I needed to do. I was very sad physically, emotionally, and mentally for my unborn baby. In my confusion, vulnerability, and desperation I decided to make appointments with the three companies that I thought would help me ease my confusion.

1. I called the "Doctor's office" to have an ultrasound because the doctor told me that the unborn baby might possibly have the Down syndrome.

2. I called a "Hope Mentor" for advice regarding what I needed to do concerning my unborn baby.

3. I called the "Abortion Clinic" for them to kill my unborn baby.

After making those threes appointment to each of them, I just hoped for the best. That night, I was crying, praying, and calling on God. In my desperation, I needed for God to let me know that He was with me. I needed God to show me what I needed to do. I needed direction from the Lord. And I needed God to answer me quickly, at that time my understanding about God was very weak. I knew that God is real but I did not have understanding about Him. I don't have a relationship with Him at that time.

UNBORN BABY IS TALKING

That night God spoke to me and He said that I need to make an appointment to the Ultra Sound first, and the following day that's what I did, I made an appointment to the Ultra Sound first. I ask the baby's daddy if he wants to come with me to the Ultra sound, and he said yes. When we were at my doctor's office, I experienced the miracle of God beyond my expectations. I saw God's hand through my unborn baby in my womb. The nurse performed an ultrasound on me, and at that time, the unborn baby was three months in my womb. While the nurse was checking my unborn baby in my stomach, suddenly, we saw from the ultrasound that my unborn baby's right hand moved. "The unborn baby's one hand was raised up high," and my unborn baby was "waving" as if like she was saying hello to me.

The nurse and I were amazed and in awe. We were both Shocked, the nurse asked me if I wanted her to take pictures of my unborn baby's hand being raised up and waving at us, and I said yes with excitement. I felt love and joy seeing that my unborn baby was safe and moving in my stomach. Then the nurse shared with me that she had never before seen any unborn baby lifted hand's up high like that at such an early period from the womb. She added that she had been working as a nurse for seventeen years. She said that there is no other unborn babies can be able to raised hand up that early stage from the fetus yet except my unborn baby, she and I were amazed.

I have so much joy from God the nurse knew that it was the Lord who perform a miracle like that in front of her. I was so glad to be able to see the five fingers of my unborn baby raised up high like that. I knew right away that I could not get an abortion. I knew that the unborn baby was a special, unique, and perfect baby for me. I immediately asked God to forgive me for even considering killing my unborn baby. God is so good.

MIRACLES FROM GOD

That night, while I was watching TV in my living room, there was a commercial about "Stop Violence," as I was watching the "hand" from the TV commercial, I remember my unborn baby hand's picture, I immediately jump from the couch and look for her picture, when I found it, I immediately put the picture close to the TV and I compare both of them. I was shocked when I saw them how identical they are. The shape, of the hand, the size and they are both "right hands." They were both wide open. I felt like I was mesmerize with her hand, her small little tiny hand were so beautiful, I felt love, joy and compassion for my unborn baby.

As I was staring at my unborn baby's hand, I noticed about her hand as if like she was talking to me saying;

"Mom, I do not want to die. Mom, please don't kill me, let me live and not die, mom, give me a life like what you have, you are the only hope I have, you are the only one who can make a decision for me to live, please let me live, I want to live, Mom, give me a chance to live, Mom, please I begged you, I want my life that is rightfully belongs to me, I want to see you face to face, I love you mom."

It was like the baby was asking me to help her, and I was the only one who could. I started to have love, peace, strength, and compassion for my unborn baby. I started thinking that I should not get abortion and that I should give her a chance to be here in this world like me. I knew that I was the only one who could protect her, love her, and give her life from God. I was so glad that I had an ultrasound to allow me to see my unborn baby. I have found hope with God and the Lord let me know that He is about *life* and not *death*. So I made a decision not get an abortion. I decided that I wanted to keep my unborn baby. I want her to live and not die. I want to give her life, because is the right things to do. God is about life and not death.

So I told the father of the baby that I was not going to get an abortion, I told him that I loved my baby and wanted to keep her. I told him that if he didn't want to be part of the baby's life, that was fine for me. All he needed to do was to sign a document saying that the baby did not belong to him, and we would move on. He was not very happy with my decision; he was very upset with me, knowing I was three months pregnant. He was torturing me mentally, verbally, and emotionally and physically. He was calling me, harassing and threatening me, those things goes on all the way to my five months pregnancy, but I stood by my word to protect my unborn baby, and I even cancelled my two appointments with the Hope Mentor and with the abortion clinic. I conquered the works of the devil. I was thanking God for performing miracles for me to see His love over me and for my unborn baby.

I felt so much joy for my unborn baby that no one could change my mind. I decided to break up with the man to save my unborn baby. One day, I was hoping that maybe he realized that I was telling the truth that I was not going to get an abortion; that's when he came to me and tried to propose to me by shaking my whole body and demanding me to marry him instead. Because I was verbally, mentally, and physically hurt by him, that I made the decision that I would not marry the man. I did not expect for him to shake me just to ask me to marry him.

I felt like being single was better than being married to a man who would hurt me later on. I felt like when two people wanted to get married, it should be based on God and not on their situation in life, but on God's purpose in their life. I didn't want to make another mistake and get hurt again one day.

Then one day, it was time for me to have the baby; He offered to take me to the hospital. I knew he couldn't wait to see the baby. I had a C-section. After having the baby, I saw that he was excited to see the baby. It seemed like he liked the baby. He asked for me and the baby to stay with him at his house so that he could take care of us. So after I left the hospital, we stayed at his house. The man and his mom took care of us. I was so glad because I really needed help at that time. After having a C-section, I was in so much pain that I could barely walk, and I was having a hard time taking care of myself and the baby. They taking care of us helped me and the baby a lot. But two weeks later, his mom had to go back home.

One week later after she left, after having the C-section, the baby was up all night, and later on we were quiet and rested, I remember the man suddenly got mad while I was lying in bed. He went on top of me and was ready to hit me with his fist. I was shocked I don't know what just happened. I was very tired and I was in so much pain that morning by the C-section.

So I got up off the bed right away and went to the bathroom; he followed me there and pushed me so hard that I fell down head first on the tub. I was so scared. I was in so much pain I thought that my head is burst open and my stitches on my stomach would come undone. I felt like my head was spinning. I was in so much pain; I felt like there was so much darkness all around me. He did not call the doctor for me. He told me not to tell anyone what he did to me. I was in so much pain from the C-section and being pushed in the tub. I did not go to the hospital. I just took pain medication instead. But for my baby's sake, I did not call the police on him because I felt like I needed his help with the baby. I didn't have anybody to help me at that time. I was silent with fear inside of me.

One day, my mother called me and told me that my father died. I was very sad and was mourning for my dad. I loved my dad so much, and I missed him. I wished that he was with me. I wished I was in the Philippines with my family. As I was heading toward my car with my baby, the man suddenly followed us and wanted to fight with me. He said that "I should follow my dad to the grave," knowing my dad had just died just two days before.

I was very devastated and upset with him saying such painful words to me. I was very hurt; my heart was crushed, and I was crying out for help. I learned that the man was prideful, arrogant, and controlling. When he embarrassed and belittled me, all his words made me stronger than ever. I decided that I would never let anyone treat me bad or speak negatively to me ever again. I tried to understand all the things that were happening to me. It was only through God's grace that I found strength. The more I was defeated, the more the strength I gained with God. Later on, I found peace in my life. I thank God that He gave me the strength to keep my baby.

God healed my heart. God wins over us from the hands of our enemies. God is with us fulfilling His promises over us. He saves us, He restores us, and He delivered us. My daughter is now sixteen years old. She is love and she has a lot to offer. I become a **Brave** and a **Hero** mother for her.

I have compassion on the man and I decided to forgive him. The man is now have love and joy having her in his arm. He was there for his daughter all those years; he decided to really connect with her. He loves her, and he is proud of her. He is trying to be good father to her until to this day, loving her, supporting her financially, emotionally, and physically. My love brings peace to all of us, a "Perfect Decision for us all!"

FORGIVENESS

Through all my tests, trials, persecution, and rejection, I learned to be like Jesus. His Word says that I have to take up my own cross to follow Him. I learned to depend on Him, wait on Him, and trust in Him. I love Jesus. He is the only one who showed me the way to His path. He is the only one whom I fix my eyes on because He is the only one who can break the chains of bad events in my life, and I am so glad that I follow His leadership over me.

JOHN 16:33

I have told you these things, so that in Me you may have peace, In this world you will have trouble. But take heart I have overcome the world.

PSALM 138:6–8

Though the LORD is exalted, He looks kindly on the lowly; though lofty, He sees them from afar. Though I walk in the midst of trouble, you preserve my life. You stretch out your hand against the anger of my foes; with your right hand you save me. The LORD will vindicate me; your love, LORD, endures forever- do not abandon the works of your hands.

As the days go by in your life, sometimes you face hardships, troubles or problems, the good things about it that you will never face them alone. God is your Father, and He will always be with you. He will never leave you nor forsake you. He will protect you, He will heal you, and He will give you assurance and confidence. He will walk with you. He will guide you, He will give you comfort and He will strengthening you. He will give you the right thoughts, words, and actions to fulfill His will for your life. He will grant you an abundance of blessings, and He will give you an opportunity to be a blessing to someone else. You will be the channel of light, faith, love and hope to the nations. God will give you a pure heart to do the tasks for His glory. God will release grace, courage, and wisdom in your life. God will create and make the new things that were possible for God because of your faithfulness to Him.

THE HEART OF THE FATHER

You are created in His image for His purpose and will over your life, and His favor upon your life is like a rainbow that has many colors; the colors of His love will bring peace to your soul.

God is above the enemies, He will fight the battles for you, and He will always win the victory. God takes care of you, nurtured you and the blessings of the Lord overshadow you, His love and power are the good things to come into your life. His Spirit in you and His Word are a lamp unto your feet, and He is alert, available, and He is willing to do exceedingly abundantly above all that you could us or think, and He had a heart to perform it.

God is now empowering you with His activity, signs, wonders, miracles and the wind of His Spirit and He is encountering you with His power where He will breathed and roar over you, and the courage and boldness will suddenly be birthed.

God has a plan for you. He has chosen you to love, to trust, and obey Him.

The Lord is faithful. He will strengthen and help you on the days of trouble. On a firm foundation, He will protect and guard you.

You are moving into the bright lights of day to see joy, peace, dreams, vision, provision, and victory in the tangible ways. He will give you the favor of His love.

Your break through have arrive.

CHAPTER 16

THE POWER OF GOD IS BEEN REVEALED

Many years later, on one Saturday, my daughter's father came to our house to pick her up; we were all talking outside my house. Suddenly, I heard the voice of God saying that I should pray for him. I was shocked why would God wanted me to ask the man if I could pray for him. I told the Lord that the man did not like Him and that he did not want to have anything to do with Him. So I asked God why He would want me to pray for him. So I asked God if He was really the One who was talking to me because I wanted to make sure that it was Him. I was very confused with God, because the man does not want to have anything to do with God. Even though I knew that the man would make fun of me if I asked him if I could pray for him, I decided to do it anyway because I wanted to be obedient to the Lord.

I tried to be bold and strong, so I looked into his eyes and asked him if he wanted me to pray for him. I told him that I heard God telling me that I should pray for him. First, he looked at me, and then he started laughing at me. But I knew that it was not going to intimidate me. I heard the voice of God continue asking me to ask him to pray for him. So I asked him a second time if he would allow me to pray for him. He looked at me again, and he laughed at me again. Then he looked back at me again, and this time, he knew that I was very serious and meant what I said. He stopped laughing at me, and to my surprise, he agreed for me to pray for him.

When he said yes, God wanted to answer my prayer for him. God said it was because he was the father to my daughter that God would perform a miracle for him. I was shocked when God told me that. So I prayed for healing and blessings over him. I didn't know what was going on and what was going to happen to him. All I knew was that God tried to pursue him intensely. God was in control. He knew everything about him. Only God knew what was going on and what was going to happen to him. God knew his future and destiny. God knew him more than he knew himself. God knew what was going to happen to him the next day, next week, next month, next year, and even five years from then. Seeking God brings life.

THE POWER OF GOD

One month later, the man decided to buy a four-wheeler; somebody was not very happy with him making the purchase. The person told him that he might have an accident buying the four-wheeler. Later on, the person's message did come true for him.

Because one day, the man and his friend decided to race his four-wheelers to see who was going to be the fastest. When they were racing on the street, the man was going too fast, which resulted in an accident. The four-wheeler turned over and went on top of him. Somebody took him to the hospital. The doctor said that he broke his ribs and legs and his pancreas would not stop bleeding—he was losing a lot of blood. The doctor was having a hard time stopping the bleeding. Also, if they tried to feed him, it would result in diabetes, and he would die immediately. He was basically dying. The doctor asked somebody to call all his family; the doctor was concerned that he could die at any minute. The person who told that he is going to have an accident called me and told me what happened to him. When I heard that, God told me not to be concerned. After two days, I came to see him. I saw him in the ICU; he was in a really bad shape. He looked like he was dead already. I saw that His body was swollen; he was almost unrecognizable, as if there was no hope left for him.

The doctor was giving them bad news. But I told them that there was good news and hope with God and I believed that God was a healer. His families were terrified and insisted that he might die because of what the doctor was telling them. The doctor and his team were doing whatever they could to stop the bleeding from his pancreas, but it seemed like there was no stopping it. Everybody was waiting to see what was going to happen to him next. I told them that I believe that God can heal him. I told them that I remember praying for him before and he said yes to the prayers. So therefore, I told them, that he will live and not die.

I told them that I was going to pray for him again. I knew without any doubt that God would heal him. I knew God was faithful. So I went inside the ICU; as I was looking at him, I saw the compassion that God had for him. I knew at that moment, even before I prayed for him, that the man would be healed. I laid my hand on him, and I started to pray healing for him. After doing so, I had confidence in God that he would perform a miracle for him because God loves to perform miracles for his people.

One day, I went to the hospital to visit him again. There, I saw God's action in his life. I saw his eyes were opened, and he was able to eat. Two weeks later, he regained his strength and was released from the hospital. In less than two weeks, he was completely healed, and He started working.

With God, there is hope. Even though he did not know God, God knew him. He loved to spare his life and healed him completely. I believe that when I was interceding for him, the God of miracles honored my prayers for His glory and purpose for his life, whatever it might be. God gave his life back. God gave him grace and mercy to be alive. And he experienced the presence of God in his life.

God is real, and He is alive and wants to perform miracles for him.

Who can compare to God, no one.

Prayer is the key to unlock God's power to perform miracles.

PRAYER

Heavenly Father thank You that your blood was shed for me, thank You that you watch over Your Word to perform it for me. It has been revealed through the appearance of my Savior, Christ Jesus, who has destroyed death and has brought life and immortality to my soul. Lord Jesus, thank You for forgiving my sins and I forgive those people who hurt me and persecute me, In Jesus' name. Amen.

HOSEA 14:4–7

"I will heal their waywardness and love them freely, for my anger has turned away from them. I will be like the dew to Israel He will blossom like a lily. Like a cedar of Lebanon He will send down His roots; His young shoots will grow. His splendor will be like an olive tree, His fragrance like a cedar of Lebanon. People will dwell again in His shade; they will flourish like the grain, they will blossom like the vine—Israel's fame will be like the wine of Lebanon.

THE HEART OF GOD

You serve a good God. He is the healer and the Anointed One, and nothing is impossible for Him. God can hear your prayers, and God is willing and able to do miracles for you. He wants to heal and rescue you. God knows you completely. He created you. He knows the number of hairs on your head. God knows the thoughts conceived in your heart before you even realize them. God comes to you for everything you ask and need in your life. God is your Jehovah-Rapha, the God who heals, and He has the final words for your destiny. He is coming to you as your heavenly Father because He loves you and is longing to hear from you. He wants to heal you and give you peace. With one touch of your body from God, you should receive healing. He will forgive your sins and cleanses your unrighteousness and begin your healing inside and out. God has the power to heal, and He wants to heal you.

Jesus is a good doctor and a great physician. He will never give the wrong diagnosis or the wrong medicine. He knows the very root of your problem. A simple blood from Jesus takes away your lost, poverty, sickness, disease, and even death. Believe and rest in His loving heart to heal you at the very core of your being today. Listen, the Lord's arm is not too weak to save you, nor is His ear too deaf to hear your call. He wants to demonstrate His love by acting and showing signs, wonders, and miracles in your life. With His love and power, nothing is impossible for Him. You will find refuge under His wings. The Holy Spirit will come upon you, and the power of the Most High will overshadow you. With His blood, you are free.

LUKE 1:68–75

"Praise be to the Lord, the God of Israel, because He has come to His people and redeemed them. He has raised up a horn of salvation for us in the house of His servant David (as He said through His holy prophets of long ago), salvation from our enemies and from the hand of all who hate us—to show mercy to our ancestors and to remember His holy covenant, the oath He swore to our father Abraham: to rescue us from the hand of our enemies, and to enable us to serve Him without fear in holiness and righteousness before Him all our days.

PRAYER

Dear heavenly Father,

You created all things, and You spoke, and it came to be. When you said, "Let there be light," and there was light. I know in all my heart and in all my soul that not one thing has failed of all the good things which the Lord my God spoke concerning me. You are my healer, my peace, my comforter, and my hero. Thank You for guiding me, directing me, and showing up in the bravest and lowest points of my life. You lifted me up and put me upon the rock and You save me. My body, my mind, and my soul are healed; and I am set free from the hands of my enemy. Lord, thank You for always finding me in my darkest moment, and with Your powerful Word, I become light. Your hands with power are in the midst of my trials and tribulations in my life. I love You, my God, my Savior, and my Jesus Christ, In Jesus' name. Amen.

CHAPTER 17

SACRIFICE, FASTING, AND OFFERING

In 2002, my older daughter's father had been picking her up from my house to take her to his church for about two months. One day, he could not pick her up because he was very busy. So I offered to take her to his church for him instead, but I had never been in his church before. Every time I took her to his church, I never went inside. But on that day, I dropped off my daughter so she could go to the children's ministry. And for the first time, I decided to go inside the church with my daughter. I wanted to know what kind of church my daughter was going to. When I got inside, I was amazed at how big and beautiful the church was. I went inside the sanctuary. I saw a lot of people, and all the seats were full. After seeing the sanctuary, I decided to bring my daughter to the children's ministry. When I saw the children's ministry, I too was amazed at how beautiful the place was, and the people were kind and helpful to us. I knew right away that this church was what I wanted my daughter and me to go to. After bringing my daughter to the children's ministry, I saw that the people had passion for and dedication to the children. I saw the band singing beautiful songs inside the sanctuary. As I was sitting on my seat, I started worshipping God from then on. At that time, I knew God, but I didn't have a relationship with Him yet. In that moment, I was compelled to know God more in my life.

OFFERING

When it was time for the offering, I only had a $20 bill at that time, and I didn't know when I was going to have more money since I didn't work because I just had a C-section and could not work for two months. Also, I was a single mom with two children, and I just thought of using that money to have lunch with my daughter after church. I knew that we would be hungry later on, and I would need the money to buy some food for me and my daughter. It was the only money I had that would last us for three weeks. So when the offering basket came toward me, I was torn between two things I needed to do. I had to make a decision immediately: *Do I give the money to the Lord, or should we use it to buy some food?* When the basket was getting closer to me, it became so intense for me. So when the offering basket was finally in my hands, without having a second thought, I picked up my purse and decided to pull out the $20 bill and put it into the offering basket.

Then I watched that basket disappeared from my sight, and I thought that was the only money that I had. I was so weak that I almost cried, knowing I would not have any more money for us to have lunch. I thought about what I was going to do that day. *What am I going to do, not having any money for us to have lunch?* I gave all the money that I had to the Lord. I was very sad, but I didn't have any regrets. So that day, I didn't eat lunch and dinner. My daughters ate at the house; they ate what we had in our house—but not me. I went to bed hungry.

When I woke up in the morning, I remember being on the couch as I was crying, remembering when my dad was asking me to send some money to him, but I didn't have anything to give him. I was feeling bad about it. I felt like I failed my dad. I was not there for my dad, and I didn't have anything to give. I started having all kinds of negative stuff on my mind—that I didn't know how I was going to take care of and support the baby I just had, knowing I was not working since I just had a C-section. I saw myself in the darkest moment of my life, and I didn't know when it would end. I was still feeling sick from having the baby. I could barely walk and had no one to help me.

Finally, one of my friends came, and I thought she was there to help me. Instead, she was the one who criticized me and bringing me down.

She thought that my life was over and blamed me for everything that happened in my life. I was very hurt that somebody could be so unkind toward me. I knew that God was with me and that my life was just beginning. I was so glad that God was talking to me. He was there comforting me the whole time. I knew that God was real, and there were so many times that I wanted God to show Himself to me. At that time, I didn't know Him very well, so I asked God why I had to experience pain and hardship in my life. I also asked if I did anything wrong to my friend for her to criticize me. I had never asked any help from people before; when some of my friends came to me and asked for help, I was always there for them. I was a very kind and generous person to all my friends. I realized I found out who my true friends were when bad things happened to me; true friends would be there willing to help and stay for better or for worse and would always stand by me. But at that moment, I did not see my friend being there for me. I was a single mother of two children, and it was not very easy for me. But I knew that God was with me.

OBEDIENCE

I started to get very depressed at that time. I knew that I didn't have relationship with God, nor could I hear from God; but then, at the same time, I knew that He was with me the whole time. But I was blind that I felt like I had not seen Him perform miracles for me before, knowing I was covered with full of miracles from the Lord. I was desperate for God. In my agony and pain, I started to call out to God for help.

Suddenly, I heard a voice that sounded like love and peace saying to me that I needed to get the phone book. When I heard the voice, I knew right away that was God. I wanted to be obedient to the Lord, so I did what He asked me to do. I started flipping the pages of the phone book as if I knew what to look for, but I didn't really know why I was doing it in the first place; it was just the way that God wanted me to do it.

MIRACLES FROM GOD

SACRIFICE

I was just being obedient to God. I stopped flipping the pages, and then what I saw in front of me was the mortgage company. I thought, *Wow*, because I had bad credit, I didn't have a job, and I didn't have money in the bank. Also, I already tried to go to the mortgage company before, and I wasn't qualified for anything.

So I asked myself what all this meant. Then I heard the voice of God again saying that I should call them. Without hesitation, I picked up the phone and called them. I told the mortgage company everything that I didn't have. I asked them if there was anything they could do for me, and they said yes and that they would try their best to help me; then they asked me all the information they needed for me to be qualified to refinance my town house. The man put me on hold for ten minutes.

When he got back to me, *I saw the lights of God in my life*; the man said that he was able to help me. He was able to lower the interest on my town house and give me $8,000. Also, my payment for the house was only $400 instead of $750, and I thought, *Wow*. At that time, I was not saved yet, so I used the word "lucky" instead of "blessed." But either way, God knew my heart.

Looking back, I now know that God was the one who was performing signs, wonders, and miracles for me. He was the one who was giving me hope, joy, and blessings in my life. I was being obedient to God without even knowing it.

I gave my sacrificial offering (when I gave $20 in church).

I was fasting (not eating lunch and dinner).

And I made a sacrifice (when I went to church) unto the Lord.

I was praying to bless me.

Because I was being obedient to the Lord, God showed me a favor. After receiving the money, the first thing I thought about was coming to church and giving an offering. I also thought about how I could help other people. I thought about my family back home in the Philippines and how I wanted to bless them abundantly and send them some money. For some reason, I didn't have any desires for myself, even pampering myself; all I wanted to do was to help other people.

One day, I was talking to the mother of my daughter's friend. She was very depressed, scared, and worried. I was concerned for her, so I asked her if she was okay. Then she started opening her vulnerable heart to me; she told me that their apartment management was kicking them out because she could not pay rent. I was feeling sad for her and her two children. I didn't want to see my daughter's friend living on the street with her mom and her younger sister because they didn't have any money to pay the rent. So I decided to give her the money. After I helped them out, everybody was at peace, especially my daughter's friend. God loves to help and performs miracles for His children.

The miracles of God happen when we are being obedient to the Lord and seek His kingdom first.

MATTHEW 6:33–34

But seek first His kingdom and His righteousness, and all these things will be given to you as well. Therefore do not worry about tomorrow, for tomorrow will worry about itself. Each day has enough trouble of its own.

A LOVE LETTER FROM GOD

I AM YOUR HEAVENLY FATHER

I AM your light, and I AM your salvation, whom you shall fear. I AM of whom shall you be afraid. I AM the Lord, the stronghold of your life, of whom shall you be afraid. When evil men advance against you to devour your flesh, when your enemies and your foes attack you, they will stumble and fall. Though an army besieges you, your heart will not fear. Though war breaks out against you, even then will you be confident. One thing I ask you is that you will seek Me that you may dwell in My house all the days of your life, to gaze upon My beauty and to seek Me in My temple. For in the day of trouble, I will keep you safe in My dwelling. I will hide you in the shelter of My tabernacle, and I will set you high upon a rock. Then your head will be exalted above the enemies who surround you. At My tabernacle, you will sacrifice with shouts of joy. You will sing and make music for Me. When you call Me, I will hear you. I will be merciful to you and answer you. Your heart will seek My face. I will not hide My face from you. You are My servant, and I will not be angry with you. I AM your helper. I will not reject you or forsake you. I AM your God, your Savior. Though your father and mother forsake you, I will receive you. I will teach you My way. I will lead you in a straight path because of your oppressors. I will not turn you over to the desire of your foes, for false witnesses rise up against you, breathing out violence. You will still have confidence. You will see My goodness in the land of the living. Wait for Me. Be strong and take heart and wait for Me.

This is your God,

Your Heavenly Father-abba

CHAPTER 18

I HAVE BEEN SAVED BY GOD

One day, I felt like there is a missing in my life, and I tried to find it from this world to Satisfied my needs and wants. I didn't know what I need and how to make things happen to myself and where to find these desires in my flesh. I thought to be able to satisfied myself is to get another job, so I tried to get a second job, but it does not satisfied me, I tried to go to school to comfort me, I even tried to go shopping with my friends every weekend to buy everything I want to satisfied me. I even tried to go on vacation to ease my confusion about what is missing in my life. And I even tried to get a date and tried to find love by men, but for some reason all of those things still did not work. l was still hungry and craving for something, I was trying to understand what was happening to me until one day, I meet David, and after meeting him, then I understood what is missing in my life. David brought me to the churches to know God in my life. I realized that it was God that whole time that was missing in my life. God is the only one who can satisfy me. I was so hungry and thirsty for Him. At the same time I have found God through David.

I AM SOLD OUT FOR GOD

SONG OF SOLOMOM

The journey of my relationship with God,

I met the one who held my eyes one day in 2006; He swept me off my feet, and my heart melted seeing his beautiful smile. He shared with me that he was a minister, and I did not know the meaning of the word "minister" before. I thought it meant a beautiful name, like a person who had a higher position or something. He didn't really tell me about God, but he took me to a lot of different churches. That was how I started going to different churches, and I was trying to find my way with God. David and I started to get to know each other better.

SONG OF SOLOMON 5:1

I have come into My garden, My sister, My bride; I have gathered My Myrrh with My spice; I have eaten My honeycomb with My honey; I have drunk My wine with My milk. Friends eat, and drink; drink your fill of love.

SONG OF SOLOMON 5:2

I slept but my heart was awake. Listen! My beloved is knocking: "Open to me, my sister, my darling, my dove, my flawless one. My head is drenched with dew, my hair with the dampness of the night."

One day, I had the chance to see his passions, which is watching the gospel songs on TV, listening to worship CDs, and praising God in my house and also in the car. I would see him lifting his hands up and worshipping God, and I was amazed by that because I had never seen any men lifted their hand's up for God before, sometimes he would have my children watch the movies about Jesus, and my children and I would actually sit down on the couch in the living room and watched the Jesus movie; it was a new thing for all of us because I never thought about having my children watch movies about Jesus before.

He was just blowing my mind, seeing how much he loved God. I had never met or even seen any one like him before from the men I dated. I was fascinated by him and how much he brought a melting pot in my heart. *I thought I saw God in him, and I wanted to have what he had. I noticed myself becoming jealous of him. I wanted to do the same thing like he was doing which is to love God. I wanted to feel the presence of God in my life like he did. I saw the light in him that encouraged me to want to know his God. I was trying to find his God whom I didn't know, yet I knew that He was real. I started to be hungry for God. I wanted to know how to worship Him.*

SONG OF SOLOMON 4:16

Awake, O North wind, and come, south wind! Blow on my garden that its fragrance may spread everywhere. Let my beloved come into His garden and taste its choice fruits.

SONG OF SOLOMON 3:2–4

All night long on my bed, I looked for the one my heart loves; I looked for Him but did not find Him. I will get up now and go about the city, through its streets and squares; I will search for the one my heart loves. So I looked for Him but did not find Him. The watchmen found me as they made their rounds in the city. "Have you seen the one my heart loves?" [4] *Scarcely had I passed them when I found the one my heart loves. I held Him and would not let Him go till I had brought Him to my mother's house, to the room of the one who conceived me.*

Every time we went to church, I would see people praying as if God was going to answer their prayers. I watched how people prayed, and at the back of my mind, I asked myself if God could really hear the prayers. It was always been a puzzled to me about that, *because I didn't know how to pray and could not see God at that time.* These are the questions I asked God, "Where are you God? Can You really hear me? How can I listen to You? Can you reveal Yourself to me? Are You really real like everybody says about You?

I saw people were praying as if God was real to them. And have understanding that God is going to answer their prayers. I was amazed by that. I starting to have eagerness, and thriving in my heart wanting to know Him. I wanted to know God for myself—if God really was real. I want to know so that I could worship Him.

SONG OF SOLOMON 5:4-5

My beloved thrust His hand through the latch-opening; my heart began to pound for Him. I arose to open for my beloved, and my hands dripped with myrrh, my fingers with flowing myrrh, on the handles of the bolt.

SONG OF SOLOMON 5–6

I opened for my beloved, but my beloved had left; He was gone. My heart sank at His departure. I looked for Him but did not find Him. I called Him but He did not answer.

I remember every time we went to church, the pastor would make the altar call. I always wanted to go to the altar for prayer. I didn't want to mist God. And later on, I thought I always needed to go to the altar every time the pastor made the altar call because I thought I needed to do something to feel His presence. I always wanted to know what was like to feel His love over me, and I also wanted to know if He was really real. I was desperate to know God. I was so hungry and thirsty for Him. I wanted Him to show me that He was real in my life and that He was with me. *But for some reason, I was not there yet. I had never seen, heard, or even felt Him. I felt like I needed proof that He was real. Not having understanding of God brought confusion in me.* But that whole time, I knew that God was already with me.

SONG OF SOLOMON 3:9–11

King Solomon made for himself the carriage; He made it of wood from Lebanon. Its posts He made of silver, its base of gold. Its seat was upholstered with purple, its interior inlaid with love. Daughters of Jerusalem, come out, and look, you daughters of Zion. Look on King Solomon wearing a crown, the crown with which His mother crowned Him on the day of His wedding, the day His heart rejoiced.

SONG OF SOLOMON 4:10

*How delightful is your love, my sister, my bride! How much more pleasing is
your love than wine, and the fragrance of your perfume more than any spice!*

I was started to have feelings for David. Later on, I was falling in love
with him, and he was also falling in love with me. Our love for each
other was getting so very strong that we decided to get married. We got
married on my birthday, October 25, 2006. I was the happiest woman
in the whole world. I fell in love with God through him.

SONG OF SOLOMON 1:9–10

*I liken you, my darling, to a mare among Pharaoh's chariot horses. Your
cheeks are beautiful with earrings, your neck with strings of jewels.*

SONG OF SOLOMON 1:7

*Tell me, you whom I love, where you graze your flock and where you rest
your sheep at midday. Why should I be like a veiled woman beside the flocks
of your friends?*

SONG OF SOLOMON 1:8

*If you do not know, most beautiful of women, follow the tracks of the sheep
and graze your young goats by the tents of the shepherds.*

One day, in 2007, David and I went to church. There was a guest
speaker, his name is Pastor (Afshin Ziafat) a powerful man of God,
and through him, I started to have understanding about Jesus Christ
in my life. I listened to his messages and even bought his CDs. I found
myself listening to his CDs a hundred times a day. I listened to his
CD in my house, in my job and in my car as if I couldn't get enough
of his stories about God. He was sharing the powerful testimonies in
his life and how he gave his life to God and surrendered himself to
Jesus. It was not easy for him, but He did it—He surrendered himself
and gave it all to God. The guest speaker's story was about him being
a Muslim and then finding Jesus; His parents disowned him, and the
man stood the truth for Jesus. After the hardship, persecution, and

rejection by his family, the Pastor still focused on Jesus. My heart was filling with courage, love, and excitement wanting more of God in my life. I wanted to experience the same power of love that the speaker Pastor (Afshin Ziafat) experienced with God. The Pastor experienced God in an intimate way, and I wanted the same thing—for me to be able to have a relationship with God.

But when I got to know God a little bit, I realized that it was not really that easy for me to give up everything for Him. To be able to follow Him, I realized there was a cost. I didn't realize that to be able to feel His presence, I needed to experience what He did on the cross for me.

SONG OF SOLOMON 3:6–8

Who is this coming up from the wilderness like a column of smoke, perfumed with myrrh and incense made from all the spices of the merchant? Look! It is Solomon's carriage, escorted by sixty warriors, the noblest of Israel, all of them wearing the sword, all experienced in battle, each with His sword at His side, prepared for the terrors of the night.

SONG OF SOLOMON 1:5

Dark am I, yet lovely, daughters of Jerusalem, dark like the tents of Kedar, like the tent curtains of Solomon.

As the days went by, I continued listening to his CDs. I realized that I was changing in the way I thought that God is the only one that could do it, the way I saw things about Him, and the way I presented myself to other people. I knew right away that God was changing me. God the Father was teaching me and giving me the knowledge about Jesus. When I started to understand more about who Jesus was and what He did for me, I starting to have pain and that pain was so deep into my heart knowing the reality of who He was and the suffering, blood, death, and resurrection that He experienced just for me. I cried a lot when I started to understand more of who He was and what He did for my life.

"I remember telling Jesus that I was a sinner and that I was not worthy to enter into His kingdom. I always asked Jesus why He died for a sinner like

me and what the meaning of all that was. But I was so glad that He saw me as His broken bride and that He was full of mercy and love over me."

SONG OF SOLOMON 4:1

How beautiful you are, my darling! Oh, how beautiful! Your eyes behind your veil are doves. Your hair is like a flock of goats descending from the hills of Gilead.

SONG OF SOLOMON 2:14 *My dove in the clefts of the rock, in the hiding places on the mountainside, show me your face, let me hear your voice; for your voice is sweet, and your face is lovely.*

SONG OF SOLOMON 7:10

I belong to my beloved, and His desire is for me.

SONG OF SONG 4:15

You are a garden fountain, a well of flowing water streaming down from Lebanon.

The more I understood God, the more fear I had of Him. The more I knew Him, the more I fell in love with Him. I thought I was going crazy, to actually fall in love with God, whom I could not even see, yet He is real. One day, I asked God, "Who are You, Lord?" And one day, He answered me, saying, "I AM your Loving Heavenly Father who saved you." I thought for the first time in my life that I actually heard His voice. It was a good feeling knowing that Jesus and I were communicating with each other. God had a tender heart, and He affirmed to me about His beauty and desires over me. It was so good to know that He was real and alive into my soul. Everything I touched and saw was beautiful. I saw the glory of God in my life. *I have found God, yet God chose me first.*

SONG OF SOLOMON 3:9–11

King Solomon made for himself the carriage; He made it of wood from Lebanon. Its posts He made of silver, its base of gold. Its seat was upholstered with purple, its interior inlaid with love. Daughters of Jerusalem, come out and look, you daughters of Zion. Look on King Solomon wearing a crown, the crown with which His mother crowned Him on the day of His wedding, the day His heart rejoiced.

One day, David and I went back to the same church. I was feeling peace and comfort and was full of love that day. There was a man on the pulpit preaching, and his message that day was ingrained into my soul. Then the man from the front of the altar asked everyone to come to the front if they wanted to give their lives to God. *Without hesitation, I stood up and went to the front; and this time, I actually gave my life to God for good with understanding about Him.* When I got to the front, another man gave me a white candle, and he lit it up. *I felt the fire coming from the glory of God.* As I went back to my seat, I was feeling the fire and the burning sensation in my heart. Tears were pouring down my face; and my whole body was shaking from the love, presence, and power of God in my life. And at that moment, I felt the fire of the Holy Spirit within my soul.

SONG OF SOLOMON 8:6

Place me like a seal over your heart, like a seal on your arm; for love is as strong as death, its jealousy unyielding as the grave. It burns like blazing fire, like a mighty flame. Many waters cannot quench love; river cannot sweep it away. If one were to give all the wealth of one's house for love, It would be utterly scorned.

And when the pastor was praying for the congregation, His prayer touched my heart, and I felt like a bolt of lightning of His power came into my soul. I felt like I was about to explode like fireworks, and out of my mouth I said yes to Jesus—to give my life and surrender all to Him. And I found myself going deeper and being abandoned by God. I was feeling revived, refreshed, renewed, and reborn. That day, I was saved by His love for me. I felt like a newborn baby with a pure and innocent heart. It was such a good and beautiful feeling knowing God was with me. I was crying, and tears just kept flowing down my cheeks; my heart was full of rainbows with many colors. The love of Jesus was just overflowing in me like a river. It was a feeling I had never experienced in my entire life, and I loved it. I wanted more of Him. I was so excited that

I could not get enough of Him. I was very excited about the relationship I had with Jesus that I just had to tell all my friends, to the neighbors, to the cities, to the communities, and the whole world about the goodness of God in my life. *God said, "Let us make our own image."*

You—yes, you who are reading this!—*you are the Image of God, and He loves you.*

SONG OF SOLOMON 8:14

Come away, my beloved, and be like a gazelle or like a young stag on the spice-laden mountains.

SONG OF SOLOMON 1:4

Take me away with you—let us hurry! Let the king bring me into His chambers. We rejoice and delight in you; we will praise your love more than wine. How right they are to adore you.

REVELATION 22:17

The Spirit and the bride say, "Come!" And let the one who hears say, "Come!" Let the one who is thirsty come; and let the one who wishes take the free gift of the water of life.

GOD'S GRACE AND MERCY

ROMANS 5:1–5

Therefore, since we have been justified through faith, we have peace with God through our Lord Jesus Christ, through whom we have gained access by faith into this grace in which we now stand. And we boast in the hope of the glory of God. Not only so, but we also glory in our sufferings, because we know that suffering produces perseverance; perseverance, character; and character, hope. And hope does not put us to shame, because God's love has been poured out into our hearts through the Holy Spirit, who has been given to us.

When you were still weak, hopeless, and powerless, Jesus Christ died for you. Not many people want to die for you except the righteous Man, Jesus Christ. But God demonstrated His own love and compassion for you in this; while you were still sinners, Christ died for you.

Since you are now justified by His blood, how much more will you be saved from God's wrath through Him? For if and when you were God's enemies, you were reconciled to Him through death of His Son, how much more, having reconciled, shall you be saved through His life? Not only is this so, but you received reconciliation.

Jesus is not counting the number of your sins. He died so you can be with Him and to be reconciled with your heavenly Father. His death and His resurrection is the only ultimate way of expressing His love for you. If you receive the gift of His Son Jesus Christ, our heavenly Father will receive you. And your name will be written in the Book of Life. And He will reign with you.

PRAYER

Dear heavenly Father,

Thank You for your grace and mercy toward us. Thank You for Your love and compassion, which led us to righteousness before You. Thank You for dying on the cross for us; without You, we are nothing. We will just be the dust from the ground without life. We thank You for saving us and lifting us up from the raging fires of hell. Thank You for keeping us and taking us to Your heavenly mansion. Thank, Lord, that Your eyes are on us—watching us, protecting us, and leading us to your throne. We love You, Jesus.

In Jesus' name, amen.

CHAPTER 19

THE WONDERS OF GOD

On February 14, 2008, God spoke to me. He told me that *He wanted me to have a Bible study in my house.* I was shocked by that because I didn't know anybody to have Bible study with. At that time, most of my friends went to clubs and bars and knew nothing about having Bible study. Having Bible study in my house was not on my mind either, but God said that He would send me a new friends. I trust that it was God that was talking to me. I knew that He would make a way. I just kept all the messages from God in my heart even though I did not have any understanding.

The condominium that we lived in was too small for all of us, so we decided to look for another house. We searched and saw three hundred houses but still could not find the right one for us. I started sharing to David that we needed a bigger house because God wanted us to have Bible study in our house, it sounds impossible but I knew nothing is impossible with God. David agreed with me.

One day, we found a house that we liked; the house looked nice, and we really liked it. We told the Realtor that we wanted to buy it. One afternoon, God spoke to me to stop by the house first, so I told David that I wanted to look at it one more time to make sure it was the right house for us before we bought it. When we were on our way to see the house, I heard the voice of God telling me that the house was not the one for us. I didn't know what He meant. Even before I could go inside the house, I saw a black cat beside the door, and it was staring at me. I started to feel bad; all the hairs on my arm stood on end. I did not even try to go inside. I felt like there was a demon in the house. I started walking away from the house. Then I tried getting out of the neighborhood; right before I turned left, I saw a cemetery across the street in front of the subdivision. I felt like the house is not for us, for some reason, we did not notice the cemetery before, and it was too close to the house. I was just noticing it for the first time. I was just seeing everything for the first time. When I told David what happened, He agreed with me not to buy the house. So we looked and looked again for our new home.

One day, God opened the door for us; we found our new home, and we were very happy in it. Six months into living in our new home, I started to feel lonely and alone. I did not have any friends, and I was getting bored. One day I remembered that God was supposed to give me new friends and we were supposed to have a Bible study in my house, I was waiting, and I was confused as to when God was going to bring the people for me to have Bible study with. I was very happy at the same time because I knew that God would fulfill His promises to me.

Then one day, I met a wonderful woman, and she invited me to go to a get-together with other women. And it just so happened that the group was the one for Bible study. I was amazed at how God let me meet these people. I made friends with them, and I started going to their Bible study sessions. There were many people. I was so shocked to see how much my schedule over the weekend had changed. I saw myself being close to the Lord and being connected to God's people. Instead of me going to the club with my other friends, I was connected with people who loved God and loved talking about God and having Bible study every weekend instead. As the months went by with me going to their Bible study sessions, *I started having Bible study in my house and everyone came. And the promises of God about me having Bible study in my house had been fulfilled. God is faithful. God will do what He says He will do.*

THE MOVE OF GOD

Earlier one day in 2008, we found out about this wonderful church. It was located forty minutes from our home. We decided to start going to the church. We had been coming to the church for a while. But the whole time we were there, I was very confused as to why God would let us come to that church knowing it was forty minutes away from our home even though there was one closer. But later on, we decided to be connected to the church.

One day, I had a burning desire to volunteer at the church. I called the church to see if I could volunteer in the children's ministry or if I could be an usher or greeter. As I was talking to one of the ministers in the church, I was thinking, *"How can I get involved with the church knowing they are so far away from us?"* It was also hard for me to drive that far by myself. As I was thinking this, *the minister mentioned to me that they had just moved, and it was just happen that it was from God. The place that they had just moved to it was the place close to where we lived.* I was shocked when she told me that. The people don't know that we have just moved also but yet God performed signs and wonders right before my eyes. I told her, "Wow." Then I realized and understood that God was really in control and that He wanted us to be connected to that church and to be kingdom-minded.

One day, we went to a new building for the first time. After seeing it, God whispered into my ear, saying that the new building was not the building for them. I shared with David that it was not the building for them, there is another one just for them. But He didn't believe me. Until one day . . .

The pastor was very excited about the building, which was leased to them, and they wanted to buy the building. But I told David that I was very sure that God told me that the building was not the one for them. But he still didn't want to believe me. He thought I was going out of my mind. But not with God, six months later, when it was time to buy the building, the pastor realized they could not buy the building because the owner wanted more money than what the building was worth. So the mortgage company could not buy the building for them, and so the pastor could not buy the building. When David found out about it, he was shocked. He wanted to understand me, but he was very skeptical. He thought that it was just a coincidence the whole time. But I knew that God was talking to us that day.

Jesus said, "Who can know the Father except the one who knows Him?"

DREAM

One night, I had a dream. I saw this huge building. It looked like a regular building from the outside, but in the inside, there was a church. I remember being outside the door, standing on top of the stairs of the building. I was trying to open the door, hoping that I could get in. *But there was an unknown spirit's hands trying to push me out while I was standing in front of the door.* After the hands pushed me out, suddenly, I noticed that I was on the ground. *I was holding a bowl of the anointing water. I immediately went all around the building and sprinkled it with water, and I was praying at the same time.* I was praying the Lord's Prayer. I thanked God for everything He had done to the building.

After I prayed, I noticed that I was on top of the building again; and this time, *before I tried to open the door, the door immediately opened by itself.* I tried to come in. I was so glad that I had the courage to come into the building. By the help of God, I was able to go inside. I remember being at the upper level of the building, and I saw people from the bottom coming inside. They were all looking like they had been hypnotized. They were looking like zombies, and they were all in one line to enter the building. I noticed that there were no chairs in the four walls of the building. I only saw people who were hypnotized. I was terrified of what I saw, and then I woke up.

And I said, "Wow, what a dream!" because I could not believe what I saw.

Because the pastor could not buy the building, they tried to buy another. After buying the new building, they realized they could not move into it because they found out later on that the electric wires were stolen; vandals stole the wires from all over the building. The electric company told the pastor that they could not turn the electricity on because all the wires were gone. Workers could not work to fix the building because the whole place was dark. So the building was basically useless at that time.

GOD SPOKE

Later on, God spoke to me concerning the building. I came to the pastor and shared with him what God told me. I told him that he needed $300,000, and God wanted to bless him with that. Also, God wanted to remove all the vandals who wanted to steal the wires and destroy the building. God wanted to restore the building, and he wanted to bless and help the pastor.

God spoke to me again, and He told me to anoint the building with water. He told me very specifically what kinds of water to get. He said to me to find "paddle water." I was confused as to where to get the paddle water, knowing that all the cities were experiencing drought. The water from the lake was going down, and we were losing a lot of water. Also, it had not rained for a long time.

I thought maybe God wanted me to get water from the rain or maybe water from the street. But God said no. I thought that maybe I could get it from the store or maybe from the faucet or the refrigerator, but God said no. I was disturbed by that. I asked my friend where I could get paddle water, knowing I didn't see any water anywhere. My friend told me to look around the street as I drove, hoping that I would maybe see paddle water.

One day, I spoke with one of the pastors from the church. I asked her if she saw paddle water anywhere. To my surprise, she said yes; she said that the new building that the pastor just bought had a creek behind the building. When I heard that, I was very excited because I knew that my search was over. I immediately got my children ready to go to the new building. While I was driving to get there, I was excited to see the creek. When I arrived, I saw it right away. I was very excited getting out of the car. I told my children to stay in the car.

THE PRESENCE OF GOD

When I was actually by the creek, looking at the water, I was amazed by God. I noticed the paddle water right away. When I saw it right there in front of me, I was in awe because I could not believe that I was actually seeing paddle water, knowing that the whole city's lakes were drying up. Then I started looking around, and I noticed that the creek was a little bit dark even during the day because it was surrounded by trees. The place was very quiet, and the water was still. I started to pray. I asked God if he was with me at that time. I asked if He was the one who brought me there. I asked God to reveal himself to me if He was with me. Right after I prayed, suddenly, I looked up and saw a bird flying over me. While I was there, I felt the presence of the Holy Spirit. He was moving with His love and power toward me. God told me to get the bucket from the car, and I started filling it with water.

God spoke to me again, and *He told me to anoint the building with water.* After I filled up the bucket with water, I went back home first and I started praying for the water and the building in my prayer closet. Later that same day, I went back to the building, and *God told me to sprinkle the water all around the building. So I started doing just that, accompanied by prayers. I was praying the Lord's Prayer.*

MATTHEW 6:9-13

This, then, is how you should pray: "Our Father in heaven, hollowed be your name, your kingdom come, your will be done, on earth as it is in heaven. Give us today our daily bread. And forgive us our debts, as aw also have forgiven our debtors. And lead us not into temptation, but deliver us from evil one.

I sprinkled all around the building and I was expecting signs, wonders, and miracles from God. I felt the glory of God as I was praying and sprinkling all around the building. After I finished sprinkling the building with water, I waited to see what was going to happen next. I waited upon the Lord.

LUKE 11:20

But if I drive out demons by the finger of God, then the kingdom of God has come upon you.

Less than a week after, every time I read the Bible, God always brought me to Genesis 1:1–4. I didn't understand it at that time. One day, I was reading a devotional book, and the same scripture was there. I bought the powerful book from a thrift store for only 25$, and the author was a famous Evangelist. God led me again to the same scripture from his book: Genesis 1:1–4. I felt like God was talking to me, so I finally I tried to listen to what He was saying to me.

GENESIS 1:1–4

In the beginning God created the heavens and the earth. Now the earth was formless and empty, darkness was over the surface of the deep, and the Spirit of God was hovering over the waters. And God said, "Let there be light," and there was light. God saw that the light was good and He separated the light from the darkness.

When I read Genesis 1:1–4, I was left in awe. I felt like I was part of the passage. I didn't know how to explain it. But I decided to share with David that I was in Genesis 1:1–4, that I actually experienced being in the passage. He looked at me, and he criticized me instead. He told me that the words from Genesis spoke of what happened billions of years ago, so it would be impossible for me to be in Genesis 1:1–4. I was very sad when he said that to me. I did not understand everything that was happening to me. But later on, God spoke to me again and He told me that He made the scripture to be alive for me and that He was the one who created all things. God spoke to me through His Word and He confirmed it with His Word, and there was no other way. After God told me that, His Word became *a live* within my soul. Then I understood that I was walking in genuine reality with His Word. After God spoke to me, I have found peace with Him.

DREAM FULLFILLED

In Genesis 1:2 now the earth was formless and empty, darkness was over the surface of the deep, and the Spirit of God was hovering over the waters.

When I was in the creek, it was dark, void, and empty is the place that no one wants to be in, but yet God send me there.

In Genesis 1:3 And God said, "Let there be light," and there was light.

The power company said to the pastor that **they could not turn on the lights** from the building because the wires were gone and the vandalized people took all the wires.

But one week later, after *I prayed and sprinkling water all around the building, God performed miracles before everybody's eyes. God was faithful. **The lights** from the building miraculously **turned on.***

One weekend later, the pastor saw that the light was on in the building; he was amazed and in awe of the Lord Jesus Christ.

That scripture brought confidence to me knowing that God was with me. God performed miracles for that building. **The Word of God is alive.**

GENESIS 1:2

Now the earth was formless and empty, darkness was over the surface of the deep, and the spirit of God was hovering over the waters.

I felt this when I was standing in front of the water, praying to the Lord, and when the bird was flying above me.

And God said, "Let there be light," and there was light. When God spoke to me and that was when I prayed for the building and sprinkled it with the water. God was cleaning, cleansing, washing, and making a new thing for the building. God was performing miracles. *The electricity in the building miraculously* **turned on.**

God was hovering over the building the whole time. He performed miracles beyond my understanding. To God be the glory!

When the pastor saw that the lights in the building were on, he announced it to the whole congregation. Workers were able to work in the building from then on they cannot worked on the building before because it was very dark, and the pastor was thanking God for the miracle that took place.

On Tuesday the following week, at around six in the morning, we had a prayer meeting. The pastor called me to go to the altar with him, and he announced to the whole congregation that I had a prophetic voice. At that time, I did not know about "prophetic voice" and what the meaning of "prophetic" was. But I just kept the word from the pastor in my heart. On Tuesday two weeks later, still at around six o'clock in the morning, the pastor came to me again and told me to also tell him whatever God is saying to me. He said to me that *we were one,* and I said yes to him.

I was so glad that I was able to do what God asked me to do. God is a good God. He didn't want to put me to shame. He would always fulfill all His promises in my life. From that moment on, I trusted God that He was with me and was hovering over me. "Not by might nor by power, but by the Spirit, says the Lord."

NUMBERS 12:6

He said, "Listen to My words: 'When there is a prophet among you, I the Lord, reveal Myself to them in visions, I speak to them in dreams.'"

I AM MAKING EVERYTHING NEW

LUKE 11:20

But if I drive out demons by the finger of God, then the kingdom of God has come upon you.

Ten years later, on March 15, 2018, God spoke to me. He asked me to come back to the same building. At first, I told God that I didn't want to return to the building. But God was very persistent that I needed to come back to the building. So I said yes to the Lord. I told God that I was going to come to the building just for Him.

I decided to come back on March 20, 2018, and I brought somebody with me. When we got to the building, I saw a new sign in front of the building that said "KING JESUS" on it. When I saw that, I thought, *Wow.* I could not explain what I saw in words. The building, which used to be dark and empty, and demons are occupying the building, but now had lights and was occupied by Jesus and His disciples. The building looked beautiful. God was hovering over the building. With God's finger, He made the building His kingdom. God is awesome.

THE ACTIVITY OF GOD

It was a Father's Day in 2009. God told me to go to the church that was thirty minutes from our home, because God wanted to give me something. I shared that with David, but he was not very happy about it; He thought that I just wanted to do my own thing. But God was very persistent to me, so I decided to listen to Him since He was my heavenly Father.

On the way to church, I was crying. I asked myself is to why would God wants me to go to the church by myself. Why God is not allowing me to stay with David on Father's Day, so I could go to the same church with him? I was very confused with God. I was very hurt and sad while I was driving to church. When I got there, there was a man at the door. He told me to go upstairs room, and I did. There, I saw a woman coming toward me. Then I heard the voice of the Lord saying to me that "I needed to listen to her and do what she asked me to do." She asked me if I was lost. I smiled and told her that I might be. I asked the woman is to what was the name of the place we were in. "Because I was wondering is to what is the reason God wants me to be there." The woman replied, telling me that the place was called "God's Chosen People." Then she gave me information about the meeting, and then she asked me to follow her. Then she told me to sit down beside her. I looked around, and there was no place to sit down; the room was full. A lot of people were standing up. To my amazement, the seat beside hers was empty; she asked me to sit down beside her, and I said yes. I felt like God saved the seat for me.

As I sat down, the man speaking at the front and he was asking everybody is to why they were there. Everybody shared their reason. When it was my turn to answer, I told them with tears running down my cheeks that God sent me there. I did not know at that time that I had to carry my own cross to follow Jesus.

I did not know the place was called God's Chosen People. The man handed me a bag with a DVD of prayers and other good stuff from their pastor. I was amazed that the man handed me a *Prayer with Confidence DVD*, because I didn't know how to pray at that time. At that moment, I felt like God wanted me to pray.

I remember every weekend for four weeks in a row, I have been coming to the Bible study, and everybody was asking me to pray. But I kept saying no to them because I didn't know how to pray at the time. I was so nervous just to open my mouth. So when I received the DVD from the pastor, I realized it's a message exactly what God wanted me to do—to pray and have intimacy and confidence in Him. God wanted me to connect with Him through prayer, and He wanted to teach and guide me concerning the prayer.

After that, I came home and told David what God was doing in my life, that God wanted me to go to that church to teach me how to pray. David still not believing me and he is not happy with me going to the church. That same day, I decided to bring him to a nice restaurant for Father's day. While we were having a nice dinner, David told me that he wanted us to go to downtown coming up that Saturday. He wanted us to stay in a nice hotel and go for a walk or go to a nice restaurant; he just wanted us to have a nice weekend alone together.

The following Tuesday, God spoke to me again. He told me that I was going back to that same church again; and this time, David was coming with me. I was shocked with the Lord because David was already unhappy with me going to the same church. God spoke with power over me. He wanted me to know that it was Him that I was talking to the whole time. God told me that He would perform signs and wonders for me.

I shared with David about him going to the same church with me the following weekend; after the long conversation I had with him, David still did not want to come with me because he said that God did not tell him to come. But I believe God wanted him to come. But at the same time, David thought that I was just making it up. I prayed for David and gave it all to the Lord because, after all, God is in control.

I prayed to the Lord and asked Him to give me the revelation and understanding as to what He was trying to say to me. I asked God to come to David and share it with him that God wants him to come to the same church. One day, God answer my prayer, He came to David and told him the same thing that he said to me. God spoke to me again, and He said that He would speak to David and reveal Himself to him. His voice was new to me at that time. God turned my sadness to joy and dancing because God revealed Himself to David in a mighty way. I kneeled down and prayed. I thanked God for His goodness and faithfulness towards me. God revealed to David that it was Him I was talking to and that whatever word I said was true and was from God. I learned so much about God that my confidence grew stronger than I could ever have imagined. I will never forget that *God backs me up and did not put me to shame.* God showed up and revealed Himself to David; He then realized that God was alive and real. God has all the glory. The way God reveals himself to us is beyond our understanding.

IN AWE OF GOD

God manifest Himself

A representative from his job called David on Thursday and told him that he had two tickets for the stadium, which was in downtown; he wanted to give two tickets to us. The stadium was having a gospel song performance that day; the area that we would be sitting at, had a lot of free food. David was so excited and told the man that we were planning to stay at a hotel in downtown area anyway. David was very excited because we had something meaningful to do—not just to go for a walk or eat at a nice restaurant, but to worship and glorified God at the same time in the stadium. The man also said that he was one of the members of the choir of the same church I told David that we would be going back to the church that weekend. David was shocked when he heard that from him, and he told the representative that I was just at the church over the weekend.

The man continued speaking; he said that one of the famous Gospel Singers in the America was going to be there, and he was inviting us to come to the same church that I was telling David to come. It just happened that famous singer is one of his favorite. While David was talking to the representative, he was staring right at me the whole time. He realized that I was telling the truth—that we were going to the same church that same weekend after all. David was amazed, and overwhelm with awe of God that he didn't have a choice but to say yes to the man to gives us two tickets for the stadium and for us to come to the same church that I told him that God wants us to go. Then David came to me and told me that we were going to the same church that I went to last Sunday. I smiled and said yes to him. That weekend we went to church and we praise and worship God and also to see the famous singer.

God fulfilled His promises when He said to me that David will come to church with me, God, again did not put me to shame. I was not shocked because I was expecting that from God because I knew He would perform signs and wonders for us. David knew that I was telling the truth. I did not tell him, "I told you so." Instead, I knelt down and humbled myself, and I thanked God that He did not put me to shame. God is faithful. He will do what He says He will do. He is a good Father. I was in awe of God. He really strengthened my faith with His love over me like never before. God speaks the truth with love.

When we were at the stadium, I saw a lot of people worshipping and praising God. People were hungry and thirsty for God. As I was watching them, I heard the voice of God saying that this stadium was not only for basketball, but also for His people that were going to worship Him and for them to know His love for them. And He said to me that I would one day be able to speak and share His words of healing, restoration and deliverance to His people in the stadium. People will be heal, restore and delivered. When I heard Him saying that, I was overwhelmed with His love and His plan over my life. Tears of joy came down my cheeks. I thought that was a huge project for me, but it was not my project—it was God's. Nothing is impossible with God. He is in control over me. All I need to say is yes to God. I believe God, and I believe God can perform miracles. I was amazed with God for showing up and revealing Himself to me by bringing signs, wonders, and miracles into my life.

DISCERNING THE VOICE OF GOD

REVELATION 21:3

And I heard a loud voice from the throne saying, "Look! God's dwelling place is now among the people, and He will dwell with them. They will be His people, and God himself will be with them and be their God.

LUKE 9:35

A voice came from the cloud, saying, "This is my Son, whom I have chosen; listen to Him."

MATTHEW 17:5

While He was still speaking, a bright cloud covered them, and a voice from the cloud said, "This is my Son, whom I love; with Him I am well pleased. Listen to Him!"

JOHN 12:28–30

Father, glorify your name!" Then a voice came from heaven, "I have glorified it, and will glorify it again." The crowd that was there and heard it said it had thundered; others said an angel had spoken to Him. Jesus said, "This voice was for your benefit, not mine.

PSALM 40:5

Many, Lord my God, are the wonders you have done, the things you planned for us. None can compare with you; were I to speak and tell of your deeds, they would be too many to declare.

PSALM 21:1–10

The king rejoices in your strength, Lord. How great is His joy in the victories you give! You have granted Him His heart's desire and have not withheld the request of His lips. You came to greet Him with rich blessings and placed a crown of pure gold on His head. He asked you for life, and you gave it to Him— length of days, forever and ever. Through the victories you gave, His glory is great; you have bestowed on Him splendor and majesty. Surely you have granted Him unending blessings and made Him glad with the joy of your presence. For the king trusts in the Lord; through the unfailing love of the Most High He will not be shaken. Your hand will lay hold on all your enemies; your right hand will seize your foes. When you appear for battle, you will burn them up as in a blazing furnace. The Lord will swallow them up in His wrath, and His fire will consume them. You will destroy their descendants from the earth, their posterity from mankind.

PSALM 24

The earth is the Lord's and everything in it, the world, and all who live in it; For He founded it on the seas and established it on the waters. Who may ascend the mountain of the Lord? Who may stand in His Holy place? the one who has clean hands and a pure heart, who does not trust in an idol or swear by a false god. They will receive blessing from the Lord and vindication from God their Savior. Such is the generation of those who seek Him, who seek Your face, God of Jacob. Lift up Your heads, You gates; be lifted up, You ancient doors, that the King of Glory may come in. who is this King of Glory? The Lord strong and mighty, the Lord mighty in battle. Lift up your heads, you gates; lift them up. You ancient doors, that the King of Glory may come in. who is He, this King of Glory/the Lord Almighty—He is the King of Glory.

God is the God of glory, and He loves to talk to you and tell you all the good things that are going to happen for your future and your destiny. You have been predestined to carry His glory. You have been chosen to be the one to carry His Word to the nations. People follow your leadership because of His love and glory over you.

CHAPTER 20

LOST

David and I decided to go to Florida for our first-year anniversary on October 25, 2007. We went to the "Holy Land Experience" in Florida, and it was a beautiful experience. We loved it, and we enjoyed just being able to see the Bible come to life. It brought comfort to my heart. Our anniversary brought love and peace into my heart.

On November 19, 2007, when we got back from Florida, I started to feel weak. I felt like I was going to fall down to the ground. I was so weak that I was crawling to go up the stairs towards our bedroom. I didn't know what was happening to me; fear came over me. I started to have feelings of anxiety, and I was very nervous. I felt pain all over my body. I decided to go to the doctor's office for a physical check-up. The doctor found out that my blood was not normal; he told me that I should go to a specialist doctor to check my blood. I was shocked. I started to talk to myself. I thought, *what is this doctor trying to tell me about me going to a specialist?* I started to get very concerned, and I asked myself what was going on with my body. As I was making an appointment to see the specialist, fear came over me again. I felt like I didn't want to see the doctor and for him to give me the bad news. I asked David to come with me for support, and he did; he went with me to the specialist.

BAD NEWS FROM THE DOCTOR

When we get to the doctor specialist's office, I met a nurse who was from the Philippines. We started talking to each other in our language, and she was comforting me before I went to see the doctor. When it was time for the doctor to check me, my hands were very sweaty, tingly, and shaky. The doctor diagnosed me with CML (chronic myeloid leukemia). He said to me that there was nothing that could heal the cancer, not even medicine; he said that the medicine can only maintain my body so I can be alive and continually saying that I will eventually die. The doctor said to me and to David that I was going to die within six months, especially if I did not take the medicine.

When the doctor said that I was going to die, I got even more scared. I was terrified; my heart was beating really fast with fear, knowing the doctor was telling me that I was going to die. David was very concerned; with fear, he asked the doctor a lot of questions concerning leukemia. The doctor told him what was going to happen to me; he said that the cancer could not be healed and that I would die. David was very scared and sad. The doctor wrote me a prescription of my medication, and we went to a pharmacy to buy the medicine. The man at the pharmacy said that it would take three days for the medicine to come. I was very concerned about the cancer, so I told him that I needed the medicine that same day. He said to me that it was a special medicine that had to be ordered. He suggested for me that if I ever have a fever, I should go directly to the hospital. I shouldn't even take Tylenol. When He told me that, I became even more afraid. I understood at that moment that the disease was very serious. It was a matter of life or death.

When we got home, David and I didn't know what to think. We could hardly talk to each other; we were both shocked. We couldn't believe this was actually happening to us. I remember looking at David's face, seeing that he was very distressed and worried. One night, I remember lying on the bed all by myself. I was looking back on my life, how much of my life was good and there was no stress. I didn't have to worry about the disease. In my quiet moment, I asked God, "Why me?" I thought to myself that there were so many people in this world, *but why me? Why is it cancer? My life is just beginning,* I thought. I started remembering all the good things in life, the memories that I would never forget. I was married to David for one year, and David and I are so in love and we had a beautiful life together. For the first time in my life, I thought I found a good man in my life who loved God and me. I thought my life was complete. I understand that I barely knew God, I have just gave my life to Him less than one year, I don't have a relationship with Him yet, I felt like the minute I gave my life to God, my whole life change and shakes me with His presence. I have never understood what was happening to me, I was shocked.

So my question to God was, "Why me?" I thought the journey of my life was going to be good, that I was going to have a good family and a good life. But at that moment, I realized I was wrong. I felt like the cancer stopped everything in my life. The cancer was always on my mind, and I cried so many times just thinking about it. I was very sad; there were so many times that I want to killed myself, my reason was that I was going to die anyway, and it was taking very slowly, so why not die sooner? My mind was in such a haze that I couldn't even think right. I felt like I was falling into darkness.

I thought about my children and what was going to happen to them if I died. What were they going to do? Who was going to take care of them? I also felt like the cancer was so unfair for David, knowing we just got married and had just started our new life together. I thought our one year together would be wonderful new journey for us. I was very concerned for him. I was wondering what was going on in his mind about all this bad news.

I started to blame myself, and so much negativity came to my mind and my life. I questioned myself, is to what is *really going on in my life? Is there a place for me to go? Is there anything I can do?* I found out from the doctor that there was nothing they could do for me except to wait for me to die. I just had to do what the doctor wanted me to do. I was feeling hopeless and powerless, like I was in a dead-end situation in my life.

I came to my pastor and asked him and everybody to pray for me at that time, I felt like I lost my faith. I felt very weak, and I didn't have any confidence whatsoever. I always depended on the doctor to fix my situation. At that time, I didn't know that God could heal me. One day, I went to the doctor's office, and they withdrew blood from me. They wanted me to come to the doctor's office every two weeks to check my blood to see if there were any changes in my blood and my body. Also, they would inject needles in me to give me B12 at least twice a week. I didn't like needles; they scared me. And every time they took blood from me, I felt like they took the part of me.

Darkness that it wasn't there before but at that moment was forming in my life. I also noticed that I did not have control over my life anymore. I felt like I didn't have freedom anymore. I saw myself at the doctor's office all the time, having my blood checked. I felt like the demons were tying me down to their realm of death. I felt like I had to do what the doctor wanted me to do. I had to listen to what they told me and go to places they wanted me to go. I felt like I lost my freedom. I was broken and shattered. Everything changed in my life. I felt like the demons really got me that time.

Losing control over my life prompted me to wanting to know if God was real. Now my question was, is God really real? I thought I knew God, but at that moment, I realized that I didn't know Him at all. I did not have the understanding about God. I felt like I lost myself; and I was losing hope, joy, and strength. I was in so much pain physically, emotionally, and mentally. I was hopeless, helpless, and I thought my life was over.

I questioned myself a lot, is to *how can I fix the problem? Where is God? Is there any place for me to be? Is God hiding from me? Is there any place that I can find Him?* And I realized that there was no place to go except with God, being face to face with Him.

One day, I was at work crying, and my tears were just pouring down like a flowing river on my face. I remember memories of everything that happened to me in my past flashing right there in front of me. God brought my memories back. I saw the following visions flashing by:

God showed me all the things that He did for me, how He is faithful towards me.

Is when the day I died and came back to life, is when Peter tried to kill me and I escaped from death, is when Scott tried to remove me from the face of this earth, but yet I am still alive, when the naked man almost raped me, and the angel protect me, and now the cancer, but yet I am still standing.

God reveal His love, His kindness, and faithfulness over me and how He gives me hope. That God will always be there for me to protect me from the hands of the enemies. When those memories kept flashing back again,

I realized that the enemy was trying to wipe me out from this falling world. I tried to be strong, and no matter what the enemy was trying to do to me, I knew God was always with me. God always protected me from those people and the enemy who was trying to touch my body and remove me from the face of this earth. The enemy could try, but he will not succeed because I knew that God was with me. So I started to believe and trust in God, and I believed that God could do all things for His children who loved Him. Without any doubt, I knew that God could heal me.

After remembering all those signs, wonders, and miracles from God in my past, I started to have confidence, assurance, hope, and peace with God. I knew He loved me, and I believed in Him. I tried to change my way of thinking that although I could not see God, I still knew He was real. I knew He was with me, and I trusted Him. I started to be a good person and showed love and kindness to everybody like Jesus had, which I had never done before because of my sins. I tried to be a good wife for David, like it says in Proverbs 31. I started to have fear in the Lord. I didn't want to disappoint God. I wanted to make sure I was walking with Him. I wanted to walk in the righteousness before God. I did what God told me to do, which was to read His Word, pray, and worship Him.

ISAIAH 57:15

For this is what the high and exalted says-He who lives forever, whose name is holy: I live in a high and holy place, but also with the one who is contrite and lowly in spirit, to revive the spirit of the lowly and to revive the heart of the contrite.

ISAIAH 66:2

Has not My hand made all these things, and so they came into being? declares the Lord. These are the ones I look on with favor: those who are humble and contrite in spirit, and who tremble at My word.

EPHESIANS 6:11–12

Put on the whole armor of God that you may be able to stand against the schemes of the devil. For we wrestle not against flesh and blood, but against principalities, against powers against the rulers of the darkness of this world, against spiritual wickedness in high places.

2 CORINTHIANS 2:11

In order that Satan might not outwit us. For we are not unaware of His schemes.

The enemy will try and do everything it takes in His power to prevent you from becoming who God made you to be because the enemy knows that you are a threat to his throne and to his kingdom. God sees you as a powerful instrument, workmanship, and tools for God's glory because God has an eye on you before you were born, and He wants to give you His throne. The enemy wants to twist your mind to confuse you so that you will not receive what God has ordained for you to have. But God wins every time.

If you experience being alienated, be encouraged because your gift—the power and fire of God—has already been placed in your hands.

The attacks of the enemy on your life are not about who you were in the past, but who you will be in the future, The carrier of God's glory. When bad things happen, that's when light cover you and He *shine on you. God loves you!*

CHAPTER 21

MY PAIN

One day, in 2009, David thought that the cancer would be a problem for our marriage, so he thought of not staying married to me. He thought that I was going to die soon. His behavior toward me was changing; He was trying to remove himself from me. Sometimes he would not come home until the following day. I would ask him where he was, but he would ignore me, not wanting me to know where he was. It was a very painful season for me. I asked God is to why He did that to me and why He allowed that to happen in my life—after wanting to know God, getting to know Him, and trying to emulate Proverbs 31, doing my best to be a good, loving, and submissive wife to my husband. I was shocked as to why something like this happened to me. I thought that if I gave myself to God, that He would take care of my needs. I asked God if I did anything wrong for David to have a change of heart toward me. But He did not answer me. So much trouble came my way. I was praying for David and for myself.

At around nine o'clock one evening, I remember drawing the cross while I was waiting for David to come home. As I was drawing, I noticed my tears kept falling on my drawing, and it started to have smears. I tried to call David, but he did not answer. I kept looking at the clock, wondering why he was not home yet; every night that I waited for him, I noticed that my tears kept falling. I started to feel sad and anxious because David was not home yet. I was hoping that he would come home soon. But he never did. I didn't want to lose David because for the first time in my married life, I actually understood what marriage was all about—it was about God's love over me.

David was the one who brought me and my family to God, and he brought us to different churches. Before I met him, my whole family and I barely went to church. I do not have relationships and understanding about God at that time. David was the one who brought me closer to God, and he also was the only one who brought us to church. But suddenly, he was not around anymore. I would think that in my darkest moment that my husband will be the one who will be there by my side, but I was wrong. I was so confused about what was happening to us. I asked God if He was with me. I felt like David is not the same person I once knew. I was losing hope with God. David decided to remove himself from me. He was out there in the dark, where he thought he would find something good; but later on, he realized that he was wrong that whole time. But he is still pursued darkness over light. I found out that he was cheating on me with another woman; infidelity was creeping in our marriage.

He thought that I would be a burden for him one day; He thought that I would get very sick, and he would have to take care of me. He thought that I would die one day, just thinking about all of those things that made him realize, that he could not handle it. He did not believe God was there for me—that God was the healer and that He wanted to heal me. But the reality was that he chose not to stay married to me because of the cancer. I loved God so much that I chose light and not to follow the darkness. Jesus says, "If you disown me before man, I will disown you before my father." I felt like if I followed David, who was going to the wrong way as if God was saying to me that I was following the darkness instead of light, and that I am going to disowning Him, so I followed God's way and chose light instead. The Bible says that if I follow Jesus Christ, I will be persecuted that I must die daily, so I felt like I died daily for me to experience pain and rejection. I started to pray for David and believed God for him.

One day, after I prayed for David, God performed a miracle for me by bringing him back home to me. David had asked for forgiveness from me. So I forgave him, and we tried to move on and tried to stay together. I tried to get some help, and I tried my best to be a good wife for him. I was hoping that he would have a change of heart and would be a good husband to me.

One month later, in the afternoon, my older daughter borrowed David's laptop. And there it was—she saw with her own eyes what he was doing to me. He was talking to a lot of woman on the Internet, watching pornography, and doing other stuff. My daughter came to me with tears on her face; after she saw everything that he had done to me, she told me not to buy her a car anymore. After, my daughter showed me what was on his computer, including all those women on the Internet he was talking to. When I found out more of the truth, I thought that my whole world was tumbling down over me. My self-esteem was demolished; the shame was pointed at my face. I felt like I lost all my belief, my future, and my life. I thought that my whole life and my destiny were supposed to be with him—that we would always stay married until we grow old and die and that we would serve and worship God together. But at that time, I felt lost, rejected, defeated, and weak just thinking my life without him. I thought my life was over. My question to myself was, what will I do without him? I was so broken and shattered and had no direction in life. I knew I loved him so much. I tried to forgive him again despite of his imperfections and every wrong he had done to me.

I pray and I asked God to give us another chance, and God did answer me. God brought David back to me again. Even though he did me wrong, I got back with him because of love. Also, I want to save our marriage. We had a conversation for us to get back together, and he agreed. Repentance, forgiveness, and reconciliation took place from that moment on. But later on, our relationship started to get cloudy again. For three days and three nights being with him, my heart still hurt, and I could not erase from my mind the pain that he caused me. I was asking God to give me strength to pass through the deep waters. I wanted God to heal my broken heart. I just wanted to believe David even though everything he said was a lied. I wanted to believe him because I wanted to save our marriage and also because I loved him. I was fighting for my marriage I was desperate for God's direction over my life.

One night later, God spoke to me to come to church and pray. I went to church at around eleven at night, and there, I prayed for God to guide and direct me so that I will find peace in Him. I wanted God to be near me and give me direction at that moment. After I prayed, I went back home, I saw David sleeping and I saw his laptop again. It was sitting on my side of the bed. I have never checked his laptop and cell phone before because I trusted him, but for the first in our marriage, I actually opened his laptop. I looked at him, and he was still sleeping, so I started to look at his laptop. I was shocked by what I saw with my own eyes. I saw everything he was doing behind my back while I was at the church praying to God to guide me regarding him. David was watching pornography and talking to a lot of women on the Internet that night again. I was feeling hurt, shame, fear, anxiety, betrayal, neglect, brokenness, and hopelessness. I lost it, and I thought I was the ugliest woman on the face of this earth. I lost my worth as his wife. I felt like I could not see straight. I thought everything I saw was dark. I thought I was blind.

Because of my brokenness and hurt, I acted poorly and started to fight him. That night, I said something that I would never forget, but I did not mean to say it to him. I told him that *I would put him in jail because he was holding my hands very tights that leave scars on my arms.* But I did not call the police on him. Instead, I went to church and prayed. I asked God to give me understanding, peace, and strength. I came back home, and I saw him sleeping again. I forgave him and I prayed for him again.

One day, I called his friend to ask if he knew where he was, his friend told me that he went to jail when he came to his house. I did not know that he went to jail until two days later, when he did not come home. When the police picked him up and took him to jail, I realized that I spoke about him going to jail and it was actually happening to him. I was shocked is to how my word have power. I felt like didn't really mean for him to go to jail. I felt like I was just not happy with him. But I did not know that the word I said will actually happen to him.

I tried to understand what just happened. Fear of the Lord came over me—I was shocked that God could actually do that. I repented for my sins immediately. I forgave David. I didn't want anything in my heart that was not of God after what happened to him. I wanted to be right with God.

I told to everyone that no matter what happened to them, they need to forgive and they need to give words that should edify, exalt, and comfort the people at all times. But at the same time, I felt like it was the word from God what happen to him, God is letting me know what is going to happen to him in advance. God said that He would protect me from anyone who will harm me. David humbled himself while he is in jail.

LUKE 6:29

If someone slaps you on one cheek, turn to them the other also. If someone takes your coat, do not with hold your shirt from them.

Later on, God spoke to me, and He told me that He was protecting me from David. God said to me that I was the "chosen one," and through me, God would bring justice to the people. I never understood that message, but I pondered on it in my heart.

I didn't want David to go jail. But God showed me what would take place in his life. God showed me that he was going to jail in the spirit realm. It was actually a prophecy for him, in heaven is already ordained for him to go to jail—God was just revealing it to me.

God will not be mocked and be insulted by men. He is God. I told to his friend that I told David that I would put him to jail, but that I didn't mean it; his friend was shocked and became afraid of me. He said to me that David mentioned to him that I was anointed by God, but he did not know how true that was until he saw what was happening to him. Just one word from me, and he went to jail. The Bible says, "Do not touch my anointing do my prophet no harm." All I could do was to pray for him and forgive him.

ENCOURAGING WORD

When you have been hurt, denied and betrayed by somebody, forgiveness and prayers are the best tools to have peace and strength. God loves you. He will never leave you nor forsake you. God will protect you.

1 CHRONICLES 16:22

Do not touch My anointed Ones; do My Prophets no harm.

I realized that God was fighting my battles. God gave David so many chances, but he did not obey God. God spoke to me, and He told me to let David go this time. I could not change David—only God could change him. God said to me that He would separate the light from the darkness so He could take care of the light and also God can take care of the darkness.

I did what God told me to do—I let him go. We decided to move on and go our separate ways. I remember signing the divorce papers, and it was a very hard thing for me to do. When David trying to sign the divorced paper, he mention to me that he had to go back home on time by seven o'clock in the evening, otherwise the police will take him to jail again. I was shocked when he told me that, because when we were marriage I always tell him to come home by seven o'clock in the evening so that we can have a date. The whole time, he never comes home by seven o'clock. But after we got divorced God make him to come back home by seven o'clock. I was amazed by God; He is faith full in all His ways.

God was trying to protect me from him. God was disciplining him and bringing David back to God. I had fear of God. I wanted to do the righteousness of God in my life. Fearing God means wisdom of God. David thought that I was going to die, but by the grace of God, I am still standing. I am victorious with Jesus. I have found God, and I will never let Him go in my life. I want to walk in righteousness before God because *I love Him.* I forgive and I pray for David.

IDENTITY WITH GOD

PSALM 24:3–10

Who may ascend the hill of the Lord? Who may stand in His Holy place? He who has clean hands and a pure hearth, who does not lift up His soul to an idol or swear by what is false. He will receive blessing from the Lord. And vindication from God His Savior. Such is the generation of those who seek Him, who seek your face, O God of Jacob. Lift up your heads, O you gates; be lifted up, you ancient doors, that the King of glory may come in. who is this the King of glory? The Lord strong and mighty, the Lord mighty in battle. Lift up your heads, O you gates; lift them up, you ancient doors, that the King of glory may come in. who is He, this King of glory? The Lord Almighty—He is the King of glory.

2 CORINTHIANS 4:8–9

We are hard pressed on every side, but not crushed; perplexed, but not in despair; persecuted, but not abandoned; struck down, but not destroyed.

PSALM 42:1–3

As the deer pants for streams of water, so my soul pants for You, my God. My soul thirsts for God, for the living God. When can I go and meet with God? My tears have been my food day and night, while the people say to me all day long, "Where is your God?"

PHILIPPIANS 3:13-14

Brothers and sisters, I do not consider myself yet to have taken hold of it. But one thing I do: forgetting what is behind and straining toward what is ahead. Press toward the goal to win the prize for which God has called me heavenward in Christ Jesus.

Know who you are; you are the daughter of the King. You are precious and beautiful to His eyes.

God doesn't want you to have fear because He is with you. God doesn't want you to be dismayed, for He is your God. He will strengthen you. Yes, He will uphold you with His righteous right hand. God wants you to give all your burdens to Him, and He will sustain you. He will never permit the righteous to be moved. "Come to me all who labor and are heavy-laden, and I will give you rest. Take my yoke upon you and learn from me, for I am gentle and lowly in heart, and you will find rest for your souls. For my yoke is easy, and my burden is light."

He would grant you, according to the riches of His glory, to be strengthened with might through His Spirit in the inner man, that Christ may dwell in your hearts through faith, that you, being rooted and grounded in love, may be able to comprehend with all the saints what is the width and length and depth and height—to know the love of Christ, which passes knowledge, that you may be filled with all the fullness of God. But He said to me, "My grace is sufficient for you, for my power is made perfect in weakness.

"Therefore, I will boast all the more gladly of my weakness so that the power of Christ may rest upon me. Bless those who persecute you. Bless and do not curse. Be kind and compassionate to one another, forgiving each other, just as Christ God forgave you. And when you stand praying, if you hold anything against anyone, forgive them, so that you Father in heaven may forgive you your sins. God is a God of grace and mercy. He loves you. He forgives you, and He wants to set you free because you are His sons and daughters. God does not want you to have fear, but love and a sound mind. God has a plan for you, plans for welfare and not for evil, to give you future and a hope.

You are a new creation; the old has passed away. Behold, the new has come. For as high as the heavens are above the earth so great is His love for you. You fear Him; as far as the east is from the west, so far has He removed your transgression from you. The Lord is near to the brokenhearted and saves the crushed in spirit. He heals the brokenhearted and binds up their wounds. Now may God of hope fill you with all joy and peace in believing that you may abound in hope by the power of the Holy Spirit, my Father in heaven, hallowed be your name. Your kingdom come Your will be done on earth as it is in heaven. Give me this day my daily bread and forgive me my debts, as I forgive my debtors. And do not lead me into temptation, but deliver me from evil. For yours is the kingdom and the power and the Holy Spirit and the glory forever. Amen.

BLESSINGS FROM GOD

PHILIPPIANS 4:6–7

Do not be anxious about anything, but in every situation, by prayer and petition, with thanksgiving, present your request to God. And the peace of God, which transcends all understanding, will guard your hearts and your minds in Christ Jesus.

God wants to stretch out His arms and manifest His power on you. And Jesus is saying that whatever you bind on earth will be bound in heaven, and whatever you loose on earth will be loosed in heaven. Jesus said, "Repent, for the kingdom of heaven is at hand." Jesus came to teach you His way in.

MATTHEW 5:3–11

Blessed are the poor in spirit, for theirs is the kingdom of heaven.

Blessed are those who mourn, for they will be comforted.

Blessed are the meek, for they will inherit the earth.

Blessed are those who hunger and thirst for righteousness, for they will be filled.

Blessed are the merciful for they will be shown mercy.

Blessed are the pure in heart, for they will see God.

Blessed are the peacemakers, for they will be called sons of God.

Blessed are those who are persecuted because of righteousness, for theirs is the kingdom of heaven.

Blessed are you when people insult you, persecute you and falsely say all kinds of evil against you because of me.

Rejoice and be glad, because great is your reward in heaven, for in the same way they persecuted the prophets who were before you.

Jesus rules and reigns on the earth. He teaches His disciples that the kingdom of heaven is at hand. The new rule from on High gives new love, new hope, new strength, new life, new destiny, new future, new justice, new vision, new provision, new responsibilities, new identity, and new rewards. The kingdom of God is here with you to rule over you. Jesus is in control over your life.

THE GOD WHO HEARS

God says to you, "Behold, I create a new heaven and a new earth. The former things will not be remembered, nor will they come to mind. But be glad and rejoice forever in what I will create about you is to be a delight and joy for God's people. I will rejoice over you and take delight in my people. The sound of weeping and of crying will be heard in it no more."

God says, "Before you call me, I will answer you. While you are still speaking, I will hear you. For this is the Lord saying to you: I will extend peace to you like a river and the wealth of nations like a flooding stream. You will nurse and be carried on her arm and dandled on her knees. As a mother comforts her child, so will I comfort you, and you will be comforted over the nations."

CHAPTER 22

THE MIRACLES FROM GOD

On December 15, 2012, I was experiencing pain all over my body. Death was trying to creep into my life. My body was changing. I was getting weaker and weaker. It was hard for me to open my hands after closing them. Because my hands were very stiff I was so weak that I could not even write my own name. I was losing a lot of weight, and my whole body was shaking; my bones were getting smaller and deteriorating. I was fainting; pain and despair were in front of me. I was getting worse every day, and I could not even go up the stairs or come back down.

One day, I woke up at three o'clock in the morning. I went to the bathroom; when I turned on the light, I was shocked by what I saw on the mirror. I started to cry. I didn't know what was happening to me. Looking myself in the mirror, fear and terror came over me. I felt like my whole body was drowning because the woman staring back at me in the mirror didn't look like me anymore. I thought that I was seeing a different woman;

The person I saw in the mirror had the figure and face of a very skinny old woman. But at the same time, she was me, and I was her. I asked myself, *who is this woman in the mirror?* And I started to cry. I felt like my whole body was transforming into a dead person or something. My whole body turned pale. I felt like I was whiter than the white people.

I asked God what was happening to me and why I was experiencing those things. The woman in the mirror does not look like me. Even my daughters, my neighbors, and my friends for twelve years could not recognize me. They were all shocked to see my body transforming like I was dying from leprosy. The scriptures became alive to me when God said the following to Moses:

EXODUS 4:5–7

"This," said the Lord, "is so that they may believe that the Lord the God of their fathers—the God of Abraham, the God of Isaac and Jacob- has appeared to you." Then the Lord said, "Put your hand inside your cloak." So Moses put His hand into His cloak, and when He took it out, the skin was leprous—it had become as white as snow. Now put it back into your cloak, He said. So Moses put His hand back into His cloak, and when He took it out, it was restored, like the rest of His flesh.

SHARE THE TESTIMONY

One day, one of the women I knew for many months asked me to pick her up to take her to her church. Because I had not seen her in so many months, she didn't know that I had been diagnosed with cancer. When I picked her up, she was so shocked seeing me that she did not even recognize me. She said that she doesn't want me to feel bad about what she thought about me, but I will never forget her comment. She said to me, *"Esther, don't get mad at me if I tell you that you are not a pretty woman anymore. You have changed."* She continued saying those words many times. She told me that she remembered that I didn't look like an old lady before, that *I used to be very beautiful and radiant.* But at that moment, she thought that I looked like a very old woman. She went on telling me that I had changed a lot.

Then I finally told her about the cancer. I shared with her what happened to me in 2007, about the doctor saying that I was going to die within six months. I told her about how he said that the medicine could not heal me and it would just maintain my body so I could stay alive, but he said that I would eventually die. But by the grace of God, at that time she has asked me that it was already 2012. I was still standing, and my life was just beginning for God's glory.

I told her that God was on my side. She was amazed about my testimony, and she asked me if I could share the testimony to her church, and I said yes to her. I decided to go to the church with her instead of going to the hospital. Without thinking, my whole body could've dropped dead on the ground at that very moment because I was very sick and weak, and I felt like my body would melt away at any minute. And I didn't know if I could make it through the day. But by the grace of God, He gave me the strength to do what He asked me to do. She asked her leader if I could share my testimony with the congregation. Her leader called me from the pulpit and wanted me to share my testimony. When I was on the stage, I blocked everything about my situation—going to church instead of the hospital, being very sick and weak and being ashamed of how I looked, and thinking my body would melt anytime and that I could die that day. Instead, I brought the message of God upon the congregation—about the healing, blessings, deliverance, and salvation of the Lord for them. I let them know that God was real and alive and that He walked among us. I told the congregation that there was nothing like Him. I told them that God was the God of salvation, power and love. And who can know Him? After I shared the goodness of God with everyone, everyone was blessed and healed.

After I shared my testimony with the congregation, God restored my life. To God be the glory!

TRUSTING IN GOD

On Christmas Eve of 2012, I went to my friend's house for dinner. I knew my friend for twenty-one years. When everybody saw me, they were shocked. They were all concerned for me; they did not recognize me—I needed the blood and the resurrection power of Jesus Christ. I did not tell everyone that it might be my last Christmas with them because I was very sick. But I still had hope that God would make a way for me, that He would come and heal my body one day. I was very strong with the Lord because I knew that He was my healer. And I knew that one day He would come to me and heal my body. I didn't want to be moved by what I saw happening to my body, but by my belief that God was my healer and that He wanted to heal me.

RESTORED

One day on 2012, I was one of the members of the prayer teams at my friend's church, and they e-mailed me about the name of the person that I was going to pray for. When I read the name, I stretched out my hands toward the screen monitor; and I started to pray for him, not knowing who the person was. Three days later, I was invited to go to one of the Bible study sessions, but the owner of the house was sick. It just so happen that he was the one that I had been praying for the whole time. *I thought what a small world.* When I came to his house, I was urged by the Holy Spirit to pray for him. I had asked his wife, who was also from the Philippines, if I could pray for him. She looked at me; and it seemed like she was thinking that I looked like a ghost because I looked very pale, sick, and scary looking. But of course, she didn't want to tell me that because she was scared of me. I did not have a chance to share with her that I had been diagnosed with cancer and that was why I looked like a ghost. But she did not give me a chance to pray for her husband, so I just pray for him from my heart that night.

Many years later, in 2014, by the grace of God, God touched my whole body. I found peace with God; my body, mind, and soul were back to normal. God restored me. The woman saw me again years later, and she was amazed at how I looked. She thought that I was a beautiful woman, and radiance, and she knew right away that God was with me. Seeing that difference in me gave her a confidence toward God. She started to have more confidence in God, and she was not scared of me anymore. We became very good friends; she wanted to be close with God and decided to come to my church. She also went to school at my church. God is good. Who can know Him except His Son Jesus Christ of Nazareth.

HEALING

On New Year's Eves in 2012, I went to my friend's church, and he was a pastor there. When I came in, I noticed about the sign with a scripture from the pulpit, and it said the following:

2 KINGS 20:5

Turn back, and say to Hezekiah the leader of my people, thus says the Lord, the God of David your Father; I have heard your prayer; I have seen your tears. Behold I will heal you. On the third day you shall go up to the house of the Lord.

I kept that message in my heart, and I believed God would make a way in my life. I knew that God would restore me. The following day, I had an appointment to go to the doctor's office; it had been a while since I had seen my doctor. The doctor was shocked to see me being transformed into an older woman. I had so many questions to ask the doctor. Why did I look like an older woman? Why was I weak? Why did I look like a ghost? And what was happening to my body? I felt like I was dying. And the doctor said to me, "Esther, what do you expect? You have leukemia. You have a deadly disease, and in your situation, it's better to look older than being dead." I was shocked with his response. I remember I saw the scripture from the pulpit at the church about 2 Kings 20:5—that I was already healed, and I claimed that scriptures over my life. So I kept the Word of God in my heart that He already healed me at that moment.

In 2013, I mentioned to the woman about the same scripture that God was getting ready to heal me because I believed in signs, wonders, and miracles. But she was very skeptical because she believed that nothing could heal cancer. I shared with her that the Word of God was alive and active and I believed that God would heal me. But she continued not to believe me.

One day, God spoke to me, and He said, "My daughter, it was just a test. It was not about you—it was about me." God continued saying that the reason I was experiencing hardship was because I was bringing glory to His name. God said to me that I was the carrier of His glory.

I believe that Jesus is the healer, and I will stand on His word that by His stripes I'm already healed.

BEHOLD, I WILL HEAL YOU

One afternoon in 2014, I was telling some of my friends that God was getting ready to heal me. Three months later, my blood was changing. The doctor did not know what was happening to me, so he asked me to go back to the hospital for my bone marrow checked. So I went to the hospital; they put me on the machine and checked me, and they took some bone from the bottom of my back. They did other procedures with my body, including a CAT scan. The result was negative for leukemia. The doctor was shocked; they could not believe what was happening to me. My blood returned to normal. I was so happy, and I thanked God for His faithfulness. God did not put me to shame. He was telling the truth. My friend was amazed for me, and she asked me if I could pray for her and her family.

DEATH IS IN FRONT OF ME

But in 2015, the cancer came back, and I experienced my bones getting smaller and smaller again. I felt pain all over my body. I was having short of breath and I was very weak. I was feeling numbness in my hands and legs; the fatigue was slowing me down. The pain paralyzed my whole body; death was in front of me. It was the lowest point of my life. I really needed to hear from God at that moment. I was so glad that He was near me, and I found hope in Him. I continued praying and believing in God for my life because He was the only one that I could count on. As the months went by, God maintained my body by me focusing on Him.

I LOST MY VOICE

In the beginning of 2016, I started to feel worse than ever before. I was getting weaker. My throat was in really bad condition. I was in so much pain, and I could barely talk. Later on, I actually lost my voice. I went to the doctor; He put a long tube in my nose all the way down on my throat, and diagnosed me with the lymph node. While I was at the throat doctor's office, he told me that I was going to need a surgery. I started to ask God why I had to lose my voice knowing I needed it to pray for people, to preach, and to worship Him. But God wanted to take care of me first. I really needed to hear from God. All I could do was to pray for my complete healing.

I went to the hospital for surgery. They gave me anesthesia to put me to sleep, and the throat doctor performed the surgery on. After the surgery, I had a hard time talking. But I continued going back to the doctor until I was finally healed. I thanked God for bringing my voice back to normal. I had so much joy that I could praise and worship Him again.

GOD CALLS US TO MOVE OUT OF OUR HOME

After God healed my voice, I heard Him speak to me, saying I needed to move out from my home. I started to get worried because I didn't have anywhere to go. But I wanted to be obedient to God, so I decided to pack our stuff little by little. I heard God's voice telling me again to let go of all my stuff; the only things He wanted me to take were our clothes and pictures. I was having a hard time understanding God. I was trying to figure out where we were going to live. I had a good-enough salary to pay for rent and other stuff, and also, my furniture and all my other stuff were worth at least $20,000. But God did not want me to take them, so I had to let them go. At that time, God was the only one I was relying on for our lives and our future. I was asking God where He wanted us to go and what we needed to do. I tried to be alert and awake to hear from God because it was a big decision for me. And It is not my will, but God's will in my life.

One day, I started to have a hard time walking up the stairs and back down. My whole body was very weak, and I was in so much pain. I was having a hard time opening my hands because my fingers were very stiff. My whole body was shaking. My bones were deteriorating and I was having a hard time to breathe. While all of those things were happening to me, I still had to be concerned about my everyday life.

I was so glad that God did not stop me from sharing the Gospel, preaching, praying for people, and worshipping and praising Him. He was worthy of it all. I focused on God and His faithfulness toward me. God is my healer.

SEEKING REST AND PEACE

Because of the cancer trying to dig into my body, my mind is staring to shake; it brought my world to the core of hardship. Later on, I found out that I could not work anymore after all those things was happening to me. I saw myself trusting and believing in God like never before. We moved out from our home, and my daughter and I stayed with my friend to accompany her. Later on, my older daughter asked us to move in with them so that we could be with them and I could also take care of my grandchildren while they went to work. I felt so much joy when my daughter asked us to live with them. I was thanking God that He continued blessing us. But sometimes there were times that I missed having my own home. It was different when I had my own house, so I felt homesick. I wanted my own home. Sometimes I felt sad because I missed my bed, especially since I slept on the floor in the living room of my daughter's house; it was very uncomfortable for me, and my body was in so much pain, God really humbling me at that time.

On November 15, 2016, I was very sick. I started to feel very weak and tired. I vomited so many times, I was dehydrated and my whole body was in pain; my feet and hands were tingling, and I thought that it was the end of my life. My body was changing. So much chaos was happening to my body. At the same time, I was always awake very early in the morning and slept very late at night. I saw myself being tired and weary. There was a time that I thought about staying in a hotel over the weekend so I could get some rest. But I could not do it because I was suffering from so much pain in my body, and the pain was getting worse and worse.

So later on, I decided to call my on-call doctor, and I told him what I was feeling. He asked me to go to the hospital because he thought that it was a very serious situation. The doctor did not want me to take a chance, so I went to the hospital. And it was Thanksgiving Day at that time. When I got to the hospital, they admitted me right away. The nurse brought me to my room; when I lay down on the bed, I felt rested at that moment. I thought everything in my surroundings was very quiet. I did not hear people talking, and I did not hear babies crying. I did not see anybody walking. I was actually by myself in my room. I was all alone, and it was very quiet. I was sleeping on the comfortable soft bed. I thought, *Wow, I don't have to stay in a hotel to get some rest after all.* I felt rested and spoiled at the hospital. The nurse gave me anything that I needed, which included food. I was feeling joy at that moment. But later on, little did I know that I had to pay for all the comfort and rest I was receiving.

The following morning, the nurse brought me to get x-rays and a CAT scan; and they found a lot of fluids on two parts of my body. The doctor said to me that the fluids came from my lungs, and I also I had fluids around my heart. The doctor told me that they needed to remove the fluids from my body before it got worse and I might die. I was so scared by what the doctor found inside my body. They prepared me for the procedure to remove the fluids from my body. The nurse gave me a paper to sign. It was a living will. I was very confused as to why the nurse gave me the living will as if I was going to die or something, but for some reason, I forgot to sign it. I thought that the procedure was going to be easy. I started to pray for the Lord to heal me and touch me and to make the procedure easy.

When I was in the procedure room, I asked the doctor to take pictures of me first because I wanted to see myself before and after the procedure just for fun. I was smiling and feeling good. The doctor said yes. A nurse took the pictures. That whole time, I was thinking that the doctor didn't usually allow people to have cameras in the room and take pictures. I felt like I was blessed.

After they took my pictures, the doctor started with the procedure. While they were moving the fluids from my body, I felt like I was drowning little by little. I tried to breathe, but I felt like there was no air coming in and out of my lungs. I was feeling helpless and powerless, and I kept trying to breathe and talk to the doctor and the nurses at the same time, but there was no sound coming out of my mouth. I actually could not breathe; there was no air in my lungs. I started to panic. I was afraid that I was going to die at that moment. As he was trying to get the fluid from my body, I was getting weak at the same time.

After the doctor finished the procedure, I noticed that the doctor and the nurses left me by myself on the bed. I was very scared because I felt like the doctor and the nurse didn't know what was happening to me—that I was having a hard time to breathe and could not talk. I felt like I was actually drowning at that moment. I thought that I was going to die that day. I was very scared. Even though I was weak, I tried to wave my hand so I could get the nurses' attention, but they did not answer me; they were gone.

There, I was in the quiet room all by myself. I was panicking and helpless. I started to make noise by moving the bed, hoping that the nurse from outside the room would notice me. I started to pray silently through my heart that God would help me, heal me, and breathe life into me. I thanked God that He answered my prayers. Because later on, the other nurse heard the noise and she came and helped me. I was so glad that the nurse noticed me. I moved my hand as some form of sign language. I tried telling her to stay in the room with me, and the nurse did; she watched the monitor for me to make sure that I was okay. The whole time, I thought about Jesus, and I was calling His name. I felt like the nurse was my angel. After calling God's name, I saw a miracle happen—that I was able to breathe and talk little by little until I was fully healed. I even sang, and that was how happy and joyful I was. To God be the glory!

I was very happy that I can be able to breathe again. I thanked God for my healing and keeping me alive. I was in so much joy that I started to sing, and I even shared it on my Facebook. To God be the glory! God is so good. Miracles do happen. Thank you, Jesus.

My friends ask me what happened to me. I told them that God is good. My dry bones situation was so hard, but God is faithful to me and I escaped the grave that was in front of me. The Spirit of God poured out His Spirit and He breathed on me, and He gave me my life back.

I was thanking God for all the things that I have experience, I knew without God I will be fading away from this earth.

SUPERNATURAL BALLOONS

While I was at the hospital, there were three women that I knew came and visited me. They gave me three balloons; each balloon had a word. One balloon said "Get well." Another balloon said "I love you." And the last said "Take care." When I came back from the hospital, I put the balloons in my granddaughter's room. Two days later, two balloons were deflated, so I had to throw them away. But the one balloon that said "I love you" was still good, so I left it in my granddaughter's bedroom.

I had not seen the balloon for one week. I did not know where it went. I asked my children and my granddaughter if they knew where the balloon was; everybody said that they had not seen it. But ten days later, while I was sleeping on the couch downstairs in the living room, it was around three thirty in the morning, and the lights were not on. But for some reason, I woke up, and I was shocked, because I noticed something floating above me. I thought it was a person or something. As my eyes adapted to the dark, I noticed that it was a balloon floating above me. When I saw the balloon was just floating above me, the first thing I thought was that; how the balloon got down in the living room and landed right above me, knowing it was supposed to stay upstairs in my granddaughter's room. The words from the balloon said "I love you." I knew right away that it was from the Lord wanting to visit me. Everybody was still sleeping. I was the only one who was awake. The following day, I asked my granddaughter if she saw the balloon before in her room, but she said that she did not see the balloon, that day I put the balloon back at my granddaughter's room. I felt like God supernaturally reveal wonders to me as such as time as this, because I needed Him. Two weeks later the balloon is gone, my children and I cannot find the balloon anywhere. The balloon disappeared, only God knew where it was.

One day, God spoke to me and He said that He will bless me. I feel peace and love from God and I hold on to His promises over my life. On November, 2017 God fulfilled His promises over me. He restored me, and He delivered me. God blessed me with thirty thousand dollars and I bought a car paid off and He gave me a place to live, and until to this day, God is the one who provide for me. I put everything in my heart because I knew only God could do that. He is in control of my life. God is my good Father who loves me.

*I remember having a dream of a bright light floating above me.

DREAM

In 2010, I had a dream about a bright light floating above me, while I was walking through the water and I was trying to catch the bright light.

It reminds me about the balloon with the words says "I love you" floating slowly over my head, and I was trying to catch it. So when I saw the balloon floating above me on the couch where I slept that early morning, it reminded me of the light of God hovering over me, telling me that God loves me.

I immediately knelt down and prayed to God that early morning, and I cried out to the Lord. I was thanking Him for protecting me, blessing me, giving me peace, and healing my body while I was in the hospital. To God be the glory!

THE WONDERS OF GOD'S EYES

One day, I was driving in the city. I saw this beautiful cloud, and I immediately got my cell phone so I could take a picture of the cloud. To my surprise, I did not know that I accidently took a video of the odometer, and I witnessed things that shocked me. "I saw two beautiful green eyes," and they were staring right at me. As I was looking at the video intensely, I noticed that the eyes blinked at me." I was shocked, knowing that I was the only one in the driver's seat and my daughter was at the backseat. When I saw the eyes, I knew right away it was the Lord's (Jesus Christ). I was very excited about the beauty of God in my life as He revealed himself to me. I didn't want to lose the video, so I gave my cell phone to my daughter to save the video for me. My whole body melted when my daughter told me that she accidently erased it. I was thinking that maybe His eyes were just for me to see. God is so good.

GOD'S OUTSTRETCHED ARM

One day in 2017, God spoke to me He told me that He wants to appear Himself to me. I just didn't know how, but I trust Him. One day, the whole world was waiting for the Solar Eclipse to come. I was one of them. I was so excited that I wanted to take pictures of it. I remember taking a lot of pictures of the eclipse; but there were three pictures that captured my heart. One picture looked normal; in to my surprise, on the second picture, "I saw a little cross is at the edge of the middle of the Solar Eclipse." I thought, Wow. God was so good for me to able to see the Solar Eclipse with a cross on it. One person said He saw Jesus at the edge of the Solar Eclipse. I thought "wow" I had never seen anything like that before in my life. I was amazed.

As I was looking at the three pictures of the Solar Eclipse, I could not understand why it was shaped differently; it wasn't shaped like those two other eclipses. I did not think anything of it, and I just moved on. Two weeks later, God spoke to me and He wants me to check the Solar Eclipse again, I thought is to why the eclipse shape different, and I asked myself is to why is it that the shape of the Solar Eclipse is not the same like the others. I decided to look at the picture again. Then I realized as I was staring at the picture that it was actually shape like the "Outstretched arm and the right hand of God," not the left hand, but the right hand. I thought, *Wow.* God shocked me all the time. God told me to put His picture in the cover of the book. Because I want to be obedient to the Lord, so I did put the Solar Eclipse "Outstretch Arm" on the cover of the book. He loved to talk to me using signs, wonders, and miracles. I was so glad that He allowed me to see His beauty through the Solar Eclipse.

God is a God of miracles. I believe Him! Jesus is the light, and He wants us to walk in the light with Him.

You have been chosen to carry His glory and light.

REVELATION 1:19

Write, therefore, what you have seen, what is now and what will take place later.

NUMBERS 14:14

And they will tell the inhabitants of this land about it. They have already heard that You, Lord, are with these people and that You, Lord have been seen Face to Face, that Your cloud stays over them, and that You go before them in a pillar of cloud by day and in a pillar of Fire by night.

DEUTERONOMY 5:4

The Lord spoke to you Face to face out of the Fire on the mountain.

REVELATION 1:17–18

When I saw Him, I feel at His feet as though dead. Then He placed His right hand on Me and said: "Do not be afraid. I am the first and the Last. I AM the living One; I was dead, and behold I AM alive forever and ever! And I hold the keys of death and Hades."

YOUR IDENTITY WITH GOD

ISAIAH 43:1–4

But now, this is what the LORD says— He who created you, Jacob, He who formed you, Israel: "Do not fear, for I have redeemed you; I have summoned you by name; you are mine. When you pass through the waters, I will be with you; and when you pass through the rivers, they will not sweep over you. When you walk through the fire, you w ill not be burned; the flames will not set you ablaze. For I am the LORD your God, the Holy One of Israel, your Savior; I give Egypt for your ransom, Cush and Seba in your stead. Since you are precious and honored in my sight, and because I love you, I will give people in exchange for you, nations in exchange for your life.

YOUR LIFE EXPERIENCED

Sometimes living in this world is not very easy. Sometime we can experience tragic in our lives, even hardships, sometimes life is so unfair, sometimes it can be very difficult, perplex and painful. Sometimes you feel trap, confused, anxious, trouble, numb, and being invisible from this world. Sometimes you feel upset, angry and hatred. Sometimes you feel unqualified, disqualified, unworthy, unwanted, unfit, undeserving and even sometime lost.

Sometimes the situation in your life and the challenges in your life just melt you down in the inner core of your heart. Sometimes you feel like your soul is weak, sleeping, drowning and fighting. Sometimes you can be very drawn, sad, a lone, depress, and lost control. Sometimes you feel unsettled within your soul. Sometimes you feel that your world is very unsuitable, unstable, uncertain and unfair. Sometimes your life can be very unpredictable and unknown. Sometimes you feel darkness and cloudy and is creeping all around you. Sometimes you feel disturbed—struggles, strife, and defeat just crippling you in. Sometimes you feel worry, and your whole body will shake like tsunami, not knowing what is to come.

Sometimes you are feeling wondering, and having anxiety and fear just digging the ground all the way to the point of death. Sometimes you are facing bad news from the doctor, sickness, disease, and even death trying to come in. Sometimes you are having stress and feeling abandonment and it was slowing you down.

Sometimes you are experiencing the pain, the hurt, the rejection, the desertion, the persecution, and even affliction just bringing you down to the grave. The land of brokenness and wilderness with nowhere to go and nowhere to escape brings confusion to the core of our soul. Sometimes the unexpected decision, trauma, diagnosis, the loss of a loved one, and financial difficulty just keeps coming and you don't know when is going to stop, the trouble in your life that keeps you in the prison weakened your Identity.

Just getting through life can be very hard like a mountain that is difficult to climb. The tragedies of your life are like raging waves that are not easy to stop. You have experienced being abused, rejection, persecution, afflicted, bent, broken, alone, and shattered.

Sometimes you may realize that your love, peace, faith, hope, needs to grow and be strengthened when life is not easy for you. It's very hard to walk through it when you're in the midst of it all. God will not put you in the situation that you cannot handle. He will be there for you and He make a war for you.

I AM THE WAY THE TRUTH AND THE LIFE

As you walk through the blood of Jesus Christ, you will see the victory of God over your life. That whole time, God keeps you very strong to conquer all things and even keeps you alive. God is with you to strengthen and sustain you, and He has a great power to bring you out from the raging waves of death and set you upon the rock. God does it because He loves you.

You long for faith, hope, peace, and strength in your life. God will take your hands and lead you straight into His brightest light to bring greater love, power, revelation, expectation, position, character, knowledge, trust, beauty, wisdom, hope, and perseverance to the deepest part of your soul. You are not called to live in defeat. You are called to be a warrior to win the victory. Heaven has no defeat to give you—only His love, His comfort and His affection over you. There is no sickness, disease, hopeless, depression, or despair in heaven. Always speak the Word of God in your life, and you will be set free. You will always need God in your mind. Trust in the Word of God to protect, guide, lead, and direct you. Having your perfect peace comes from knowing God. You are forgiven when you confess your sins and thank Him for His Grace and mercy.

Your tongue is used to speak positively to decree and declare the power of God to feel and see having the moment with God. Your tongue is called to be prophetic and powerful in releasing the Word of the Lord to edify, exalt, and comfort you. Speak the storm and death out of your life and command that storm and death to move from here to there, and it will move, and nothing will be impossible for you.

Prophesy to your situation and challenges in your life. God wants to perform miracles for you.

The Lord has mantled you with His authority, Word, wisdom, revelation, and knowledge of Him. God will speak to you through your spirit, mind, and soul. As you read the Word of God, He will navigate you to the place where He is. His presence will renew your mind, and the His timing will always be with you. God's will sanctifies you according to His love and perfect will. God is your master creator, and in Him, you will be clean as whiter as snow. He will leave you a sparkling new spirit, a new character, a new you, a new beginning, a new revelation, and new wisdom over your life. He will give you more than you ever had. God will be faithful, creating a new you.

Know this: God will not abandon you like an orphan. You will not be in the midst of the lifeless. He will take care of you, and He promises that. He not only promises that but also He delivers it. His desire for your life is ultimately to make you have eternal life and be more like Him. He wants to have intimacy with you and to have a relationship with you. You will know the way, you will know the truth, and you will have life in Him. He will not leave you sitting and waiting in the dark, but you will have love, faith, hope, assurance, and confidence in Him. He will walk with you through the storm until you come out on the other side.

God will revive, will renew, and will refresh you; and you will not be move and be shaken. God has a plan and purpose for your life. God has given you a fresh love, hope, and faith; and you are not alone. You are never forgotten. He will always be there for you. God loves you. He desires you, and you are important to Him. You have been given a new power and a fresh glimpse of His glory and presence. With His whispers in your ears, you hear Him saying that He loves you.

God is trustworthy. He is all you need. He is powerful. He is able to do exceedingly above all that you could ask or think. He is your God that cares and watches over you. He is your God in any situation, no matter how difficult it may seem. He is your healer, provider, deliverer, redeemer, and restorer; and nothing is difficult or impossible for Him. God loves to comfort you when you cry. He gives you peace, and you feel His presence to cover your mind and thoughts. He keeps you safe in His presence forever. God's ways are greater than yours, and His thoughts are bigger than yours.

Don't give up . . . don't give in . . . because your breakthrough is here now.

JOB 10:12

YOU GAVE ME LIFE AND SHOWED ME KINDNESS, AND IN YOUR PROVIDENCE WATCH OVER MY SPIRIT.

ISAIAH 53:5

That You are wounded for my transgression, bruised for my iniquities, the chastisement of my peace was upon You and with Your stripes, I am healed.

PRAYER

Dear heavenly Father,

You are the Alpha and Omega, the beginning and the end. You are the First and the Last—who Was, who Is, and who is to Come—*the Almighty God.*

Lord, you are my great physician. You are my healer. You are my medicine. You are my deliverer. You are my way maker. You are my signs, wonders, and miracles. Lord Jesus, with you on my side, I am healed, prospered, blessed, and restored.

You are my rock and my salvation, and there is none like you. I come to You to see your goodness in my life. Thank You for lifting me up and carrying me to Your throne. Thank You for fueling me for the task that You have given me that my joy will be complete. Consume the weakness in my life and make me stronger again. I want to mount up with wings like an eagle. I want to soar with You. I ask You to give me strength and fill me with Your supernatural power to overcome each obstacle in my path.

My eyes are on You, Lord. Thank You for walking beside with me and working through me. I can make it with You being by my side. Thank You for your shadow of love over me and I found favor in Your sight. You are my peace, love, and strength. I trust and have faith in You, and I thank You that You are my refuge and healer. Thank You that You filled me with Your love and compassion, and thank You for flowing through me. Thank You for giving me wisdom, revelation, and knowledge coming from Your throne, in Jesus' name. Amen.

I LOVE YOU, JESUS

Lord Jesus, You are my strong heart and my strong mind, my body, my soul and my tower; and nothing can shake, move, and break me from this world.

Through You, I am tough, I am strong I am rock, and I am steel. I overcome obstacles in my life and persevered trials and difficulties. And I cannot be easily bent. You gave me a humble spirit that I am able to conquer all things. I am loved all the way to the point of death by you, Jesus Christ. You have been giving me the word coming from Your heart. I have found the wisdom, revelation, and the knowledge you gave me from the love of your cross. I am courageous and bold through your fire that burns inside of me; you have been giving me the deep impartation and dependence in Your word. I am the masterpiece and craftsmanship that you created. *I am your child, I love You, my Father in heaven.*

CHAPTER 23

MY JOB

Cleaning houses was my specialty. I loved to clean people's houses. I met so many people who love for me to clean their houses; all my customers were very nice, loving, and compassionate. I worked for some of them for ten years and sometimes fifteen years; the shortest was four years. All of them were good people and I love them. The customer I had been working for, for four years found a good business in another state and decided to move out. I was very sad when I found out that they were moving because I loved them and didn't want to lose them as my customer. They were the ones who helped me when I just had a baby. It was so hard for them to let me go, so they asked me if I wanted to come and work for them in the other state they were moving to. They said that they would buy me a house and a car if I would move with them. It was a very hard decision for me because I already own a condominium, and I didn't know what to do with it if I went with them. In my sadness, I said no to them. "I thought to myself that I still had a lot of customers that I didn't need to move anywhere." I miss them a lot, and they are always in my heart.

Years went by, and my living situation changed. I decided to just get a job instead of building a business. I went to an agency, and they found me a new boss. I could not say that they were my customers because they were not. I actually had a boss; experience for being having a boss was very hard for me. I felt like working for a boss meant that I was going to need God. Lord Jesus, help me. Here are some stories about me having a boss.

On November 2007, I started to work as a housekeeper and a house manager. Working for somebody was difficult most of the time. It was then I needed to hear the voice of God very clearly. After I got saved in 2007, for the first time in my life (in 2008), I was able to understand and hear the voice of God. At that time, I did not know that God could actually talk, and He was actually talking me. I knew that I had so much to learn about God then. I was just so glad that God was with me—guiding, protecting, and blessing me. While I was working for these people, I felt like I was ready to quit.

There were so many times that I thought they wanted to fired me, but God spoke to me, and He said to me that they could not fire me and I could not quit. But God spoke to me, and He will be the one who will remove me from them. When He removed me from them, then I will be working for God. I embraced those words from the Lord because they were encouraging for me. I held on to the beautiful voice of God and His promises into my life. I felt comfort, assurance, and love from the Lord. After eight years working for them, God removed me from them, and I started to work for the Lord—exactly the same words that He promised me.

NO RAIN

One day, while I was working. They were going to have a party outside in their backyard, and it was supposed to rain that Saturday. The man asked me if I could pray for them so that it would not rain, and I said yes to him. I prayed to the Lord, asking Him not to let it rain that Saturday. God answered my prayer—it did not rain that Saturday. So they were able to have the party outdoors. The man came to me and acknowledged that God answered my prayer. The man knew that I loved God and loved to pray, and God loved to answer my prayers.

LOVE AND UNITY

One day, I gave the woman a devotional book about God, but she did not read it. I gave her another devotional book about the bread of God, and she did not read it either. Then I gave her a devotional book about loving God and loving husband, and she did not read it also. So I kept asking God to help them.

I remember going down to the basement, and I started to pray for them. By the time I was finished, I went upstairs, and I knew that God was already intervening for them in whatever that was happening to them, I saw love and unity in them; they were making peace with one another. I thanked God for everything He had done for the family.

But one day, I started to fear the woman. I felt like she was trying to put fear on me. Just for her saying a word to me, it made my whole body shake. I have never understood that. And at the same time, I would hear God's voice saying, "Give your burden to Me, and I will give you rest." God always gave me peace and rest in Him, and then I would be shocked because the message that God gave me is in the Bible at that same time. I was learning to hear the voice of God. Every time God spoke to me, He always confirmed it through His word, "Bible." God always shocks me. He is such a powerful God. His Word is alive and active. God always leaves me in awe.

THE POWER OF PRAYER

PSALM 91:3–7

Surely He will save you from the fowler's snare and from the deadly pestilence. He will cover you with His feathers, and under His wings you will find refuge, His faithfulness will be your shield and rampart. You will not fear the terror of night, nor the arrow that flies by day, nor pestilence that stalks in the darkness, nor the plague that destroys at midday. A thousand may fall at your right side, ten thousand at your right hand, but it will not come near you.

THE MIRACLES OF GOD

One day later, I was at the basement cleaning. I heard the voice of God telling me to go upstairs, and I did. I went straight to the laundry room. The woman came in from jogging outside, and she went straight to the kitchen. She took one big vitamin pill and tried to swallow it, but it got stuck in her throat. I heard her choking all the way from the laundry room. I was very concerned, so I rushed to her to see what happened. When I saw her, I could tell she was choking. She couldn't talk; she was just holding her throat, hoping the pill would come out. I immediately positioned myself to give her the Heimlich maneuver. I started to make a fist and placed it against her upper abdomen. Then I started pressing into her upper abdomen many times, but the pill still did not come out. I thought that I should try it again, hoping that the vitamin would come out. But it never did! Her face started to look like pale, and she became very weak.

I started to panic, so I left her so I could call 911. Halfway between her and the telephone, I looked back to see how she was doing. I saw her slowly going down to the floor, and her hands were moving as if she was looking for me to see if I was close to her. I saw fear came over her; she knew that her death was just around the corner. She knew that she could die in the blink of an eye. She depended on me to keep her alive; she was hopeless in her situation. I was so scared for her at the same time. I knew I was the only one in the house who could help her.

I thought about her husband. What would he think if she died? I knew that her husband would blame me. I was torn between making the phone call to 911 and continue doing the Heimlich maneuver. I thought that by the time I called 911, it might be too late for her and that she might die. But I thought that if I came back to her, I might be able to remove the pill from her throat.

So I took a chance and came back to help her. I started to make a fist again, and before I put my fist back to her upper abdomen, I knew *it was out of my control*. I knew that this time, *God was in control*. I closed my eyes, and I prayed to the Lord. I said, "Lord, help." After I said that, I put my two fists to her upper abdomen, and I press it again. *Then the pill miraculously came out of her mouth*. After that, tears of joy came to her; with just one press to her upper abdomen, the vitamin came out of her mouth, and she was able to breathe again, and she started to calm herself down; she realized that she was saved, and we rejoiced together. With tears running down her face, she told me that she was scared because she knew that she was going to die at that hour. And she was thanking

God that He saved her life; she was also thanking me for saving her life. She knew that was only God who could protect her.

I knew that I could not do it without God by my side. God was the only one who could save the woman. I started to feel joy. The whole time, God was comforting me. He let me know that He was beside me and that He was able. God loved me, and peace came over me. God is real. *He performs miracles to let us know that He is* able.

HEBREWS 4:16

Let us therefore come boldly unto the throne of Grace that we might obtain Mercy and Grace to help in time of need.

MATERIAL THINGS

One day, instead of them focusing on things above instead, they were focusing on the material things from their home. One day, God spoke to me and He said to me that they would be hiring a cleaning crew for their house. I was shocked, thinking that maybe they were going to replace me. I was very disturbed by it because I didn't want them to replace me. So every day, I would be looking out the windows waiting for the cleaning crew to come; but it had already been a week, and the cleaning crew had not arrived yet. I thought that maybe they were going to hire the cleaning crew for their party. I asked myself is to why would they do that, knowing I could do all the cleaning myself? So I continued looking out the windows. It was already two weeks, but the cleaning crew has not arrived yet.

Then one day, I came to work; the woman called me and told me that she hired window cleaners and that they were coming to clean all the windows around the house. After she said that, I understood God. She hired a window cleaner. I realized that she is not going to replaced me. They were just the ones who were going to clean all the windows outside the house. I tell God that I got it. God is good. He loves mystery. So when the cleaning crew came, I watched them to see what they were going to do, I have never understand is to why I have to watch them, If I knew then what I knew now, I will have pray for the people instead.

Because the people loved to worship and praise their house so much, they also put so many idols and everything that was not of God in their house. God was not very happy with that. He wanted them to worship and praise only Him because God is a jealous God. I tried to understand God and His ways concerning the people. I understood that God was in control. When I saw what was happening to their house, I trembled before God with fear, knowing that He could also bring disaster to the people. God is a jealous God, and we need to praise and worship only Him and no one and nothing else. He is the Almighty God.

I watched the cleaning crew almost sweep their house away. While they were cleaning the windows and also the bricks and copper from the roof, I saw that the whole house started to have a mark of holes in each brick, including the stairs and all around the house. It was coming from the pressures of the water. The copper from the roof was turning into a slimy green because of the chemicals they were using to clean it. They also had a huge grill on the patio that was made of silver, and while they were cleaning it, the chemicals they were using kept dripping on the huge silver grill. And it was destroyed; because it had spots created by the chemicals everywhere.

When I saw what was happening, I was shocked. I started having fear of the Lord. I knew He was real, but I didn't know how real He was until I saw what was happening in front of me. After seeing that, I started to kneel down before God and cried out for mercy, grace, and forgiveness for my life and also for those people. I could not explain it in words. I prayed to them and I tried giving them more devotional books, hoping they would read them. I knew God would make a way for them one day.

DIFFICULT TIME

One day, the man could not find His cuff links; He was very upset with me. He accused me of stealing the cuff links, and he wanted to call the police on me. I was very sad. But instead of being upset with him, I decided to come to the Lord to ask for help. I prayed and asked Him to find the cuff links for me because I didn't know where they were; the minute I prayed, God told me to get the man's luggage, and I did. I found the cuff links and the rest of his stuff in the little packet inside his luggage. At that time, he was about to leave the house. He was in front of the door, ready to walk out. So I immediately called his name before he left; he came towards me, and I showed him his cuff links. When he realized I found his cuff links, he was glad, and he wanted me to put them inside his closet. It was a relief knowing that I have found his lost cuff links, and I knew that God will talk to him. I thanked God for helping me and getting me out of that trouble. All I could do was to pray. The more I saw my boss, the more I fixed my eyes on the Lord. The more my boss was angry, the more I bowed down and prayed for my boss. I forgave my boss.

EXODUS 14:14

The Lord will fight for you; you need only to be still.

SODOM AND GOMORRAH

One day, I was sharing with my boss the story about Sodom and Gomorrah and how the people were being punished by God for being wicked. Lot and his family escaped from Sodom and Gomorrah, and the angel of the Lord told Lot and his family not to look back. But his wife looked back, and she turned into a pillar of salt.

GENESIS 19:24–26

Then the Lord rained down burning sulfur on Sodom and Gomorrah— from the Lord out of the heavens. Thus He overthrew those cities and the entire plain, including all those living in the cities—and also the vegetation in the land. But Lot's wife looked back, and she became a pillar of salt.

When I shared that story with the man, he did not listen, not knowing how special the Bible was. The Bible was not just a regular book—it was the Word from God. The message I shared with him about Sodom and Gomorrah was actually a prophecy for him that it was actually going to happen to him in the future. If he would humble himself and listen to God's Word, if he would come to God and seek Him, and if he would bow down to God and ask for His forgiveness, If only will surrender to Him, the man would be able to see the grace, mercy, and goodness of God upon his life. But instead, he rejected God, and he did not listen to the Word of the Lord. I left, and all I could do is prayed for them.

BOW DOWN TO GOD

One day, as I was cleaning, God spoke to me. And He told me that He did not forget how my boss had been treating me. God let me know that He was sad. He told me that He would make my boss bow down to Him and that I would see it with my own eyes. God will make him humble himself to me. I did not know what God was saying at that time; all I could do was to pray for them. Later on, something happened. God let me know that I was not alone, that He was by my side and wanted to protect me. God let me know that I was His child and that He loved me. I was so glad that God was with me, loving me and taking care of me. It was so true when God said, *"Do not touch my anointing do My prophet no harm.* The man lost so much stuff and he also "lost His significant other," God humbled the man. God does not want to be mocked and to be insulted by man. He is God; and He is the one who created the heaven, the earth, and under the earth. He is the alpha and omega, the beginning and the end. Who was and who is and who is to come, the Almighty God. We must have fear in God. He is real, and He walks among us. *God told me that my enemy would bow down to me.* **God does not want any bad things to happen to the people. He wants to bless the people.**

One morning the man was cooking pancakes, and he asked me if I wanted one. I was shocked; my mouth was wide open, and then I said yes to him. After he gave me a pancake, he asked me if I wanted syrup for my pancake. With my humble voice, I said yes to him again. I was in awe of God. The man then poured syrup on my pancake. I was thanking God for my boss. I started to cried because I felt like God put a humble spirit within him. I saw my boss being humble to God, the man starting serving God and also to me. And also God's promised to me was granted when He said that my boss will bow down to Him and also to me. I felt like everything was going to be good from then on.

Later on, love grew in them, and I learned to love them. At the end, they became good people to me, giving and sharing their hearts to me. I learned so much about God through them by being crucified, rejected, and loved by them at the same time.

I worked for them for eight years. After eight years, God removed me from them, and I am now working for God like He promised to me. To this day, I continue praying for them. I want good things to happen to them. I love them, and I forgive them.

God is the protector and the healer

PROVERBS 11:4

Wealth is worthless in the day of wrath, but righteousness delivers from death.

ROMANS 1:18

The wrath of God is being revealed from heaven against all the godlessness and wickedness of men, who suppress the truth by their wickedness.

There is nothing to compare about the world, the amount of wealth, and money, to erase the wrath of God. The Arrogant, the pride and vanity is a sin that create pain in the heart of God. Humility is a way to see God face to face, and to hear the voice of God and to touch His vision and provision on the earth. Only Jesus Christ and His precious blood can take away our sins. And no amount of goodness or kindness will be able to save us—only through His blood, and His love on the cross. No one is perfect, but Jesus alone. But through His obedience to the heavenly Father and by accepting the agony of being on the cross, our sins are wiped away, and we are able to stand on the throne of God with us being blameless and spotless before Him.

MATTHEW 6:19-24

Do not store up for yourselves treasures on earth, where moth and rust destroy, and where thieves break in and steal. But store up yourselves treasures in heaven, where moth and rust do not destroy, and where thieves do not break in and steal. For where your treasure is, there your heart will be also. The eye is the lamp of the body. If your eyes are good, your whole body will be full of light. But if your eyes are bad, your whole be full of darkness. If then the light within you is darkness, how great is that darkness! No one can serve two masters. Either He will hate the one and love the other, or He will be devoted to the one and despise the other. You cannot serve both God and money.

2 CHRONICLES 7:13–14

When I shut up the heavens so that there is no rain, or command locust to devour the land or send a plague among My people. If My people, who are called by My name, will humble themselves and pray and seek My face and turn from their wicked ways, then will I hear from heaven and will forgive their sin and will heal their land.

MATTHEW 11:28–30

Come to Me, all who are weary and heavy-laden, and I will give you rest. Take My yoke upon you and learn from Me, for I am gentle and humble in heart, and you will find rest for your souls.

Jesus is a very humble Man, and He wants us to be humble before Him.

PRAYER

Dear heavenly Father,

Forgive us for the things we have done wrong, knowingly and unknowingly. We ask Lord that you will touch us, wash us, cleanse us, and mold us into your scarred hands. Lord, we understand now that you are in control of our life. We ask, Lord, to have your way in us. Thank you for humbling us and giving us wisdom to make the right decision so that we may bring glory to your name. Thank you for your grace and mercy and for protecting us from every fiery dart of the enemy and from the temptation of this world. Lord Jesus, your grace has been given to us to bring down any pride in us, and your love preserves us with humility and humbleness within our soul. Thank you, Jesus, for sharing with us how to live in the way that pleases you. Thank you that your eyes are on us and your Word sets us free, In Jesus' Name. Amen.

CHAPTER 24

GOD IS PERSISTENT FOR MAN

One day, I went to a family's house to have a fellowship, and I met the leader and his wife; they were a wonderful couple. I also had a chance to meet everybody at the fellowship, and it was very nice to have friends who also loved to talk about God. After going to the fellowship for a while, I heard the voice of God telling me to pray for the leader. I didn't understand God at first because my thought was that he was the leader—if anything, he should be the one to pray for me because I didn't have any understanding about praying and didn't even know how to pray back then. My faith in God was very weak and poor. I barely knew God at that time, and I didn't know any scripture, and I also just got saved. I still needed to know more about God. I needed to study His Word and have knowledge of Him. I knew for me to pray for the leader was from heaven because it was something that I could not do by myself, and it was a blessing from God.

So finally, one day, God asked me to pray for the leader again. I did what God told me to do because I wanted to be obedient to the Lord. I came up to the leader and asked him if he wanted me to pray for him; he looked at me and he looked around, and when he noticed that there were so many people around us, he hesitated to say yes. So I was very shocked that he said no to the prayer. So I did not pray for him that night, and I moved on.

One weekend, I saw the leader again, and God told me to pray for him again. I was thinking not to ask the leader if I could pray for him because I knew that he would say no to me again anyway. But I heard God telling me to pray for him again. I wanted to be obedient to the Lord, so when I noticed that he was by himself, I came up to him and asked him again if I could pray for him. And for the second time, he looked around again and he said no to me. I gave him a smile and said, "Okay." I asked God if it was Him who kept talking to me because the leader kept saying no to me. I started to get embarrassed asking the leader if I could pray for him. So finally, I asked God is why He wanted me to pray for the leader so bad, knowing he didn't want the prayer. I asked God to give me a sign as to why He wanted me to pray for him.

Later on, God spoke to me concerning the leader. God told me that His angels and the demons were at war in the midair. That was why He wanted me to pray for him. God was fighting for him. I don't know what was happening to him, all I know that I needed to pray for him.

One day, somebody asked me to have a fellowship in my house, and I said yes. One weekend later, I saw the leader. God spoke to me again, telling me to ask the leader if I could pray for him at my house instead. When I asked the leader if I could pray for him at my house, this time, he said yes. So the leader made an appointment with the Holy Spirit. God spoke to me, saying, "I love my son, and I want to heal him." After God said that to me, I said, "Wow." I thought God was funny. He was not offended, but He was a persistent God for His children. God loved the leader.

THE MIRACLE AND THE LOVE OF GOD

Three days before we had the fellowship in my house, God spoke to me again, asking me if I trusted Him. I said yes to the Lord. I have never understood is to why God asked me if I trusted Him.

One day, after the fellowship, I noticed that the leader was sitting on the chair at the table by himself I thought that it was a good opportunity for me to ask him if I could pray for him then. But when I came up to him, the leader could not speak anymore; no word came out from his mouth, his body was frozen sitting on the chair; he was trying to get up and walk, but he could not. He was stuck on the chair; he was just looking right at me, and he was moving his hands as if he was trying to say something to me. I knew then that something was wrong. I noticed that he accidently wet his pants. When I saw all those things, I did not have time to tell everybody what happened to him. Everybody was talking, at the back of my mind I knew that I needed to pray for him immediately. I was eager with confidence that I must definitely pray over him for God to make a way for him, to heal him. I saw the enemy was attacking him with force. I noticed that the Holy Spirit was rising over me. I felt the angels were all around me, as if God and the demons were getting ready to fight to see who would win the battle. All I thought about was that I must pray for the leader; he and I needed to have an agreement with each other for prayer. I was hoping that he would not say no to me again. The leader was having a stroke, and I was amazed with God that He knew what was going to happen to the leader before he had a stroke. God was already moving to rescue him. God is on time, He never late and He is in control.

CONFIDENCE WITH PRAYER

So my confidence in God became stronger than I could ever imagine; after the leader knew what was happening to him, he nudged his head, saying yes for me to pray for him. I was thanking God when he said yes for me to pray for him, and then I prayed for him. I told him to stand up and start walking. I told him that God wanted to heal him, and he did. He got up, and he started walking, but earlier, he had a hard time walking or even talking. But after I prayed, the miracles took place in his life. The leader was able to walk and talk and he started walking toward the bathroom. While he was in the bathroom, it gave me the time to tell his wife and to everybody what was happening to him earlier. When they saw what happened to him, everybody couldn't believe what happened, everybody decided to go home.

When it was time for everybody to go home, the leader tried to take one step on the stairs outside the door to go outside, but he could not put his foot on the stairs; his legs were very stiff, and he could not move them. I asked God the meaning of all that was happening. He spoke to me and told me to call 911 because God wanted to heal him. He said that the leader would be healed as he went. If the leader left my house, the enemy will attack him on his way between my house and his. God was saying that He didn't want him to leave my house because God wanted to protect him and heal him. I believed that God already healed him. But since he could not put his leg on the stairs, God did not allow him to go home. So I mentioned to everybody to call 911. One man called 911, and then the ambulance came and took him to the hospital.

After everybody left, my house was silent. I recalled what just happened to the leader. I felt like there was emptiness in my soul; they were so many things I wanted to ask God: is to "why God did not heal the leader immediately as I prayed for him?" "Why did the leader have to go to the hospital?" And "why was he not healed already?" At that time, I was very confused with God. Being new Christian and having strong faith in the Lord, I knew that God would make a way. I was expecting the leader to be healed as I prayed for him at that time. But He did not get healed completely right away. I asked God is to why He did not answer me. God gave this scripture to me instead:

JOHN 9:6–7

After saying this, He spit on the ground, made some mud with the saliva, and put it on the man's eyes. "Go" He told Him "wash in the pool of Siloam" (this word means "sent"). So the man went and washed, and came home seeing.

God said to me, "My daughter;

"The leader was already healed as he went. I just wanted him to be obedient to Me, believe and trust in Me. I healed him because I love him, and you are also being obedient to Me. And you have passion and much persistence to pray for him. You did not let me down because of your faith for him to be healed. I will answer your prayer because you call upon Me and trust Me. Therefore, I will answer you."

After God told me that, I had peace with Him.

Four days later, I found out that the leader was at his church for his wife's birthday party. He was healed and was dancing with his wife. I thought, *Wow, to God be the glory!* That was God telling me that the leader was healed as he went. Since then, I understood that I was not the healer—God was the healer. I could only pray and believe God, that He would make a way. After the leader was healed, I asked him every time I saw him if he wanted me to pray for him; He always immediately said yes to me with a smile on his face because the leader knew and understood that God was with me. The leader needed to find in his heart to trust and have faith in the Lord Jesus. The leader and his wife loved to call me an angel.

My faith in God is now greater than I ever could've imagined. I was so glad that God did not put me to shame. God will do what He says He will do. He is faithful. I learned so much about Jesus healing ministry. He is in control

The question is; do you trust Him?

PRAYER

Prayer is the key to unlock the treasures from heaven; through prayer, you can have confidence that God will perform miracles for you. Prayer is the assurance that God knows your request. Through your prayer, God can manifest Himself. Your prayer is very important to God; your prayer is a beautiful burning incense of fire from His throne. Prayer is being face-to-face with God.

TRUSTING GOD

PROVERBS 3:5

Trust in the Lord with all your heart and lean not on your own understanding; in all your ways acknowledge Him and He will make your paths straight.

JEREMIAH 17:7–8

But blessed is the man who trust in the Lord, whose confidence is in Him. He will be like a tree planted by the water that sends out its roots by the stream. It does not fear when heat comes. Its leaves are always green. It has no worries in a year of drought and never fails to bear fruits.

BELIEVE GOD

It is very important to trust God to know His love for you. When you pray, believe that God has already answered your prayers and that you should have them. God is willing and able to lead and rescue you. He has the power and authority to make all things new for you. When you pray, you understand that His ways are always right and greater than you could ever imagine. Surrendering to and trusting God is the key to see the activity and the beauty of God in your life. Knowing, trusting, and having confidence in Him will give you the strength to conquer the pain, the hurt, poverty, and the difficulties in your life. God is with you. He will never leave you nor forsake you. *You are* the *unshakable* and *immovable* one.

When God is in the center of your life, there is nothing that the enemy can do to you that God cannot do. He is greater than anything in this falling world. With God, you will find healing, blessings, and abundance of life. Even in the midst of trials and hardships, you can count on God that He will stay with you to shape you and see the manifestation of God's glory in your life. He is your heavenly Father. God's love for you is immeasurable, undeniable, unceasing, and unconditional.

Stay focused on Him.

CHAPTER 25

THE WOMAN REFUSES TO PRAY

One early morning in 2012, God spoke to me concerning a woman who needs to come to the church and stay over the weekend. She would pray, seek His face, and just stay in His presence to have one night with the King. God wanted to talk to her, and it was very important. God wanted her to pray for her family. I didn't understand why I had to ask the woman for her to pray; all I knew was that I wanted to be obedient to the Lord. I had fear of God.

So I called her right away and told her what God told me—for her to pray for herself, for her family, and for her friends. I invited her to come to the church so she could pray to the Lord. After I told her that, she said yes. She told me that she loved to pray in the night, so she made an agreement with the Holy Spirit that she was going to the church to pray over the weekend. She invited two more people to come and pray with us. That Friday night, along with other friends, decided to come to the fellowship first. After fellowship, we were supposed to go straight to the church so we could pray; but right when we were supposed to go to church, the woman suddenly changed her mind. She didn't want to go to the church, to pray, and she does not want to spend the night with the King anymore. She just wanted to come back home. I took her home instead of us praying in the church. I was sad, but it was okay with me. I came back to the church, where I spent the weekend to worship, praise, pray and seek God's face. I want to do what God asked me to do.

Later on, before the weekend began, I received a text from the woman saying that she was very afraid and she was having anxiety. She asked me if I could pray for her and her family immediately; it sounded like something bad happened to them that I needed to pray for them right away, especially for her grandson. So I start praying for them and believed that God would make a way for them.

The following morning, the woman started to share with me about what happened to her grandson; he was supposed to go to his high school prom that night, but instead, he decided to go to the restaurant, where he invited his two friends, who were sisters. While he was driving, the car flipped over. They had an accident. One of the girl passengers died, and one was in a coma. Her grandson was badly hurt, and the hospital took care of him. But eventually, he later went to jail.

One week later, my partner in prayer and I visited the young girl that was in the coma. While we were in her room, I heard from the Lord to play the Psalm 91 prayer that I had been working on for the past two weeks for my project, it was still in my cell phone. God told me that if the children will listen to Psalm 91, they would be healed, blessed, and protected by God. I want to be obedient to the Lord so I decided to put my cell phone beside the girl's ears, and I played Psalm 91 to her from my phone. I did not know that the nurse was watching me the whole time the nurse came over and told us that we should not make noise because the young girl had a tube in her brain, and she is also going to have an operation. I was trying to apologize to the nurse because I thought I was making noise. But God spoke to me, saying that He was the one who was making noise. I thought if God was the one who is making noise that means that there were be the miracles. I was very excited. I knew that God would perform miracles for the young girl. His Word says the following:

JOB 36:33

Its Noise declares His presence, the cattle also, concerning what is coming up.

EZEKIEL 37:6–10

"I will attach tendons to you and make flesh come upon you and cover you with skin; I will put breath in you, and you will come to life. Then you will know that I AM the Lord."' So I prophesied as I was commanded. And as I was prophesying, there was a noise, a rattling sound, and the bones came together, bone to bone. I looked, and tendons and flesh appeared on them and skin covered them, but there was no breath in them. Then He said to me, "Prophesy to the breath; prophesy son of man, and say to it, 'This is what the Sovereign Lord says; Come from the four winds, O breath, and breathe into these slain, that they may live.'" So I prophesied as He commanded me, and breath entered them; they came to Life" and stood up on their feet—a vast army.

One week later, the woman and her friend came to visit the young girl; she didn't know that we already came to visit to the hospital and prayed for the young girl the week before. During their visit, they noticed that the young girl was moving, and the nurse told them that a miracle happened to the young girl. The nurse was amazed; she said it was a miracle that they have to remove the tube from the young girl's brain and that she didn't need an operation anymore. The young girl was healed and restored. And the nurse said that she doesn't need the operation anymore. Jesus healed her. That was the same thing the nurse told me, but in an opposite way, that was confirmation from the Lord. I believe that the young girl was healed because of the Psalm 91.

God knew that the enemy would attack, and He knew what was going to happen to the woman. God wanted to intervene; that was why He wanted the woman to pray. God wanted to rescue her and her family from the attack of the enemy. He knew that the enemy was trying to take over their lives, and God wanted to stop the works of the enemy through prayer. But she decided not to pray. God truly wanted His children to pray. After witnessing all this, I was shocked, and I started to have fear of the Lord. I learned to bow down to God more than ever. God is actually real, and He is actually alive. I always tell people that we don't know what our future will bring; we don't know what is going to happen tomorrow or one week, one month, one year, or five years from now. God is the only one who can control our lives.

PRAYERS,

Only God knows our future and destiny. Through your prayers, God can rend the heavens and come down to fulfill His promises toward you. Your prayers are very important to God. Your prayers are a powerful tools and instrument to have the channel of God in your life. Your prayers can reach the throne of God to fight the battles for you. Your prayers can bring the sword to come alive and to stop the works of the enemy in your life. When you don't pray, the enemy will attack, and He will kill and destroy and bring destruction. God wants you to be alert, awake, and active at all times. Seeking God and God alone bring peace into your soul because God is the only one who can navigate you. Prayers are the love and activity of God; prayer is the way to communicate with God. Prayer is talking to God face-to-face. It's very important to pray; through prayer, you are able to see the result of what you ask for. God answers your prayers; and He wants to manifest himself through your prayers by signs, wonders, and miracles. His glory takes place when you pray.

MATTHEW 26:40–41

Then He returned to His disciples and found them sleeping, "could you men not keep watch with me for one hour?" He asked Peter. "Watch and pray so that you will not fall into temptation. The Spirit is willing, but the body is weak."

DEUTERONOMY 20:4

For the Lord your God is the One who goes with you to fight for you against your enemies to give you victory.

1 CORINTHIANS 15:57

But thanks be to God He gives us the victory through our Lord Jesus Christ.

When God speaks we must listen, three weeks later, the woman's daughter decided to move out of their house and left the woman without a home; she became homeless. I felt so bad for her not having a home because I knew that she would be living on the streets. We asked her if she would like to live with us, and she said yes. So the woman lived with us.

DIVINITY OF GOD

Years later, God spoke to me, and He told me to move out from the place we were staying at the time. At first, I did not understand that. I was asking God is to where we are going to live because I had not found a house or a place for us to live yet. But I was obedient to Him, so I started to pack our stuff as if we had a place to live already. One day, God showed me the house that we would be living in.

Two weeks later, one of my friends and I decided to go to the open area to share the Gospel. There, we met this powerful woman of God. A week later, the same woman texted me and asked me if I could pray for the opening prayer for the event that they were having. Without hesitation, I said yes. I didn't think that I would get nervous praying in front of people. She also wanted me to sing in the choir, to which I also said yes. I thought wow, God is so good.

Later on, I was shocked because I just found out that it was the same high school this young boy and young girls went. I was amazed with how much God loved the children in that high school for me to pray and sing there. At the same time, I had just moved one week prior to the same city. I thought, *Wow that was Divine Providence from the Lord.*

THE BRIGHT LIGHT

My friend was taking a video of me while I was praying on the stage at the high school. I saw the video of me praying on the stage, I saw and I noticed about the bright lights around me. The bright light was brighter than the sun. I could not see myself because of the brightness around me. I knew that the podium was made out of dark wood, but the podium itself was bright, which was unique. It was me and the podium is the only have this bright lights. The bright light from the podium was not the same light from the building; nothing could compare to how it looked. I thought maybe it was just a coincidence, that something was wrong with the light. But everybody said it was a miracle; they all saw the podium with the bright light of Jesus in the video.

I AM THE LIGHT

I was amazed when I saw another video of me as one of the choir members singing on the stage. I compared the light with the light in the other video, and it was almost the same. When the spotlight was aimed at us while we were singing, all of us had a light from the building light, but I was the only one that has a radiance bright light. Everyone else did not have a light like mine. I was shocked, when it came to me, the only things I could see were my green blouse and my black skirt, and the rest of my body was covered in light. I could not see my shoes even though they were black. I could not see my face because it was covered in light. I could not see my hands because they too were covered in light. I could not see my legs and feet because they were also covered in light. I could see the shoes of the woman behind me, and I could see everybody but me, I could not see myself. I felt like my feet was floating, and was not touching the ground while I was singing that day.

Everything about that day was beautiful and bright. It was a cloud of glory that came down from heaven. I could see everybody's faces and the clothes they were wearing except mine. I showed the video to everybody to witness God's glory, and everybody was astonished with the beauty of God.

I was amazed about everything that took place that day—how God turned me into the bright light. I gave it all the glory to God. Because of His grace and mercy, I was able to experience His glory over me.

I asked God about the connection and what He had for me to do. God was like a puzzle. He loved to put things together. God is like a dot— just follow the dots to get His wisdom and revelation. God told me that I was the light to the world. Thank you Lord. I thanked God for giving me an opportunity to experience His beauty.

I pray that you will experience God, greater than what I experience. May the Lord touch you and overwhelm you with His fire. In Jesus' name Amen.

MATTHEW 5:14–16

You are the light of the world. A town built on a hill cannot be hidden. Neither do people light a lamp and put it under a bowl. Instead they put it on its stand, and it gives light to everyone in the house. In the same way, let your light shine before others, that they may see your good deeds and glorify your Father in heaven.

2 CORINTHIANS 4:6

For God, who said, "Let light shine out of darkness," made His light shine in our hearts to give us the light of the knowledge of God's glory displayed in the face of Christ.

PRAYER

Dear heavenly Father,

Your love, peace, goodness, and kindness to Your Son bring peace and light into my soul. Through just knowing you, I have eternal life. Lord, I praise and glorify you. Thank you for removing the veil of darkness over me. Thank you for giving me understanding of who You are in my life. Your Word is a lamp to my feet and a lamp to my path. Thank You for coming into my life to remove every obstacle and to block my heart from the things of this world that is not of You so that I can fix my eyes and see You. Thank you for setting me free and giving me freedom to fly and soar I can be with You. Thank you for revealing yourself to me that I may be a light to others. Thank you for giving me the courage, and boldness to stand with you to share the light for your people. Thank you for placing me here on earth to show Your love and glory to that ones who need you and to filled the world with love, hope, and peace so that in your name they will see You in me. In Jesus' name Amen.

EXODUS 14:14

The Lord will fight for you; you need only to be still.

PSALM 105:15

Do not touch My anointed ones; do My Prophets no harm.

The Word of God is a prophecy of Jesus Christ, and it comes from the breath of God. His Word has Spirit and it has life. The prophet is a voice of God, and He is face-to-face with God. And we must respect His servant. Everything is good and lovely, and also, wrath is from God. God gave grace and mercy for His people.

PRAYER

Dear heavenly Father,

Thank You, Lord for protecting me and watching over me. Thank you for pouring out Your love and anointing for me, and without You, I would be nothing. Thank you for all the promises and plans for my life. You are always faithful to me. Your love is magnificent, and I am speechless of the goodness of Your countenance over me. Thank you, Lord, that you saw my tears, grief, hardship, and desperation. You breathed new life within me, and I am alive in you. In Jesus' name Amen.

CHAPTER 26

HALO ABOVE MY HEAD

One time, I was watching television, and I saw a Bishop praying to the people. Healing was taking place in his ministry. I was fascinated by his ministry, so I decided to call his church one day. I found out that they also had a church where I lived, so I went there with my friends. One week before I went to the church, the specialist doctor diagnosed me with chronic myeloid leukemia. He told me that I was going to die within six months, especially if I did not take the medicine he prescribed to me that I will die sooner. I was terrified of the bad news; fear forced its way down to the core of my heart. I was very scared.

The leader of the church didn't know what the specialist had said to me prior. The leader prophesied to me, and I was shocked with his prophecy; he told me that I was not going to die and that I should not fear. I was shocked is to how he knew what the doctor told me, knowing that nobody knew except me, God, and the specialist. I started to cried in front of the leader, and my whole body starting to shake. I felt the presence of the Lord that night. The leader continued prophesying to me about what he saw—he said to me that he saw TV, cameras, and the Miracles Crusade. I don't understand everything he said, but I was amazed about the prophecy over my life, and I embraced and put it in my heart. I was amazed with the move of God in my life. God spoke to me, telling me that the church was our new home church.

My whole family started going to their church, and we became members in less than two months. We were faithful to God and to our leader; the minute we became members, we wanted to serve God. David had become an elder at the church, and I become an intercessory, armor-bearer (I made a cup of water, coffee, and tea) to put in the pulpit for the leader to drink. I made sure that the leader's wife "Lady" was taken care of. The leader asked me if can prayed for the family and I said yes. I prayed for him and his family every day. I cleaned their house with love and care as a way of serving God. I was also in the children's ministry and cleaned the whole church, and we also did evangelism.

We became closer to the leader and his family. David was always with him as his Elder; and David was leading, teaching, and encouraging the people. I cleaned the sanctuary vacuuming. After I vacuumed, I would pick up the broom, start sweeping, and make a fine line on the carpet. After that, the carpet would look beautiful, like it was a work of art. Whoever walked on the carpet would feel like they were kings and queens. The fine lines on the carpet were very beautiful.

One day, the leader came to me and asked me if I could pray a private prayer for him and his family and I said yes. I felt like it was an honor. But there was a question on my mind that I had to ask God about. I asked God why the leader wanted me to pray for them knowing I didn't know how to pray at that time. Even when somebody would ask me to pray during fellowship, I will say no. It was not that I didn't want to pray; it was because I didn't know how to pray at that time.

Also, one of the leaders' wives that I knew asked me to pray for the opening prayer at their church. Two leaders who didn't know each other wanted me to go to the intercessory meeting as if they knew something about me that I didn't. I praised the Lord. By going to that church, I learned so much about what God called me to do—to speak to people of God and to lay hands on people for healing, blessings, restoration, and deliverance. I started to have confidence knowing that God was with me; as I prayed and prophesied to the people, I encountered God beyond my understanding. People were being healed, and the Word of God was right in their lives. It was so amazing to see the activity of God in the church. I devoted my life to God. I was seeking His face, wanting more of Him. I was hungry for God, and I needed Him in my life.

HALO ABOVE MY HEAD

One day, the Bishop and his wife came from another state and visited the church; they also owned the building. While the Bishop was at the pulpit, he told the whole congregation that he saw demons all over the place and that there were so many of them. I started to get concerned while he was speaking. I thought that if he saw demons everywhere. Who it is then that was following me? And right when I was thinking that, his wife got up from her chair and came toward the Bishop while he was speaking. She whispered in his left ear, telling him that she saw a "*halo above my head.*" After the Bishop finished preaching, they went to the office, and the Bishop's wife told my leader and his wife that she saw a halo above my head; she said that it looked like a ring of cloud above me. After they shared that with me, I felt relieved, and I thanked God that He—and not the demons—was with me. We continued serving God in the church for two more years, and good things were happening in our lives. Blessing after blessing came our way. One day, I saw a vision about a house, and God spoke to me that He was going to bless us with a beautiful house with a swimming pool and a gazebo in it. I was amazed by God, and I just wanted to trust Him and believe that God would make it happen for us.

I noticed that everything that God said to me was happening to my pastor first, and then all the blessings from God also happened to us. I was amazed by the activity of God in our lives.

God blessed our leader with a beautiful house with a swimming pool in it. Also, our leader was wearing a black Gaza. At the same time, God told me that I would be wearing the same Gaza, but mine would be white. He also said that we would have a beautiful house with a swimming pool and a gazebo. I was shocked I was not expecting those things. But I was amazed with God. I saw His kindness toward us. God is good. There were so many things that God told me that I would be doing and also what He wanted to bless me with. I thought, *Wow, God is a good God. He really does wonders.* God did perform miracles for us He blesses us with a good house with a gazebo and a swimming pool. I am still waiting for the white Gaza. God is so good all the time. To God be the glory!

THE HEART OF JESUS

JOHN 14:11–14

Believe Me when I say that I am in the Father and the father is in Me, or at least believe on the evidence of the miracles themselves. I tell you the truth, anyone who has faith in Me will do what I have been doing. He will do even greater things than these, because I am going to the Father. And I will do whatever you ask in my name, and I will do it.

ISAIAH 57:15

For this is what the high and exalted one says—He who lives forever, whose name is holy: I live in a high and holy place, but also with the one who is contrite and lowly in spirit, to revive the spirit of the lowly and to revive the heart of the contrite

I will give thanks to the Lord with all my heart. I will tell of all His wonders. God said His presence shall go with you, and He will give you rest. God will make known to you the path of life. In His presence is fullness of joy. In His right hand are pleasures forever. "Just as the Father has loved me, I have also loved you. Abide in my love." Jesus said, "You will seek Me and find Me when you search for Me with all your heart." Where can you go from His Spirit or where can you flee from His presence?

I love you, O Lord, my strength. You are my rock, my fortress, my redeemer and my deliverer. You are God my rock in whom I take refuge. You are my shield and the horn of my salvation, my stronghold. I call to the Lord, who is worthy of my praise, and I am saved from my enemies.

CHAPTER 27

UNDERSTANDING GOD

GOD BLESS THEM

Out of all the people in the church, the leader chose me to pray for him and his family. I felt honored to pray for them, and I did pray for all of them. Signs, wonders, and miracles were taking place in their life. God poured out blessings after blessings upon them.

One day, I prophesied to the leader's wife "Lady" about Paul being in jail, Paul received gifts from the congregation, and it pleased God. After I prophesied to his wife about Paul being in jail, and I shares with her that the blessings of the Lord were also hovering over her; God wants to bless her. The following Sunday the whole congregation was blessing her with many gifts and cards with money, the same word that I told her what is going to happen to her. That God will bless her.

One day, I spoke to the leader in front of the congregation for the blessings of the Lord to come upon his life. I prophesied to him that he would have a car; three weeks later, the whole congregation bought him a brand-new car. The blessings of the Lord were hovering over him. I prayed for the whole congregation, and it was multiplying, from twenty-five members to four hundred members. God was blessing the whole congregation and showing his power over them.

I was calling my leader my spiritual father and his wife my spiritual mother and we were feeling love and bless from them. I had never experienced the love from spiritual parents before, and I loved it. I called the congregation my spiritual family from God and my brothers and sisters in Christ.

WORRIED AND CONCERNED

One day, David did not come home for two days I was worried and concerned for him. I felt like I need somebody to reach out for him, something happened to David; his heart started to harden. I was in desperate for help from the elders and brothers from the church to find out if they heard from David because I had not heard from him for the past two days. David was always with the Pastor, elders, Deacon and they always did things for the church before. He was in church almost every week doing things for the church for over two years. The Pastor, Pastor elect, the Elder, the Minister, and the Deacons were friends with him. So I thought that they might want to minister to him. I felt like David needed God and prayers in his life.

So I asked the elders if they could call David to make sure that he was all right, and two days later, one of the elders got back to me, and he said to me that the leader of the church did not want him to call David. I was very sad. I really needed help concerning David. I felt like somebody needed to minister to him. David decided not to come home, and I was very sad. And people from the church did not want to reach out to him, which made me even sadder, and I started to cry out and pray to the Lord for help.

David and I usually sat at the front of the sanctuary, but I noticed that the people from the church didn't want me to sit at the same spot anymore. I felt like everybody was talking about us. I became the talk of the town. I did not feel the love of people that day. I was hurt. I felt rejected and persecuted by the people. I cried every day because I had fallen in love with people the same way that I had with God. I had never experienced being in so much pain in my heart from other people before. I had never served God in any church before in my life; being saved was a new thing for me. I felt like a little child full of hope as I served God. But at that time, I was lost among my brothers and sisters in Christ. I needed help.

Growing up, I didn't usually go to church. I went only when there was an occasion or during holidays. When I got to know God a little bit, I decided to serve Him, but I did not know that it was not easy. I experienced the difficulties of serving God by being around with other people who I thought were my brothers and sisters in Christ at that time. I questioned God a lot about my situation because I was confused. I thought that when I had a problem, it would be easy for me to come to them. But I was wrong. I realized that I had to come to the Lord to get help.

All I wanted to do was to love everyone and to serve God. I asked God why all those things were happening to me. I felt like my heart for people was sinking, that I lost my trust in people. I searched my heart, to make sure we did the right thing in the church. I knew we were paying our tithes, we gave more than fourteen thousand a year and we go to church every weekend and do all of our duties. I asked God is to what went wrong. So I tried to find the answer from God. I desperately needed to hear God's voice in my brokenness.

One day, David came back home, and I forgave him; and we decided to move on and not to come back to the same church. When the leader found out about it, he said to the whole congregation to "*not ever call me and not to even pray for me and for my whole family.*" I was shocked, and I was very hurt because I had a loving heart toward him, to his family, and all the people from the church. When the people from the church heard that from the leader's mouth, they called me immediately and asked me if I was okay. I said yes, and they decided not to come back to the church. When I found out about that, I was hurt even more because I didn't want to see a divided church. God did not want an unhealthy and divided church. God wanted love, unity and restoration in the body of Christ. I was asking God to give me understanding, peace, and strength. I was praying for the church to have love and unity as the body of Christ.

GOD SHOWS ME HIS WAYS

One day, my friend asked me to go with her to the church that was open 24/7. I was reluctant at first, but I said yes to her even though I didn't know where the church was. One month later, something happened that shocked me and my family. In the blink of our eyes, the beautiful home that we leased purchased was gone before our eyes. It happened so fast. We had to move out from our house because the owner wanted more money than the house was worth. The mortgage company could not buy the house for us. We decided to try to find a house in five locations. But we couldn't find one that we wanted to live in, so we decided to stay in a hotel until we found a house that we like. While we were searching for a house, we found a basement for rent; we thought that we should stay there for awhile until we found a house that we really liked instead of staying in a hotel because the hotel cost us one hundred dollars a night. We decided to stay in the basement for awhile, and it was the only place available for us at that time. So my family agreed. The basement had two bedrooms, and we were all satisfied. Not knowing that God had a plan for us.

One day, I was on my way to the store, and I kept passing by this unique church, which was two minutes away from our place. At that time, I forgot about my friend inviting me to go to the church that was open 24/7. Every time I passed by the church, there were always a lot of people during the day and even at night. It was always a puzzle to me as to what kind of church was open all day and all night. I did not realize that it was the same church that my friend was inviting me to go to. How fascinating it was to know that it was a divine appointment that God set before us. God found us a place to live, and it was only two minutes away from the church that my friend invited me to come. Instead of my friend brings me to the church that she was talking about, but God Himself who is the One who brought me to the church, how fascinating that was to see God move for us. I love God.

God moved us from our house to somebody's basement, and God's wisdom and plan for us were beyond my understanding. God was so good. God used the house with the basement to connect us to the church that was open 24/7.

And God spoke to me that the church would be our new home as our new church. Sad to say that later on, David continued being disobedient and kept sinning against God. Finally, God had to remove him from my life. We got a divorce, and I moved on with my life. Then my journey with God had begun. To God be the glory!

My new church gave me a recommendation letter for my old church to sign; when I brought it to my old leader for him to sign so that we would be released from the church, he told me that he was not going to sign the letter because he believed that we belonged to their church. He asked me why we left the church. I told him that when our marriage was falling apart, no one reached out to us—not even him. I told him that David was very disobedient to God and he was lost, and somebody needed to reach out to him. David needed God, but no one contacted him.

I shared with the leader about the shepherd needing to reach out to the lost sheep. He told me that the shepherd also broke the sheep's legs. I told him that when the sheep was lost and the shepherd did not reach out to the one lost sheep, God the Father would not bring any more sheep to the shepherd.

MATTHEW 18:12

What do you think? If a man owns a hundred sheep, and one of them wanders away, will He not leave the ninety-nine on the hills and go to look for the one that wandered off?

After sharing our feelings toward the situation, we shook hands with smiles on our faces, and we prayed for each other. Then I left.

LUKE 6:27–29

But to you who are listening I say: Love your enemies, do good to those who hate you. Bless those who curse you, pray for those who mistreat you. If someone slaps you on one cheek, turn to them the other also. If someone takes your coat, do not demand it back. Do to others as you would have them do to you.

Not knowing that my words became a prophecy for him. Something happened to him that shocked him. Before we became members of the church, they only had twenty-five members. Their number increased to four hundred members while we were members of the church; after we left, the church members decreased to twenty-five people again. Before, they had a huge building. After we left, they moved to a really small office building. And later on, he lost his wife.

The word of God is alive and active. God did not bring any more sheep to the shepherd.

My story and my life are about God's message for the leader. Humbleness and humility are the key and treasures for God's kingdom.

Years later, I visited the church to let them know that I had forgiven them, and I shared a powerful testimony with them. I wanted God to restore them and bless the church. I prayed for the leader and to the whole congregation to have love, peace, unity, restoration, and blessings from heaven.

GOD GIVES GRACE AND MERCY TO THE HUMBLE

JOHN 17:11

I will remain in the world no longer, but they are still in the world, and I am coming to you, Holy Father, protect them by the power of Your name the name You gave me so that they may be one as We are One.

2 JOHN 1:3

Grace, mercy and peace from God the Father and from Jesus Christ, the Father's Son, will be with us in truth and love.

PRAYER

Dear heavenly Father,

Your name, Jesus, is powerful and astonishing. Your name is above every name. Your name is rich, and nothing in this universe can compare to it. Your name brings awe to the core of my being, and in my heart, You stand.

With Your love, You reconciled me to Yourself and gave me the right to stand with You. Lord Jesus, You are my God who washed away my sins, and it is through You that I am now saved. Lord Jesus, thank you for using me as an instrument of Your Word for Your people. Let the whole world be amazed by You and by the kindness and goodness of Your love that bring unity for your people.

Lord Jesus, I love you! in Jesus' name, amen.

CHAPTER 28

MY NAME IS WRITTEN ON THE WALL

While I was working, God gave me a vision of the house that He was going to give to us. He gave me a description of the house—it would have a gazebo, a swimming pool, and a huge land. At that time, I thought it was impossible because we had just moved into our new place three months prior, and we were not planning to move out. My friends were so excited for us to live close to them. But I told them with assurance from God that we would not stay in the house very long. I told them that we would move to a different house again because that was where God told me that we would live. I even showed the backyard to my friend to prove that the house did not have a swimming pool. I told her that I was very sure that our new house would have a pool. At that time swimming pool is not on my mind at all, I'm not sure if I want a swimming. But God said that He wants me to have them, and I'm being obedient to the Lord.

One night, I had a vision about the lions, and I started talking about them for one month. I even asked the pastor and the leader of the fellowship group if they knew the meaning of the lions that I saw in my vision, but they didn't know the meaning of it either, so I just kept it to myself. One month later, I had a vision of this beautiful house, and I told David about it, it just so happen at the same time that he was talking to his friend about the house that his friend was fixing. One day, David asked me to go to the house and see what I thought about it. I said yes to him. The following day, while I was working, God spoke to me about an angel, who was a woman. I started thanking God for the angel, and then I praised and worshipped Him. At that time, I didn't know that God was going to tell me about the angel. I was just glad that He was communicating with me, and I was very happy knowing God's presence was with me.

I remember telling God that I knew about the angel, and I said "thank you to the Lord." That day, I came to the house that David wanted me to see; the first thing I noticed about it was the beautiful fountain that had the faces of seventeen lions in front of the house. I was amazed because God told me about the lions even before I saw them. I went toward the front door, and I noticed a beautiful huge statue of a lion's head on top of the door. At that time, I felt the presence of God. When I opened the door, I saw the living room right away, and I was amazed at how huge and beautiful it was; the living room looked like a chapel. I was very excited. I went around to the right side, and I saw a fireplace. Then I looked up with amazement in my heart because I just saw this beautiful huge mural on the wall with a woman angel standing on top of a fountain. I started talking to the picture on the wall and I said, "I remember you from yesterday." God told me about you." Then I turned around toward the kitchen, and I saw my name was written on the wall under the island; there were three murals of flower vases, and in the middle of the two was this huge vase with my name, Esther, written on the wall. I was amazed because of all three hundred houses we looked at this was the only one that had my name written on the wall.

I was very shocked and amazed with God, and I asked myself, *about what kind of a house is this?* I went outside the balcony, and it had a gazebo. I also saw a long swimming pool with lions' heads all around it. After seeing all these, I was fascinated by God; the house was exactly the same as the one in my vision. God is so good. He wanted to bless me mightily. God opened the door for us to live there, and later on, I became the host for the fellowship. There were two people saved and two people healed. I was amazed with God for His faithfulness to His children.

VISION FROM GOD

ACTS 2:17–21

In the last days, God says, I will pour out My Spirit on all people. Your sons and daughters will prophesy, you young men will see visions, your old men will dream dreams. Even on My servants, both men and women, I will pour out My Spirit in those days, and they will prophesy. I will show wonders in the heaven above and signs on the earth below, blood and fire and billows of smoke. The sun will be turned to darkness and the moon to blood before the coming of the great and glorious day of the Lord. And every one who calls on the name of the Lord will be saved.

PRAYER

Dear heavenly Father,

You are the greatest Father that I have ever had, and You bring miracles to the core of my being. I praise You, Lord, and I glorify You. Lord, Your Word is alive within my soul. You created me full of Your love, and You established me to be the watchman on the wall. Lord, when I call You, You answer me without waiting to let me know that You are near me. And for that, I want to say thank You. You are the one who brings wonder to my soul In Jesus' name. Amen.

CHAPTER 29

THE ANGEL IS REAL

PSALM 91:11

FOR HE WILL COMMND HIS ANGELS CONCERNING YOU TO GUARD YOU IN ALL YOUR WAYS.

One day, at around 9:15 am, I was on my way to work. I heard the voice of God saying that I should call Joshua, who was also a servant of God. God spoke to me in a very clear and firm voice, saying that I should pray for him. God wanted me to tell him about the angel of the Lord, the Psalm 91. At that time, I was running late for work, and I didn't have time to really pray for him. But God was very persistent in wanting me to pray for him at that moment. So I stopped my car, and I called the man. I was so glad that he answered my phone call. I asked him if he wanted me to pray for him, and he said yes. So I started praying for him, and God led me to pray Psalm 91 over his life.

God wanted to protect him and put him under his wing so Joshua could find refuge in God. Because the man was faithful to the Lord, God had a purpose for him. I didn't know what was about to happen to him, but God did. God could see the works of the enemy from afar, and God was willing and able to protect him from the woks of the enemy. So Psalm 91 is about protection and peace for his servant. God intervened whatever the enemy was trying to do to the servant of God. After I prayed for him, I went straight to work.

Around three o'clock in the afternoon, I started getting worried about Joshua, so I prayed for him again. I was expecting him to be at the Christmas party for the ministry, but he did not show up on time. He called one of the leaders to let him know that he had been in an accident. I was shocked, and I prayed some more for him.

The following day, Joshua called me to tell me what happened to him. He shared his testimony with me. " He said that he was driving an eighteen-wheeler truck on the highway that day. Suddenly, a car on the right side of him just pulled over in front of him; He tried to change lanes so that he would not hit the other car. But it happened so fast that he lost control of the steering wheel. Still, he tried not to hit the car in front of him. He tried to turn the wheel really fast, but he was having a hard time controlling it and the brakes. So the truck moved really fast, heading to the bridge.

While all this was happening, he was starring the wheel that whole time. At the back of his mind, he knew that he did not have the ability to control the situation. Without any doubt, he was going to hit the bridge; he knew that he could die that day. The only things that he had in front of him were the wheel, gas, and brakes. And he knew that the truck would go down the bridge, and a lot of people under the bridge would be hurt. He knew that the eighteen-wheeler would hit the bridge, and he would not be able to escape. He did not have time to pray because it was happening so fast that all he could do was hold on to the wheel very tightly and step on the brakes really hard, when he got closer to the bridge he said "My God, my God, I am going to hit the bridge." And He did hit the bridge.

The minute the truck hit the bridge, the power of God was revealed miraculously in his life because God intervened to save him. When the truck hit the bridge, the hood of his truck fell from the edge of the bridge and landed on the ground and no one was hurt. After he hit the bridge real hard, the truck bounced back, and he became unconscious; and the truck rolled away to the right side of the road. The people and the police came and helped him, while they were helping him, he woke up and he can't remember anything. He thought that he was dead. He thanked God that he was still alive. The prayers really did work, and he realized that God just answered my prayers that same day. He was so glad that no one was hurt when the hood fell from the bridge and that nothing in his body was broken because the angel of the Lord was protecting him. I was so glad that God used me to pray for him at that moment, not knowing what would happen to him; he could have died, but God saved his life instead. He thanked God for protecting him. He was very scared because he really thought that he was going to die; instead, God spared his life for his purpose, will, and glory for his life. His faith in the Lord grew even stronger. Nothing in his body were hurt instead, the company gave him the money to cover all the cost. God bless the man.

When God wants to protect His people, He will do everything in His power to make sure His job is fulfilled; the enemy will try to kill and destroy, but God is ahead of Him. He will send His angel to protect His faithful servant because God is a loving God, and He always wins in battles.

EXODUS 14:31

And when the Israelites saw the great power the Lord displayed against the Egyptians, the people feared the Lord and put their trust in Him and Moses His servant.

When the enemy tries to attack and kill, always know that God is with you. He will fights for your battles, and God wins every time. God is the only one who can make the impossible to possible. God wants to release you from captivity to freedom. God will make a way when there seems to be no way out. The bigger the challenges are in your life, the greater His ability to overcome them all. When you listen to the clarity of His voice, He will give you assurance and confidence. Always know how to be still and hear His voice. God will you lead you and direct you to the path where He is. Your obedience to His voice will always lead into blessings for your future and destiny.

Our prayers, obedience, faithfulness, and dedication to the Lord will change our life and people around us. God sees you. He sees when you are in danger or are hurting and struggling. God will never leave you nor forsake you. He will always bring good things in your life. He is the God who gives life.

CHAPTER 30

DREAMS

MY DAD AND THE CHILD

One tiring night in 2013, I was sleeping, and I started dreaming about my father. In my dream, I saw him sitting on the ground, holding this handsome little boy; my dad kept looking at me as I kept looking at him. As I was looking at the child, I noticed how curly his hair was, and he was a very handsome little boy. I had never seen the little boy before. I didn't know where the boy came from. As I was looking at them, I asked myself why they were sitting on the ground, why my dad was holding the child, and where his parents were. And then I woke up.

I CARRY THE CROSS

DREA M

One year later, in 2014, I had another dream; this one had me carrying a huge and very heavy cross. I needed to take it where it was safe. I saw this beautiful field and meadow, and I was thinking of taking the cross there. For me to be able to take the cross to that beautiful field and meadow, meant that I had to pass through the river to make it to the other side. When I looked at the meadow, I noticed that there was no other way to get to the other side, but through the river. As I was looking at the river, it was raging really fast. At that moment, I was thinking about how to take the cross to other side. I knew how important it was for me to take the cross to the other side, so that I can be able to have peace.

So I decided to carry the cross across the river, and I started walking through the water. While I was in the middle of the river, I noticed that the raging water started to rise up from my knees and all the way up to my neck really fast. The water continued to rise up high, past my head, and I knew that I could drown any minute and die. The cross was very heavy, and I was having a hard time carrying it. I started feeling helpless and powerless. I couldn't do anything, and I felt like I was stuck in the deep waters. I was going down under the water little by little. I tried to swim, but I couldn't because the cross was too heavy for me to carry on my shoulder. I felt like I was drowning from the raging deep waters.

Even though the cross was too heavy, I still carried it on my shoulder. I didn't want to let go of the cross. I didn't want to give up. I wanted the cross to stay with me, and no matter what happened to me, I wanted to hold on to the cross. But the water was getting higher and higher and rougher and rougher, and the cross was getting heavier and heavier. I was getting tired, weak, and scared; and I felt like giving up because the cross was too heavy, and it was bringing me down. I knew right away that I was going to die.

Even with all that pain and despair, I still continued trying to carry the cross to the other side of the river. And right when I was feeling weak and tired and about to give up, I suddenly saw and felt a light that looked like a hand pull me out from the waters and bring me back on the dry ground.

I looked to the other side with despair and hopelessness. I thought that I was very close to making it to the other side, but I was wrong. I felt sadness and hopelessness come over me, knowing that there was no hope that I could take the cross to the other side. I felt like coming back to the waters again with the cross on my shoulder because I didn't want to give up.

But when I looked at the river, the raging waters were very strong. I knew that they could sweep me off and drown me if I tried to go through them. I knew that I was not able to take the cross to the other side because the water was too deep and the other side was far away. I felt disappointed. I was feeling helpless and hurt. I saw myself bending my knees to the ground and crying out to the Lord. I was calling God with agony and pain.

Later on, as I was crying, I felt the presence and love of God by protecting me from the raging waters. I was very happy that I was safe, but at the same time, I was very sad that I could not take the cross to the other side. I was looking at the other side, and I said to myself that maybe I could take the cross to the other side next time. And then I woke up.

PSALM 18:16–19

He reached down from on high and took hold of me; He drew me out of deep waters. He rescued from my foes, who were too strong for me. They confronted me in the day of my disaster, He brought me out into a spacious place; He rescued me because He delighted in me.

Peace is brought into your soul through Jesus Christ, His blood, His cross, and His resurrection. He is the one who can take you out from the darkness situations and challenges in your life. He will hold you as His child and lead to you to His path. In Him, you are saved.

CHAPTER 31

GOD IS ABOVE ALL

One day, my brother called me from the Philippines. He asked me if I can send some money for him, because he was very sick and he wants to see the doctor to see what was wrong with him. I said yes. I sent him some money. I have been sending money to him for the past three weeks. He went to the doctor and the doctor diagnosed him with tuberculosis and another disease. The doctor gave him medicine hoping that he will be healed. After two weeks, my brother's wife called me to tell me that she was going to bring my brother back to the hospital again because he was having a hard time to breathe. When my sister-in-law told me that, I started to cry because I saw in the "vision" that my brother is already dead without them bringing him back to the doctor. When I went to the church that morning, I immediately kneeled down to the altar before God. I cried out to the Lord and I asked God to help my brother and heal him completely. I prayed to the Lord with tears running through my cheeks. After I prayed, I felt assurance and peace with God. The following day my sister-in-law called me again and told me that when she was bringing back my brother to the hospital, the doctor took care of him right away and the doctor told her that he didn't know what to do with him because my brother was not breathing anymore. He said that my brother is already dead. But God revealed his glory by showing to the doctor that my brother is still alive, and he starting to breathe. My brother was alive! When the doctor saw that my brother was still alive, the doctor started taking care of my brother right away. I thanked God for answering my prayer and for touching my brother for him to be alive. My brother stayed in the hospital for two weeks, and later on I sent some money for him to pay for the hospital so he can go back home.

I pray to the Lord that the hospital will give favor to the people that need healing, to have compassion and help them. When my brother got home, I shared with him about the love and the goodness of God. He embraced it and gave his life to God. I feel so much better because I knew that his name is written in the Book of Life and he will stay in God's mansion that has many rooms and I knew that one room is for him.

Two weeks later, my niece called me urgently and she told me that they needed to bring my brother back to the hospital and she was asking for some money for my brother to pay for the hospital before they admitted him. I told her to bring my brother to the hospital right away, but she told me that they needed at least some down payment to bring my brother to the hospital. At that time I didn't have any more money because I already sent all my money to him for the hospital and also for my aunt because she was also sick at the same time and I sent her some money also so she can go to the hospital, but without notice, she died right away. I was having a hard time sending any more money right away to my brother, but I knew later on that I would be able to send some money to him. I was feeling helpless and hopeless.

My niece told me if they did not bring my brother to the hospital, he will die, and if I send some money to them so they can take my brother to the hospital, then he will live. After she told me that, knowing I don't have any more money to send to them, I starting to have anxiety, feeling weak, crushed, and had fear and trouble in my heart. I felt like the brick just hit me on my head. I starting to cried out to the Lord while I was sitting on the chair at the dining table. I start asking God about, "why would God give me something to do that was too hard for me to do." I thought at that moment that God was unfair to me. I told God that I don't have any more money to give to my brother. I told God about why He would put all the burdens to me. Why is it that if I send some money to my brother, my brother will live, and if I don't send some money to my brother, that my brother will die. I don't have any control of what is happening to my brother. I told God that He is in control, so I prayed to God to heal my brother and that I want Him to perform miracles for my brother. I told God that I am surrendering my brother to Him and I want Him to have His way with my brother and give Him peace.

I remember all my tears were pouring down my face. I was feeling hurt and I was very concerned. I was thinking as to what would happen to my brother. I was praying for my brother, believing that God will heal him. I asked myself how and where I could get some money for him. I asked God to be in control of my situation because I was weak and broken at that moment.

After I hanged up the phone with my niece, I immediately called one of the persons I knew and asked for help, hoping that the person can help me with my brother, but the person said no to helping me because this person thought it was my brother's fault why he was sick. I thought the person could help me, but I was wrong. Because I was in desperate need at that time, in my desperation, at that moment of my life, I decided to turn and fix my eyes on the Lord instead.

I tried to text the family that I knew a long time ago. I knew that they were millionaires, and they have a lot of extra cars and houses all over the States and they have some land and a mansion in another country. I thought that maybe they could lend me some money. I was borrowing five hundred dollars so I could bring my brother to the hospital and I told them that I will pay them back. I was very disappointed when they said no they cannot lend me some money because they said that they don't lend money. I was very hurt when they said that because I was expecting them to help me. Because I thought that they have a lot of money and that they can afford it. I thought that they were the only ones that could help me. I thought only this family can be able to answer my problems. But I was wrong. I was devastated. I was having anxiety. I was losing hope, and I started to have fear for my brother. I felt helpless and hopeless at that moment. I continued to pray, with tears pouring down on my face. I was very weak and confused, but I knew that I am very strong and God is on my side. I thanked God for giving me the power and the strength to fight the battles that are beyond my control, my understanding, and my ability. I am relying only in God.

After being rejected a couple of times, I came back up and continued to make phone calls to my other friends. I called my friend that I knew for twenty-five years—the last person that I thought I should not call. I was thinking that my friends might not have enough money to lend me the money for my brother, but I tried to call them anyway and I asked them to help me with my brother. I told them the story of my brother, and he immediately sent some money for my brother that same night. I was very shocked because I almost did not call him to help me with my brother. I was thanking God for my friends, for being good friends to me. God makes a way and performed miracles for me. He gave me peace that night. To God be the glory.

I was very happy, overjoyed, and blessed, and I felt released from anxiety and worry, and I felt hope with God at that moment. I was thanking God for blessing me and my brother. I was thanking God for my friends, for showering their lives with many blessings, with wonderful freedom and a beautiful purpose in their lives. They are the most blessed people I know, and God has continued to bless them for the rest of their lives. Later on I paid them back for the full amount, and I thanked God for them.

After my friend sent the money for my family, I was waiting for my niece to call me back. It was getting late that night and I did not hear from her until the following morning when she called me and I told her that I already sent the money. I asked them if they can pick up the money and bring my brother to the hospital, but my niece told me that there was a bad typhoon in the city overnight, and the whole city was flooded, with the water even reaching above the houses, buildings, and even the hospitals. They cannot pick up the money, and they cannot even take my brother to the hospital. I was shocked. I asked myself as to how that just happened, that water just flooded overnight. I was just talking to my niece the night before how the waters just rise up like that and it happened real fast in one night. My niece told me that my brother was having a hard time to breathe.

My brother needed a machine to breathe with. They don't have any more machines that he can use so he can breathe. The hospital did not give them the machine enough to last for a long time. So my family tried to go to the neighborhood to see if they have the machine that my brother can use. But the neighborhood does not have the machine either. They were in despair, and they were losing hope to find h elp.

I started to cry and pray that God will make a way for my brother. I was feeling hopeless and sad. I tried my best to help, but I felt like I failed my brother. Being far away from them became even harder for me. At the same time while my brother was lying on the bed, the rain kept pouring down, and the water kept rising up. The water had almost reached inside the house. Everybody was scared that the water might go inside the house and worried for my brother. The water was raging so hard that it hit our kitchen very hard. We lost our kitchen due to the bad typhoon. My family was very scared. They didn't know what to do because the kitchen was beside my brother's bedroom. They knew any time that the typhoon can wipe away my brother's bedroom too. While these things were happening to my family, I was very concerned and scared in America at the same time. I don't remember going to sleep that night, thinking and praying for them. At the same time, all I can do is to be still and continue to wait upon the Lord. Later on, it was Sunday morning and I received the bad news from my family. They told me that my brother had died and that he gave himself to the Lord. I was mourning and feeling very sad. I cried out all night that night. I thought that night would never end. I was mourning for my brother. I love my brother and I miss him.

While they were fighting the bad storm and also fighting for my brother's death, at the same time I was fighting with darkness in my house in America. Because I had lost the power, our house does not have any electricity for two weeks. At that time, it was summer. It was so hot in the house. We had no air-conditioning. My daughter and my granddaughter decided to go to somebody's house because they cannot take the house being hot.

During that whole two weeks of darkness in my house and my brother being dead, I felt empty into my soul. I started to have fear of the Lord. I realized that God is real and alive. I thought that whole time that I knew God but I realized that I was wrong. In my brokenness and poor mind, after realizing my situation and about my brother being dead, I knew God was in control of my life and the fact that my brother was dead. With fear on the Lord, I kneeled down before Him, and at that moment I gave all my life and I surrendered all to the Lord all over again, and I knew this time will be different for me. I felt like I had just wake up from my reality that anytime I could die. This time I dedicated myself more to the Lord, my savior Jesus Christ.

Having fear of the Lord brings peace into my soul, knowing that He is on my side. With me being in the darkness and empty, God turned it around, filling me up and shining on me. I realized that God was saying something to me that I needed to be connected to the source of power, which is Jesus Christ. I thought I knew Jesus Christ at that time, but in my broken soul, God's blood brought me back together again. Having a relationship with Him brings healing and freedom into my soul. God set me free.

One week later, my younger brother called me to let me know what I want to do concerning my brother's body. I cannot answer him right away.

While I was on the phone with my family, I decided to minister and prayed for all of them. After I prayed for them, they all gave their lives to the Lord and they all had peace. They received the money. The money was supposed to be for my brother to go to the hospital, but instead, they wanted to use the money to bury my brother.

BROKEN

That night, as I was sitting at the dining table in my house, I was thinking about my brother. I felt like everything was quiet. Darkness was all around me. I couldn't see straight. Tears were just falling from my eyes. Pain, loss, and emptiness were just covering all over me. I was very hurt. I asked God as to why my brother had to die. I love my brother. He is everything to me. I cannot explain the pain that I was going through. I felt like the night was very long. I wanted the day light to come immediately and shower me with His love. But that light never came. That night, I felt guilty, confused, and weak. My heart ached and I felt broken. I felt like at that time the isolation of my soul separated me from my creator. I searched God in my heart, and I wanted Him to speak to me, to calm my soul. I needed God at that hour.

ROMANS 8:35

Who shall separate us from the love of Christ? Shall trouble or hardship or persecution or famine or nakedness or danger or sword? As it is written: For your sake we face death all day long; we are considered as sheep to be slaughtered. No in all these things we are more than conquerors through Him who loved us. For I am convinced that neither death nor life, neither angels nor demons, neither the present nor future, nor any powers, neither height nor depth, nor anything else in all creation, will be able to separate us from the love of God that is in Christ Jesus our Lord.

That night, I was doing my homework, and my homework is about "What do I think about God?" When I read that, I was shocked, because I could have that homework before or after, but instead I have the homework the same day that my brother died.

I started to cry. I have so much to ask God about my life and concerning my brother—remembering all those chaos and challenges and also signs, wonders, and miracles in my life—and it brought me down to my knees. I thanked God for keeping me alive because I could have been dead many years ago, but He has kept me alive for His purpose. So I just started praising God because He is worthy of it all. I told God that I knew that He is a good God and a good Father to me, and I trust His leadership over my life.

MY DAD AND A CHILD

Two days later, my youngest brother called me to tell me that he wanted to ask my permission to open my father's casket to put my brother's dead body on top of my father's body, so they don't have to buy a new casket. When I heard that they were going to put my brother's dead body along with my father's dead body in one casket, I was shocked. When my brother told me that, I remembered about my dream in 2013 that flashed back to my mind right away that "my dad was holding a good-looking child," and it just happened that the child is my brother, that my father was holding my brother, when they are together in one casket. I started to cry as if like I already knew what was going to happen to my brother. That his remain body will be with my dad in the same casket God was just giving me a sign in my dream. God was giving me a warning as to what is going to happen.

JOHN 14:6

Jesus answered, I AM the way and the truth and the life. No one comes to the Father except through Me.

Jesus is saying to His disciple to fully trust in Him because He knows all things.

I CARRIED THE CROSS

In my dream, when I was trying to take the cross to the other side where it can be safe, I realized that it was my brother when He died and with me trying to help Him in any way possible. When I tried my best to help my brother so He can be alive, instead as if I failed Him, I was drowning in despair. But God was talking to me that whole time that He was in control in my life. Little did I know that God already had a plan for him, that God Himself will take the cross to the other side where the cross is forever safe for eternity for my brother, it was God's plan. While I was trying my best to keep my brother alive by bringing him to the hospital, at the same time God was working on my faith. He was strengthening me. He was developing me and He was communicating with me. God was transforming me into His image at the moment of my life.

God is faithful He to continue talking to me to let me know that He is in control in my life.

GOD IS ABOVE ALL

Every time I sing about the "Above All" song, God is telling me that He is exists, that He is sitting around above the earth and He is watching over me. I was inspired by singing the song for two months. I felt like God was talking to me and preparing me for what is about to happen to my brother. I sang the song like there is no tomorrow, not knowing that my brother is going to die. I felt like that song became alive into my soul. Without even realizing it, the sweet song became a prophecy for me—the things that were happening to me were actually the way God is talking to me.

Every time I sing that song, it is as if God was saying something to me or revealing something to me, as if God is telling me something that is going to happen in the future. I feel close to the Lord knowing that God is with me. He brings comfort into my soul. I did not know until later on that song will actually manifest in my life. God is above everything in this world. He has power and authority above all things. He has the authority and control over my life. When I was singing this "Above All" song, the story about my brother is about Above All Song. Singing the song humble me before the Lord, I kneeled down before Him to let Him know that I am keeping His word and I followed His ways. I let Him know that I love Him.

One day, before I found out about my brother dying, that song "Above All" started to come to pass in my life for my brother.

STORY

ABOVE ALL KINGS

When my brother was dying and needed some money for him to go to the hospital, I came to the millionaire man and asked for him to help my brother. I called him a (King), knowing that he is a millionaire. But God is above the man. **God is above the kings**. I STAYED FOCUSED ON GOD.

ABOVE ALL WISDOM AND ALL THE WAYS OF MAN

The person I knew told me that I needed to have wisdom when I send money to my family. I have never asked the person as to why the person wanted me to use **wisdom**. I FIXED MY EYES ON JESUS.

ABOVE ALL WEALTH AND TREASURES OF THE EARTH

That song manifested to me when my friend for twenty-five years **sent money** for my brother so that my brother can go to the hospital. However, my family cannot pick up the money from the **bank** so they can take my brother to the hospital because of the strong typhoon. The water was rising up above the buildings and that included the **banks** and the hospital. God is above all created things, **wealth, and treasures**. I AM TRUSTING GOD

REJECTED AND ALONE, LIKE A ROSE TRAMPLED ON THE GROUND

That song ministered to me when I was experiencing the "**suffering**" for not knowing what is going to happen the day ahead. **The rejection from the people who insulted me, and criticize me brought me down to the ground. The fear, the anxiety, the hardship, and even trouble in my heart for my brother brought grave into my soul.** But the whole time those things were happening to me, I knew that God was with me. God is above all those things. I BELIEVE IN MIRACLES.

CRUCIFIED, LAID BEHIND THE STONE, YOU LIVED TO DIE

When my brother was experiencing crucified the agony of pain, suffering with that disease, he cannot take it anymore that he had to be with the Lord. My brother was laid behind the stone. **My brother had to live, suffered, died so that he can forever have eternity in peace with God.** God is above all. He gave life and He can take it away. GOD IS IN CONTROL OF MY LIF E.

Everything in this world belongs to God. Everything you build to look beautiful in this world belongs to God. Without God everything you have can be blown away. Everything you treasure on this earth belongs to God. Jesus Christ who died for us is the only One who can set you free. He is the only One who is in control over your life.

EPHESIANS 1:21

Far above all rule and authority, power and dominion, and every name that is Invoked, not only in the present age but also in the one to come.

God is the majesty sitting on the throne. He is omnipotent, the infinite God, the God of all powerful. He has the authority and powers of all things. He is in control. His Deity represents the Lordship over all things and others. His name is above all names. He is the Almighty God and nothing can compare to Him.

THE HEART OF JESUS

PSALM 34:18–19

The Lord is near to those who have a broken heart, and saves such as have a contrite spirit. Many are afflictions of the righteous, but the Lord delivers Him out of them all.

God is your refuge and strength, a very present help in trouble. For He Himself has said, I will never leave you nor forsake you. So I may boldly say, The Lord is your helper, and you will not have fear. What can death and man do to you, for God is with you, He loves you all the way to eternity.

2 CORITHIANS 4:8-9

We are hard pressed on every side, but not crushed; perplexed, but in despair; persecuted, but not abandoned; struck down, but not destroyed.

The trials and challenges in our life bring us closer to God.

PRAYERS

Lord Jesus, in the midst of my troubles, the suffering, and the difficulties, you showed up and rescued me. Thank You for being my God who is always there for me. Lord, in Your presence I feel peace, strength, assurance, and confidence in my heart. Thank You, Lord. As I walk through Your fire, my whole being feels Your electricity of love over me. Thank You for revealing Yourself to me, and I stood with great faith in You. Lord Jesus, through Your eyes the heavens were open and I have found Your love, peace, comfort, and Your glory over me. Thank You, Lord, and I love You In Jesus' name. Amen.

CHAPTER 32

GOD'S GENERAL STORIES, EVANGELISTS'S STORIES AND MY STORIES

MALACHI 4:5

See, I will send the Prophet Elijah to you before that great and dreadful day of the Lord comes.

One day, in 2008, the Pastor prophesied to me and said to me that **I am not going to die** knowing that the Doctor said on 2007 and he continued saying those word every two weeks I come to his office that I was going to died within six month, but by the grace of God I am still standing, I was amazed by God. The Pastor continue saying that he saw television, camera, and miracle crusade over my life. As a young Christian, I have never understood the Pastor's prophecy over me before because I didn't know the meaning of miracle crusade at that time. I was very confused about the Pastor's prophecy over me. But for all those words that he shared to me, I decided to keep it all into my heart. As the years went by, God revealed the powerful wonders to me in an intimate way beyond my understanding. All those years of my life, God always unveiled the personal encounter I had with Him. It is the way God introduced His children to me about "God's General and Evangelists" over my life. I was so glad that God always equipped, directed, and led me for His purposes. I would like to share with you of some my experiences and how I encountered the moves and activity of God over the years of my life, and being inspired and encouraged with God's beauty and His love over me through the similarity from the Prophets, Prophetess, and Evangelists.

As I found out about "God's Generals and Evangelists stories"—the pioneer prophets and the prophetess and the new-generation Prophets that God uses for His glory on the earth, and how they really inspired me, encouraging me and impacting my life—God revealed to me all the confirmation that soon will take place in my life. My heart went up greater than I could ever imagine with God. I was amazed and awe about the supernatural encounter of similarity to the pioneer Prophets in my life and into their lives in the spirit realm with God's Generals and Evangelists. God just blew my mind through these wonderful and beautiful servants of God.

Some of "God's General and Evangelists" that I am going to shared with you are already dead and some of them are still alive, and all of them experience the brokenness, test, and hardship and also they experience the victory from God over their lives. All of them are good examples, and instrument servants of God in my life and how God revealed Himself to me in the spiritual realm through them for His glory and His purposes in my life. Through God, their hearts are connecting, partnering, and impacting their hearts into my heart, into the spiritual realm. It was so beautiful to find out that their stories are similar to my stories. Their stories and my personal stories bring hope into my soul. It was an honor to experience and walk with God and also walk with them. I saw the hands of God on these people in my life. I always asked God the meaning of why these people have a connection to me in the spiritual realm. Because these are "God's Generals and Evangelists," they are not just ordinary people; they saw and experienced God in their personal walk with Him.

The "God's generals and Evangelists" blow my mind by how much passion and dedication they have with God. They mean business when it comes with God; they are serious about their calling and God was with them. All these powerful men and women of God have the same visions, purposes, dreams, and provisions, and their faith with God is very strong. They have assurance and confidence with God and God is alive within their soul. They are all one accord from the sounds of God's voice with fire, and they all have one mind to standing up in their calling, and that is to share the "Gospel of Jesus Christ" and healing all the afflictions and oppressors throughout the communities, to the cities and to the nations. Jesus Christ is the best example of all. He died so that we can have life and have it more abundantly. He is the Alpha and Omega, the First and the Last, who was, who is, and who is to come, the Almighty God.

TO GOD BE THE GLORY. Amen.

Prayer,

I pray that as you read my stories and know about God's Generals and Evangelists, that you will find the passion to seek Jesus Christ in an intimate way, the same way that I have a passion to seek Him in an intimate way, for you is greater. I pray that God will touch your heart, and I pray that God will inspire and compel you to have the burning desires to move and to act, to humble yourself to love and to serve God. The signs, wonders, and miracles are from God, so therefore we look to God, we come to God, and we walk only for God. I pray that God is holding your hands and breathed on you to have a voice for God's people. I pray as I share with you these powerful men and women of God, that God will take you to the higher dimension of His love, His relationships, and His manifesting power for you to bring forth His name, "JESUS CHRIST," to stand up boldly and confidence in this world for His name and for His glory.

HABAKKUK 3:2

Lord, I have heard of Your fame; I stand in awe of Your deeds, Lord. Repeat them in our day.

Evangelist Mike Bickle

Evangelist Mike Bickle is an American evangelical Christian leader of IHOPKC.

In my desperation, my friend came just in time, and she was telling me that there was a church that was open 24/7 and she was inviting me to come to the church with her. I have never heard the church being open 24/7 before but I said yes to her to come to church with her, but she did not have a chance to take me to the church. One month later among all the houses in Atlanta, without realizing it, my family and I decided to relocate to the same city as the church my friend was sharing with me about, where the supernatural was taking place. I noticed that this church, which is only two minutes from our new place, is always open and has a lot of people, every time I passed by while I went to the store. One day, God told me to come to that church and I did. I noticed later on that the church is the same church that my friend had asked me to come. I thought that it was just coincidence or a small world. Because of all the churches in the city, it just happened that God moved us to two minutes from the church that my friend invited me to come. I realized it was the Lord who brings me there instead.

One day in December 2010, the church was having a ministry class, and I decided to go to one of their classes, and one of the teacher mentioned that "the man prophesied to Evangelist Mike Bickle a long time ago. He says that God will move mightily in his life, and it will happen so fast like a "*comet*." And he won't even see it coming."

That "comet" stuck in my mind, so I decided to look it up just to see what the comet looks like. When I saw the comet, I was shocked because it just happened that I had a dream about the comet one week before I found out about the prophecy for evangelists Mike Bickle. My dream is about the fireball. The comet was very beautiful, and it was very bright and radiant. I thought, wow, what a coincidence. At that time my faith with the Lord is not as strong as today.

Dream

I saw a "fireball" coming from heaven. I immediately call my daughter and we followed the "fireball." As I was watching the "fireball," the "fireball" landed on the mountain. When we get closer, the fireball turned into an angel standing on the huge rock calling my name in front of people. I called the fireball a "comet" the bright light of God.

One night again, I had a dream that I saw bright lights that look like a comet, the "fireball was hovering over my head." I was so excited that I was trying to catch it, and it seems like it was very close to me and it was just floating above my head. And suddenly the bright lights went over the waters. The bright light was so beautiful that I had to walk through the waters so I can be able to reach them, and then I woke up.

I want to call a bright light into a "pillar of fire."

One day, when I found out about Mike Bickle, I was anticipating meeting him, I was so excited that I said to myself that one day I will meet him. I decided to share it with one of the persons standing beside me. The person goes to Mike Bickle's church in Kansas and he knew that it was not easy to meet Mike because he said that he was always surrounded with a lot of people. But I never gave up. I believed that one day God will make a way for me to meet him. One day, God spoke to me and He told me that I will meet him. God's word for me gives me hope. Until one day, He came to our city, and my leader introduced him to me. I was so shocked. The man with the power of God shook my hand and also gave me a hug and he allowed me to take pictures with him. I thought, "Wow, only God can do that." God did make a way for me to meet him. God is faithful, and nothing is impossible with God.

Evangelist Steve Hill

The Evangelist is known from Brownsville Revival.

One day, in 2014, I was watching Evangelist Steve Hill on YouTube from the church. I saw the Holy Spirit moved as he preached. Three years later, in 2017, I saw Evangelist Steve Hill in YouTube again while I was in my house and I started watching him again. I feel the presence of God as he preached and shared the gospel. As I continued watching him, I saw his testimony about him being humbled in his young age, cleaning the floors at his church.

I was amazed about that, because in my old church, I was the one who cleaned the floors and the carpet in the sanctuary.

I continued watching Evangelist Steve Hill for one month. In 2017, as I was watching him, I was shocked and almost fainted when I found out that he is already dead. In his funeral, his wife asked somebody to bring his two dolls, and they put his two dolls on top of his casket. His two dolls looked exactly like him. One doll was when he was young don't know the Lord yet. The second doll was when he was old and working with the Lord. God is using him mightily people are giving themselves to the Lord Jesus Christ, healing and deliverance was taking place at the Revival. I was amazed about how good God is. I love him and I prayed for his family.

In 2012, God spoke to me to invent a doll. So I immediately called the Invent Company to make it happen. Until to this day, the Invent Company is still working on the project.

One day, on Evangelist Steve Hill's service, one of the singers sang the "Mercy Seat" song. I sang that song for three weeks, and Steve Hill keeps telling people to repent and to forgive. I did not know that the song that I sang for three weeks will be alive to me, and also the message about repentance and forgiveness.

My ex-husband, who hurt and killed me thirty years ago, suddenly showed up after thirty-three years of my life. Instead of hiding from him, I decided to face him so that he can repent to the Lord for God to give him mercy, and also I can be able to forgive him and I can be able to give him mercy.

I was amazed about the goodness of God over my life, to allow me to experience Steve Hill's message, the song, the dolls, and cleaning the floor. God is so good.

Evangelist Rex Humbard, Is a Pentecostal evangelist. He was a revival preacher.

One day, I went to a garage sale and I found a huge Bible with the evangelist's name on it. But at that time I didn't know him yet. All I know is that I liked the Bible. I decided to buy it, and it was only eight dollars, but I did not look or read the huge Bible until two years later. I just put the Bible in the box and I forgot all about it.

Two years later, I found the Bible from the storage inside the big box when we were moving. One day, I put the Bible in the living room for display only. Months later, I remember sitting in the living room and I noticed the Bible being wide open standing up on top of the prayer hand decoration table. I came up and pick it up from prayer hand and I decided to put it on the dining table and I open the huge Bible. When I opened the Bible, I noticed right away about the pictures of the evangelist and with his wife and also his family. I was fascinated by it, so I continued reading the Bible. I noticed that some of their family pictures and the messages from the Bible were related to me. I was shocked and amazed by God.

While I was reading the Bible and flipping the pages and looking at the pictures from the Bible, there was an-awe in my heart and how God moved me. When I saw the picture and the message that is on the Bible, God just blew my mind away how the message is related to me.

I saw evangelist's pictures saying that the evangelist and his wife celebrated their "Anniversary" on the 25," and another picture was saying that in "1965 they went to the Holy Land."

I was fascinated with God's beauty in my life because;

I was born on the 25, 1965

Our first Anniversary was on twenty fifth, and we went to the "Holy Land," but only to Florida.

I shared with my friend about the story of the evangelist. She had asked me to look for him on the Internet. Because she thought that there is more to the story. My friend was so excited that she decided to be the one who looked for the evangelist on the Internet instead of me seeing who Rex Humbard is.

As she was searching for the Evangelist Rex Humbard, we found out that he died in 2007. My friend and I were shocked.

I was so shocked because I was just sharing to everybody that same night in our class that I gave my life to Jesus Christ in 2007. I thought,

"Wow, one died and one is born in the Spiritual realm. God is good and He is moving.

One day, the woman and I looked him up on the Internet again so I could give Rex Humbard's Bible back to him. We found his telephone, and we decided to call him up and by the grace of God, we have chance to talk to Rex Humbard's son. As I was talking to him, he told me that they have an orphanage in the Philippines. He told me that they used to have a lot of orphanages throughout the countries, but only in the Philippine s have they kept one standing. They are still supporting the orphanage in the Philippines. I was thanking him for continuing to bless the orphanage in the Philippines. I hope one day I can bless his ministry. I was amazed by how God connected me with him. I knew that is not coincidence that of all the orphanages in the countries, only "Philippines" is left for them to support. For me meeting him and being from the Philippines, I knew God has a purpose for us. I can't wait for that moment.

Evangelist Billy Graham was an American Evangelist

One day, in 2015, the pastor prophesied to me that he saw Evangelist Billy Graham was connected to me in the spiritual realm. At that time I did not know him, but later on I looked him up on the Internet and I was shocked when I found out about him. He is a powerful man of God. The famous Evangelist was sharing the good news to millions of people and to the uttermost of the world. Three months later, I went to the thrift store and I saw his book and I bought it. His book was only fifty cents, and I didn't notice that the book was his autobiography. I brought the book to my house and then the book disappeared. I could not find his book anywhere in my house, until one month later, when I saw the book lying on the chair. I don't know how it got there, but I'm just glad that I found it. This time I put his book beside my bed.

MOON

STORY

The following morning, I saw a butterfly in front of my house and the color was dark blue and it has black dots all around the butterfly wings.

The butterfly looks like a moon. My neighbor came to my house that same morning and she started talking to me about the moon. Our conversation about the moon lasted all morning long. It became very intense.

When my daughter came home from school that afternoon, she started taking out all of her notebooks and other stuff from her book bag until she reached a huge piece of paper and she showed me her drawing. Her drawing had a "Moon" on it. I was shocked because my friend and I was just talking about the moon that early morning, and now my daughter had given me her drawing with the moon on it. I asked my daughter why she drew the moon. She said to me that she didn't know, but she just felt like drawing the moon that morning in her classroom. I thought, "Wow, God was blowing my mind." I asked myself what is going on about the moon.

Later on that night, as I was getting ready for bed, and I decided to read the famous evangelist's book, and I noticed the word from the book that says, "Evangelist Billy Graham was gazing upon the Moon." I thought, "Wow!" I was shocked. I felt like God is trying to tell me something in the spiritual realm. I thought Evangelist Billy Graham and the moon story was fascinating to me, but I did not think anything about it. I thought it was just a coincidence. So I moved on.

FLU

One day, I went to the doctor's office, and one of the ladies from the front desk asked me if I want to have a flu shot. First, I said no because I don't like flu shots, but the lady told me that it was free. Because I wanted the lady to stop asking me, I said yes to her.

They gave me a flu shot,

And later on that night I was having flu. I was so sick that night I thought that I could have to go to the hospital. That night again before I went to bed, I decided to read the famous evangelist's book. As I was reading his book, I noticed a phrase that went,

"Evangelist Billy Graham is in another country and he cannot preach that day because he had flu."

I was very shocked again. I thought, how that happen, that I was reading Evangelist Billy Graham's book and it says that he has the "flu" at that same time I have the flu. I was shocked and amazes while I was his reading his book. I didn't know what to think of it in that moment. I thought at that time that Evangelist Billy Graham's book has "power from on high."

STATEMENT

One day, somebody had given me a tiny paper that has a word on it saying,

"You are the statement."

I didn't think anything by it. I just put the tiny paper away. That night, I was reading Evangelist Billy Graham's book, and I decided to look at the back of his book to see what it was saying. I thought why is it that his book is blowing my mind, and what make the evangelist's story so special. As I was reading at the back of his book, I noticed the word that says

Evangelist Billy Graham was a "statement."

God was blowing my mind every time. I was reading the book about the Statement at the same time I was holding the tiny paper it say Statement also. I was wondering about the meaning of all those things, and what was happening to me and to the Evangelist Billy Graham. God is so good. He is so faithful.

HIS DOG

One day, I went to a Bible Study in someone's house, and the owner of the house has a "dog," and the "dog" keeps barking really loud at the garage. The owner of the house told me that he thought that "he should let the dog in." I told him that is up to him to "let the dog in." Some of the people are sitting in the living room and some are in the kitchen, and I was the only one who was sitting in front of the garage door, talking to the owner of the house.

So the owner of the house decided to "let the dog in."

The minute the dog came in, I was the only one in front of the door and I was the only one that the dog first saw. The dog keeps barking right at me. I had to get up from my seat, and the minute I stood up, the dog started to knock me down on the floor. I was terrified, and I was scared. I thought that the dog was going to bite me or something. I was so glad that the dog did not bite me. I realized that the dog was just trying to get my attention.

That same night, when I was about getting ready for bed, I decided to call my friend. I was sharing with her about the Evangelist Billy Graham and how God fascinated me about his book, and his powerful story and what I was encountering with God. I shared with my friend what happened to me and the dog and I was making a joke to my friend when I told her that I will be surprised if the dog is in the book. My friend and I burst out laughing because we thought that it was impossible that the dog will be in the book.

But that night I was shocked. I was reading Billy Graham's book before I went to bed, and in my surprise I noticed the word that says

Evangelist Billy Graham had a "dog," and he opened the door to "let the dog in."

I said to myself "wow that was a divine encounter from the Lord." Every time something is happening to me, that same night I will be reading Billy Graham's book and it was happening to him also that same night. I was amazed and in awe of God. He loves to bring wonders for His children.

At the age of seven or eight years old, he was helping his dad at the farm.

At that young age, I was helping my dad in our farm also.

I was save on 2007, since I was save I have never pray for Evangelist Billy Graham, I remember that night in my prayer closet, for the first time I was praying for him. And the following morning somebody had told me that he died. I was very sad and I cried when I found out that he died, but God revived my spirit when I saw him on television with his wife and the dog. Evangelist Billy Graham had a "dog." I was so happy and I was jumping around when I saw his dog for the first time. His dog is beautiful, fluffy, and vibrant, as the dog followed them around in their yards, while people are interviewed them.

I realized that God was letting me know that it was Him speaking to me through Billy Graham. For the first time, I have hope with God. He revealed to me about His heart by showing me about Billy Graham and his dog, and who Billy Graham is in God's kingdom. I was so glad to experience the similarity of his life into mine. I miss and love Billy Graham. He will always be in my heart. I knew that I will see him and I will meet him one day in heaven. God shared with me in the intimate way about Evangelist Billy Graham's personal life and I thank God for His goodness and kindness towards me. I was praying for his family.

Evangelist Reinhard Bonnke is a German Pentecostal evangelist founder.

In 2014, I had a dream about the stadium with one of my teachers on it. I was so excited when I saw him, and I started sharing with him about the dream right away. He was so excited about the dream that he had asked me what the dream is all about. I told him it's about me and him being in the stadium. He was so excited that he asked me if I can write it down for him to keep and also to bring encouraging to him, and I said yes. I put the date and I signed my name on it.

DREAM

I told to my teacher that my dream is about him carrying the tray of foods in a stadium that is full of people. He had asked me if I want something to eat and I said yes to him. We decided to sit down on the chairs and we were both eating the food. While we were eating, for some reason I was gone, and I came back because I thought that the food was very good and I want to eat some more. But my teacher was not there anymore. I look toward the stage to see what was happening. I was shocked to see my teacher being on the stage getting ready to call my name to speak in front of all those people. I was so nervous and then I woke up.

Three months later, I heard that Evangelist Reinhard Bonnke was coming to Atlanta. God just confirmed the dream when he came to Atlanta. Me and Evangelist Reinhard Bonnke's story

FACEBOOK

One day, while I was on my Facebook page, I saw Evangelist Reinhard Bonnke accepting me as a friend on Facebook. At that time, I didn't know him. I replied to him and I thanked him for accepting me as his friend, and then he replied to me on Messenger. I was so glad that he accepted me as his friend on Facebook. Evangelist Reinhard Bonnke started to pray for me, prophesied, and gave me a Scripture from God through the Facebook Messenger.

I remember that I was at the restaurant with my friend Andy. (Andy already went with the Lord.) I told Andy at that time that Evangelist Reinhard Bonnke was messaging me while we were having breakfast. I remember Andy had a lot of patience for me, letting me respond to the messages from Evangelist Reinhard Bonnke. I was thanking God for him because all of the messages that he sent to me were lifting my spirit up at that moment. I needed those words in my life. I felt like his messages for me is a breath from God in heaven. Later on, I looked him up on the Internet to see who he was. To my surprise, I saw Evangelist Reinhard Bonnke has led more than 75 million people to Jesus Christ. I was amazed and in awe of God. Reinhard Bonnke is a very humble servant of God. I love him. I was amazed that he had the time to minister to a little person like me who just came out from one of the poorest country in the world. I was thanking God that He saw me and He makes me an important child in His eyes through His powerful servant of God.

DREAM CONFIRMATION

Later on, I found out that the Evangelist Bonnke was coming to Atlanta and again I was shocked. I was amazed that for all the teachers that we have in my church, Evangelist Bonnke chose my teacher, the one whom I gave my dream letter to. My teacher will be leading a prayer to all the pastors for the Evangelist Reinhard Bonnke's Crusade. I thought "wow." God is good.

God truly does wonders for His people. When the famous Evangelist started speaking, I was amazed. He said to all people in the stadium that he believed that "God will raise the dead in America." I was amazed when he said that because I have been raised from the dead a couple of times.

I was so excited, and also I was one of the persons who volunteered to do the altar call at the Crusade. I am full of joy with how much that moment impacted my life. God gave me encouragement and He gave me hope. When the evangelist started calling for people for salvation, the people started coming to the front to receive prayers. The Evangelist started praying for people for salvation. I saw the move of God in that place, healing and restoration and deliverance was happening to the people, the power of God was taking place. God was using Evangelist Reinhard Bonnke mightily. I remember this one person came up to me and ask me to pray for salvation and healing. Tears were just pouring down from his cheeks. As I was praying for him, he felt the love of God upon his life. He wanted the presence of God, and he felt like God is with him at that moment and God would not let him go. I knew that God is doing the miracles in his life. He is where God wants him to be. After I prayed for him, the man is healed and restored. I was thanking God and Evangelist Reinhard Bonnke for giving me the opportunity to be used for God in the "Crusade at the Stadium." My teacher and I were both at the Miracles Crusade Stadium. God confirmed my dream at that moment, and I knew there is more supernatural encounter will come forth through the revival.

Evangelist Kathryn Kulhman is an evangelist and faith healer.

One day, the pastor told me that I was like the Evangelist Kathryn Kulhman in the spiritual realm. I asked him who she was and the pastor shared with me who she was, because at that time I didn't know who she was. But the word from the pastor saying that I am like Kathryn Kuhlman did not settle in my heart at that time. But when I came into the healing room to pray for people—the healing room was in the book store at that time—and I was sitting down at the book store getting ready to pray for people, I noticed her book was right beside me.

I thought "wow" I remember picking up the book and I noticed the front page of the book was the same image and color that was inside of my purse. I was shocked. I thought maybe it was just a coincidence, so I started talking to people around me if they have the same color and the same image of the book in their purse or wallet, but no one had the same thing. I was shocked because I was the only one that has the same image on the front page of her book."

One day my friend bought her book for me and I started to read it. As I was reading the book, I noticed the phrases, that Evangelist Kathryn Kulhman was a "forerunner in the church." I was shocked and was amazed because it just happened that I just went to "Forerunner School of Ministry" for two years, and I had just graduated for two weeks and I received a diploma, and the diploma said "forerunner" on it. In my amazement, I thought about what if I did not go to school for two years as a forerunner.

I wondered if this book will have meaning to me, or if this book will be relevant to me, if I did not go to school. I was inspired by God for His activity toward me. I asked God the meaning of all those things that were happening to me. I'm always wondering if I'm supposed to do something. I was thanking God for His presence and being near to me and I thanked God for revealing Himself to me through the woman of God.

I have so much to learn about what God was trying to tell me, and I love every bit of them, thank You Jesus.

Evangelist John G. Lake is a Pentecostal evangelist of the Healing Revival.

One day, somebody told me about John G. Lake. In 2011, I decided to buy his book. At that time I was connected to the "Healing Room and the Prophecy Room" in my church. I give prophecy and pray for people's healing and see the love and miracles for people at the "Healing Room." One day, I was reading John G. Lakes' book and I noticed that Evangelist John G. Lake had a "healing room in his ministry." I was amazed about that because I am actually in a place called the "Healing Room," praying for people for over eight years. I knew right away that is not coincidence. God is actually trying to say something to me. I thought about what if I am not at the "healing room" at that time. What if I just come to church and go home and don't do anything? Maybe the book from him will not be related to me. I was so glad because I am in the "healing room," so his book became real to me. As I continued reading his book, I noticed the name "Diego." It just happened that my father's name is "Diego." I was amazed by God and how He revealed himself to me through the evangelist. I was so glad that God brought His beauty for me and for His children.

One day, I was watching a YouTube video about the pastor's church. The pastor was sharing about the story of John G. Lake. He shows the "Healing Room." Looking back to John G. Lake's day in His ministry, I saw John G. Lake's "healing room," and the healing rooms look like a hospital that has a small metal bed for people to lie down on. I saw people need miracles from God.

As I was watching the video, my tears were pouring down from my cheeks because I remember, due to my circumstances, God put me in the position where I don't have a place to go. I have found myself sleeping in my car and I prayed. The following day I was at the "women shelter." There, I was sleeping on the metal bed, and I saw all the women and children with full of pain and distress in their heart. God spoke to me to pray for all of them, to help them, to give them a word from His throne and just to love and to bless on them. And I did what God asked me to do. The women's shelter became a "healing room" for me in that place. They needed miracles from God. And God gave it to them. I believe that God Himself sent me to the shelter to help the people. I was asking the women if I can pray for them and they all said yes, and I did pray for them. One woman needed an apartment; the following day she did have an apartment. The person needed miracle for her marriage. She wants her marriage to be restored. After I prayed, she and her three children went back home and her marriage is restored. I prayed for the woman with a baby to have a place to live, after I prayed she had a home. Women are giving themselves to the Lord. I help women by giving them a ride to go places where they needed to go, and I put blessings in their hands to the two families. God was moving in that place. As I watched John G. Lake's story, I felt like I was in the healing room back in John G. Lake's day. The shelter room, become a healing room. To God be the glory. God is taking control for His people.

As I continued watching John G. Lake's video, it says that the John G. Lake ministry still continues until to this day. I noticed about the logo, it was the cross and the crown. They were together. It just so happened that I have a cross and crown inside my car hanging on my mirror. I bought the crown in 2017, and I bought the cross in 2013. I did not think any of it. I put them together and hung them in my car. I thought that they looked good together being cross and crown. When I saw their video and their logo is about Cross and Crown, I was shocked with God. God loves to blow my mind. I thank God for He keeps revealing Himself to me.

Evangelist Aimee Semple McPherson is a Canadian - American Pentecostal evangelist from the Healing Revival.

One day around 4-19-2017, I was looking at YouTube and I noticed about Evangelist Aimee McPherson pop in on my cell phone. I decided to look at the internet about her autobiography. As I was reading about her autobiography, I started to cry because I noticed the similarities of her life and also in my life and how they are almost identical.

"Evangelist McPherson was born in October."

I was born in October.

"She was married three times." I was married three times.

"She has two children."

I have two children.

"As a child she would gather all her dolls and she will preach at them.

She also had her own doll that looks like her.

In 2012 God gave me a vision about the "doll" as my invention reaching out to the cities and communities and bringing the word of God and comfort for the children throughout the nations. Through the invention will have an opportunity to open an-orphanages throughout the countries, and helping the people that are in needs.

"Evangelist was wearing a beautiful gown flowing all the way down from her waist."

I was amazed about that because my "doll gown was all the way down to her waist also."

"Evangelist prayed for people and God's manifestation was so heavy that everybody got healed and restored."

I also prayed for healing to people and I will see the healing and the movement of God upon their lives also.

As I continued reading her story, I noticed that "she gave and fed 1.5 million of people during the Depression in America." I saw her picture that she was surrounded by all of those breads and other foods for her to give to people.

I was amazed about that because before I have found out and I read about her autobiography, two weeks before I had just connected myself to volunteer to the "Bread of Life" to give away food for the people, and also I had just taken a picture that I was surrounded with the breads and desserts also.

God is so good God. Who can compare to Him? I was so glad that God inspires me through Evangelist Mcpherson. God is so good. She inspired me.

Evangelist William M. Branham is an American Christian minister of the Healing Revival. He is known by being Elijah the prophet.

One day, on 4-28-2017. I saw him on YouTube. At that time I didn't know the Evangelist Branham, and I had never heard of him before, so I had second thoughts if I wanted to watch him on YouTube or not. I thought to myself that maybe I might get bored watching him, but something in my heart says that I should watch him and I did. As I was watching his story, my heart was amazed with God, and how we had the same life story.

Evangelist William M. Branham died in 1965.

I was born in 1965.

The Evangelist and his brother were very poor. When they were just young, William Branham and his brother were always hungry and they didn't have anything to eat.

My brother and I grew up very poor in our country. And we always hungry and we always looked for food in the market.

The Evangelist's brother died.

"My brother died, and when my brother died, I experienced the difficulty, hardships, and even the feeling of being lost. I thought I knew God. I realized that I don't know God completely, so when my brother died, I told God that I surrendered all my life to Him. This time I realized that I cannot play with God. I decided that I am going to do whatever He wants me to do because I realized that with God, there is nowhere to go and nowhere to escape. God put me on the corner and silenced me, and the only thing I have in my hands is His Word."

The Evangelist heard the "voice" that told Him, "Don't you ever drink, smoke, or defile your body in any way. There'll be work for you to do when you get older."

"After my brother died, I heard the voice of God saying to me that He wants me to be blameless and spotless before His throne for He will use me for His glory.

Evangelist William Branham was set apart. When he was born, there was a "fireball" that flew around him and his mother, and "lights" were hovering and whirling over them.

One day I had a dream. My daughter was with me in my dream. My dream was that "I was looking up from heaven and I saw the bright lights that look like a "fireball from heaven," and it was coming very fast. My eyes cannot even blink looking at this "fireball." I was fascinated by these beautiful "lights" from heaven. I thought for a moment that the "fireball" is coming toward me, but I was so glad that the "fireball" landed on the mountain. My daughter and I decided to follow the "fireball," and when we got to the mountain, I saw a lot of people looking at this huge angel standing on a huge rock. Right when I was getting closer to the angel, I heard His voice calling my name and He asked everyone if they saw me. When I heard Him calling my name, I trembled in His presence. I asked my daughter to make sure if the angel really called my name and she said yes. I panicked and I told my daughter for us to run and hide in my car. While we were in the car, I was wondering as to why the angel was calling my name, and then I woke up.

Wow, that was intense dream, I pounder my dream into my heart.

As the years went by in my life, I now understand my calling. I thank God for speaking to me through dreams.

One day, I saw Evangelist William Branham's video again on YouTube, and I saw his picture with a halo above his head.

One day, in my old church, the bishop was telling the whole congregation that he saw demons all over the place. And he said that they were so many of them. When I heard that, I was very concerned about what he saw. While the bishop was speaking from the pulpit, his wife the "prophetess" came toward him from the pulpit and whispered to his ear and she said to him that she saw the "halo above my head." I was thanking God that He was with me and He allowed the prophetess to see the "halo above my head." God loves to bring witness for me.

The angel told the Evangelist, "If you get the people to believe you and be sincere when you pray, nothing shall stand before your prayers, "not even the cancer."

I was so glad to hear that God was speaking to the Evangelist about cancer because I was diagnosed of cancer since 2007. The doctor was predicting that I was going to die within six months. With God's fire and by His Grace and mercy over my life, "I am still standing."

Before I found out about the story of the Evangelist William Branham, I always found pennies on the ground. I will go to the church, and in front of the door there will be a penny. I will go to the store and I will find a penny on the ground. Before I open the door to my car, I will find a penny on the ground. Pennies keep popping everywhere. I will be sitting in the corner and I will find a penny staring right at me. So finally, I sat down and I tried to listen to the Lord as to what He was saying to me. I keep the pennies and I take a picture of the penny that night. I felt like there was meaning about the penny and the Evangelist William Branham, and in my surprise I saw the scripture in;

Genesis 32:30

So Jacob called the place "Peniel," saying, it is because I saw "God face-to-face," and yet my life was spared.

One day, I was talking to the man, and I shared with Him about me finding pennies everywhere I go. The man asked me if I knew who was in the face on the penny. My answer was no to him. I don't know who is on the face that was on the penny. The man told me that it was Abraham Lincoln. I was very embarrassed because I knew who Abraham Lincoln is I just didn't know that his face is on the penny.

After the man mentioned that to me, I started to have a burning desire to search for Abraham Lincoln. As I was searching about Abraham Lincoln and William Branham, I found out about the two powerful men of God that have a similar outcome in their lives.

Abraham Lincoln was born in the year 1809, and he was born in a log cabin.

William Branham was born in the year of 1909, and he was born in a log cabin.

I found out that William M. Branham was born in the same state where Abraham Lincoln was born, in Kentucky. (Abraham Lincoln's face is on the penny.)

Abraham Lincoln died in 1865 at the age of 56.

William Branham died in 1965 at the age of 56.

Abraham Lincoln's face is carved on the Rushmore Mountain and his face has a similarity with William Branham. There were four carved faces on the Rushmore Mountain.

They were three curved faces Stone Mountain the

Evangelist William Branham called to be a Healing "Revival."

Abraham Lincoln was called "Freed the Slavery."

These are the two powerful men that God used for His glory.

The "Revival man," and the "freed the slavery man" being together for God's kingdom.

I was amazed with God is how He put Abraham Lincoln and William Branham together in my path and the two mountains that have faces carved. I was amazed with the similarity of the move of God with these two powerful men of God and the mountains in my life. My heart stands in awe of God. After experiencing this move of God and the confirmation in my life, I want to say that I am sold out with God. There's nothing in my flesh but the Holy Spirit in me. God has my heart crying with joy. I don't know yet what God wants me to do. All I know is that I am saying yes to Him, and I am ready for Him.

Hallelujah, God is so good. God is like a dot. He makes everything simple for me to understand.

Smith Wigglesworth Prophecy on 1947

"When the word and the Spirit come together, there will be the biggest movement of the Holy Spirit that the nation, and indeed the world, has ever seen. It will mark the beginning of a Revival that will **Eclipse** anything that has been witnessed within these shores."

When Smith Wigglesworth mention about the **Eclipse** in his prophecy, I was amazed with awe of God. On 2017, I took three pictures and God appeared to me in the form of the **Eclipse** and shape of "His **Outstretched arm.**" And also at the edge of the **Eclipse** God appeared to me in the form of His **Cross.**

The Welsh Revival

*The Welsh Revival of 1904-1905 influenced the Emerging Pentecost Movement, Led, in part, by a 26-years old **Collier** turned trainee minister, Evan Roberts (1878-1951) the Revival emphasized the need for personal self-surrender and obedience to the prompting of the Holy Spirit.*

I am amazed "The Welsh Revival" just to mention the name **Collier,** because **Collier** was my last name, (2008).

Prophet T.B. Joshua (SCOAN)

One day, in 2016, I went to the garage sale. I saw this huge bowl full of decorative fruits and vegetables. I was so excited when I bought the bowl with fruits and vegetables. When I came home, I tried to find the place where I can put them.

First, I tried to put it in the kitchen, but for some reason the bowl of fruits and vegetables does not look good in the kitchen.

Second, I tried to put it in the dining room. I tried to put the bowl in the middle of the dining table, but for some reason the bowl do not look good on the dining table either.

I don't understand as to why the bowl of fruits does not look good everywhere I put them. I was getting sad because I really liked the bowl of fruits, but I don't have any place to put them where they will look nice in the room. I almost give up is to where to put the bowl. I don't want to put the bowl in the box.

Until one day, I was sitting in the dining room. And I was looking at the altar from the living room with the Bible being in the middle, and it was also my "sanctuary." For some reason, I heard the voice of God saying to me that I need to put the bowl of fruits beside the altar. After I heard the voice of God, I want to be obedient to Him. So I picked up the bowl from the dining table and I put the bowl of fruits and vegetables in the living room where my altar is. After I put the bowl of fruits and vegetables beside the bible, I was shocked when the bowl was perfect being in the altar. I questioned myself as to why the bowl looks good in the living room than the kitchen or dining room knowing that the bowl is supposed to be in the kitchen or the dining room. Because the bowl looks perfect in the altar, I decided to keep the bowl in the altar which is "my sanctuary."

After I put the fruits and vegetables beside my bible at the altar, in my sanctuary, I decided to browse on YouTube from my cell phone, when suddenly The Man of God appeared on my screen. I didn't know the Man of God at that time, but I decided to start watching him. I was amazed about the movement of God in his life. By watching him I felt like I was seeing Jesus Christ walking on the earth.

As I continued watching him on you tube, suddenly I saw the fruits and the vegetables being in the middle of the altar and bringing the sanctuary to come alive in the church as I was watching him. I was shocked I cannot believe that I was actually seeing the fruits and the vegetables in the middle of the sanctuary. As I was watching him preaching and seeing the fruits and the vegetables at the same time, I was also looking at my fruits and vegetables beside the bible in my sanctuary in my living room. I was shocked that I have to actually sit down. I was overwhelmed with God's love over me. I was so excited trying to understand the meaning of all those things that were happening to me. I have been going to different churches before, but I have never seen a church that has fruits and vegetables in the sanctuary before, except the Man of God's sanctuary.

One week later, I continued watching him on you tube when suddenly I saw him holding water as an instrument for God. As he ministered to people with the water, miracles were taking place on people. People were getting healed and set free. I was shocked again because God was giving me water since 2008 to give away to the people as instrument for His glory. People were getting heal and bless through the water. I was amazed how God connected me to this powerful Man of God in the spirit realm, how God revealed Himself to me and what He is like and who He is in my life.

As I continued watching the Man of God, my tears started to run down from my cheeks because I saw the way he ministered to God's people. He ministered to them with passion, dedication, and humility and love to the Lord. God gave him power and strength as he prayed for people. Signs, wonders, and miracles were taking place. He had so much power when he laid hands on a millions of people. God's power has been released, and miracles are taking place on people. And also he had a heart for those that are in need. I saw his ministry blessings all the people. The Man of God has a giving heart. I was captivating about the beauty of God upon His life. Man of God is truly a powerful, humble servant of God.

As I continued watched his ministry, I was praying to the Lord that God will give me the same strength to fulfill my calling of what God asks me to do. I was inspired by the Man of God. I want to thank God for him.

I may not have the understanding of all those things that were happening to me concerning "God's Servant." I know one day that God will reveal them to me. I want to thank God for giving me the opportunity to be able to experience the "seen and the unseen of His glory" in my life, and be able to see through Man of God, the faithful servant of God.

HOSEA 12:10

I have spoken by the Prophets, and have multiplied vision; I have been given symbols through the witness of the prophets.

DEUTERENOMY 18:18

I will raise up for them a Prophet like you from among their fellow Israelites, and I will put My words in His mouth. He will tell them everything I command Him.

ISAIAH 52:13–15

See, My Servant will act wisely; He will be raised and lifted up and highly exalted. Just as there were many who were appalled at Him, His appearance was so disfigured beyond that of any human being and His form marred beyond human likeness so He will sprinkle many nations, and kings will shut their mouths because of Him. For what they were not told, they will see, and what they have not heard, they will understand.

ISAIAH 9–6

For to us a child is born, to us a Son is given, and the government will rest on His shoulders. And His name shall be called Wonderful, Counselor, Mighty God, Eternal Father, the Prince of Peace.

LUKE 4:18–21

And He was handed the book of the Prophet Isaiah. And when He had opened the book, He found the place where it was written:

"The Spirit of the Lord is upon Me, because He has anointed Me to preach the Gospel to the poor.

He has sent Me to heal the brokenhearted.

To proclaim liberty to the captives and recovery of sight to the blind

To set at liberty those who are oppressed.

To proclaim the acceptable year of the Lord.

Then He closed the book and gave it back to the attendant and sat down. And the eyes of all who were in the synagogue were fixed on Him. And He began to say to them, "Today this Scripture is fulfilled in your hearing."

JESUS CHRIST, the Son of God, He is the Image of the invisible God. He is fully God and fully Man He is the Prophet, He is the Priest, He is the King, He is the God of the Universe and He is the God without limit. Through Jesus Christ's blood, His death, His resurrection, and His word was made flesh and that flesh lives among us.

The gift from God is been given to His disciples. The powerful "violent rushing wind" that impacted the surroundings and they are all feel the presence of God. His "tongues of fire" rested on each and every one of His disciples (Acts 2:2).

Through God's Gift "the Power, the Wind and the Fire" is how the disciples can show the world that God still exists, He is still alive, and He is still real. God uses His children to have His voice and His power through His signs, wonders, and miracles, until Jesus comes back. "God's Chosen People" serve Him to share the "Gospel of Jesus Christ," accompanied by His power and His glory. God connected His Son Jesus Christ from Him to mankind.

ACTS 1:8

But you will receive power when the Holy Spirit comes on you; and you will be my witnesses and in all in Jerusalem, and all Judea and Samaria, and to the ends of the earth.

Peter being boldness with the "Fire on His voice" and have the assurance and the confidence with God, that He shakes the place by sharing the "Gospel of Jesus Christ of Nazareth" without fear, and doubt, but with the manifestation of God's power, and everyone was save and healed.

ACTS 2:14

Then Peter stood up with the Eleven, raised His voice and addressed the crowd: fellow Jews and all of you who live in Jerusalem, let me explain this to you; listen carefully to what I say.

ACTS 2:41

Those who accepted His message were baptized, and about three thousand were added to their number that day.

ACTS 3:6–8

Then Peter said, Silver and gold I do not have, but what I have I give you. In the name of Jesus Christ of Nazareth, walk. Taking Him by the right hand, He helped Him up, and instantly the man's feet and ankles became strong. He jumped to His feet and He began to walk.

CHAPTER 33

CALLING ON ELIJAH'S LIFE

1 KINGS 17:1–9

Now Elijah, who was from Tishbe in Gilead, told King Ahab, "As surely as the Lord, the God of Israel, lives—the God I serve—there will be no dew or rain during the next few years until I give the word! Then the Lord said to Elijah, "Go to the east and hide by Kerith Brook, near where it enters the Jordan River. Drink from the brook and eat what the ravens bring you, for I have command them to bring you food." So Elijah did as the Lord told Him and camped beside Kerith Brook, east of the Jordan. The ravens brought Him bread and meat each morning and evening, and He drank from the brook. But after a while the brook dried up, for there was no rainfall anywhere in the land. The Lord said to Elijah, "Go and live in the village of Zarephath, near the city of Sidon. I have instructed a widow there to feed you."

The God of Elijah is a God of wonders, signs, and miracles. Elijah's calling is beyond his understanding, but yet when he spoke the word from God, the fire came down from heaven. He speaks with power and everything he said came to pass. God prepared, taught, trained, and equipped Elijah for his ministry and God gave him boldness, passion, courage, strength, and dedication to lead God's people. Elijah is faithful and full of promises from God. Elijah is just an ordinary man just like you and I, He full of love and passion for God and with a compassion for his people and he also has a relationship with God.

God hid him, led Him, and directed him for his calling. God set him aside for his purposes, for his will, and for his glory. Elijah was by himself and alone and in the darkest moment in his life, but God was with him. In his silent moment with God, he learned to listen to God's voice and he found a relationship with him. God revealed Himself to him by humbling him. Elijah is content with wherever God takes him. He was being obedient to God and he trusted God in His leadership over his life. Wherever God brought him to the place, God is always there providing and comforting him.

ISAIAH 42:1–9

Here is My servant, whom I uphold, My chosen One in whom I delight; I will put My spirit on Him and He will bring justice to the nations. He will not shout or cry out, or raise His voice in the streets. A bruised reed He will not break, and a smoldering wick He will not snuff out. In faithfulness He will bring fort justice; He will not falter or discouraged till He establishes justice on earth. In His teaching the islands will put their hope. This is what God the Lord says—the creator of the heavens who stretches them out, who spread out the earth with all that springs from it, who gives breath to its people, and life to those who walk on it: "I, the Lord, have called You in righteousness; I will take hold of Your hand. I will keep You and will make You to be a covenant for the people and a light for the Gentiles. To open eyes that are blind, to free captives from prison and to release from the dungeon those who sit in darkness.

"I AM the Lord; that is My name! I will not yield My glory to another or My praise to Idols. See, the former things have taken place, and new things I declare; before they spring into being I announce them to You."

ESTHER'S CALLING

Through my father's prayer for all those years of my life, is when I glanced at God. God saw me, and He wants to be face-to-face with me. But with me being a rebellious child, and wanting more from the world, I did not have a chance to be face-to-face with Him at that time.

Instead of me having face to face with God, I experienced the darkness from this falling world, the hardships, the tests, and trials in my life.

The end and the core of the tunnel of darkness that it's in front of me bring confusion into my heart. I experience without direction, no lights, and no life, I was lost walking in the cruel world without life. I was at the end of the tunnels alone. But through the end of that tunnel is where I found the lights of God.

When God called me, I trembled before Him. I even almost did not recognize His voice and His presence because of all darkness and fear that enveloped me. God even separated me from everybody and even to those people that I love. I hit rock bottom of my life. God took me to the lowest point of my life, the place where I am all alone. I felt like that He hide me for a moment for His purpose and His will for my life. Throughout the difficulties in times and dry season of my life, I found myself getting excited over the greater dimension of where God is taking me. God revealed Himself to me, by Him leading me, and by Him directing me and by Him equipping me. I felt the tangible presence of God that overtakes me, and I knew that I can follow His leadership over my life.

One day, I woke up in the good mood, with passion, dedication and courage, and I heard the voice of God saying to me that it is time to bring justice to the nations. He said that He put His spirit upon me to declare the truth and His love to all His people. I was amazed and in awe of God, and I said "yes" to God, that I am ready to be used by Him.

I heard the voice of God saying to me that I He wants me to share the Gospel and let the whole world know that Jesus is real and He is alive. God was telling me that His people are losing hope in Him. God wants to give them a message to edify, comfort, and exhort them, to speak the truth and love and to encourage them, that with God they will all have salvation, hope, healing, guidance, direction, restoration, blessings, correct, rebuke, encourage, and deliverance and they will all know Him completely in His love. God is coming soon, and He wants all His people to come to Him and worship Him.

I knew that with God I can do all things through Christ who strengthens me. I don't have anything to give to people, but I knew the One who can, and His name is JESUS CHRIST OF NAZARETH.

2 TIMOTHY 4:1-2

In the presence of God and of Christ Jesus, who will judge the living and the dead, and in view of His appearing and His kingdom, I give you this charge: Preach the word; be prepared in season and out of season; correct, rebuke and encourage—with great patience careful instruction. For the time will come when men will not put up with sound doctrine. Instead, to suit their own desires, they will gather around them a great number of teachers to say what their ears wants to hear. They will turn their ears away from the truth and turn aside to myths. But you, keep your head in all situations endure hardship, do the work of an Evangelist, discharge all the duties of your ministry.

ISAIAH 49:1–6

Listen to me, you Islands; hear this, you distant nations: Before I was born the Lord called me; from my birth He has made mention of my name. He made my mouth like a sharpened sword, in the shadow of His hand He hid me; He made me into a polished arrow and concealed me in His quiver. He said to me, "You are my servant, Israel, in whom I will display My splendor." But I said, "I have labored to no purpose; I have spent my strength in vain and for nothing. Yet what is due me is in the Lord's hand, and my reward is with my God."

And now the Lord says, He who formed me in the womb to be His servant to bring Jacob back to Him and gather Israel to Himself, For I am honored in the eyes of the Lord, and my God has been my strength. He says, "It is too small a thing for you to be My servant to restore the tribes of Jacob and bring back those of Israel I have kept. I will also make you a light for the Gentiles, that you may bring My salvation to the ends of the earth."

This is what the Lord says—the Redeemer and Holy One of Israel—to Him who was despised and abhorred by the nation, to the servant of rulers: "Kings will see you and rise up, princesses will see and bow down, because of the Lord, who is faithful, the Holy One of Israel, who has chosen you."

God gave you His word to manifest Himself for His kingdom and for His glory. You have been chosen to carry His word throughout the nations. You have been called to be His Royal Priesthood, the anointing one who will set people free from the captivity of this falling world. Your love and faithfulness to the Lord will bring His power to come down to defeat the enemies for you. God honors your desires and passion for His people, your perseverance, character, attitude, endurance and your patience will brings down His wisdom and revelation for you. You have been called to be His right hand to activate His Scepter, power, and His crown to reveal Himself to humanity.

YOU ARE WHAT GOD SAYS YOU ARE! YOU ARE GOD'S CHILD. YOU COME FROM HIS HEART. GOD LOVES YOU!

RESTORATION OF ISRAEL

ISAIAH 49-8-26

This is what the Lord says:

In the name of My favor I will answer you, and in the day of salvation I will help you; I will make you and will make to be a covenant for the people, to restore the land and to reassign its desolate inheritances, to say to the captives, "Come out" and to those in darkness, "Be free!" They will feed beside the roads and find pasture on every barren hill. They will neither hunger nor thirst, nor will the desert heat or the sun beat upon them. He who has compassion on them will guide them and lead them beside springs of water. I will turn all My Mountain into roads, and My highways will be raised up. See, they will come from afar—some from the north, some from the west some from the region of Aswan.

Shout for joy, O heavens; rejoice O earth; burst into song, O mountains! For the Lord comforts His people and will have compassion on His afflicted ones.

But Zion said, the Lord has forsaken me, the Lord has forgotten me. Can a mother forget the baby at her breast and have no compassion on the child she has borne? Though she may forget, I will not forget you! See I have engraved you on the palms of My hands; your walls are ever before me. Your sons hasten back, and those who laid you waste depart from you. Lift up your eyes and look around; all your sons gather and come to you. As surely as I live, declares the Lord, you will wear them on, like a bride. Though you were ruined and made desolate and your land laid waste, now you will be too small for your people, and those who devoured you will be far away. The children born during your bereavement will yet say in your hearing. This place is too small for us; give us more space to live in. Then you will say to your heart, who bore me these? I was barren; I was exiled and rejected. Who brought these up? I was left alone, but these—where have they come from? This is what the Sovereign Lord says, "See, I will beckon to the Gentile," I will lift up My banner to the peoples; they will bring your sons in their arms and carry your daughters on their shoulders. Kings will be your foster fathers, and their queens your nursing mothers. They will bow down before you with their faces to the ground; they will lick the dust at your feet. Then you will know that I am the Lord; those who hope in Me will not be disappointed." Can plunder be taken from warriors, or captives rescued from the fierce?

But this is what the Lord says:

"Yes, captives will be taken from warriors, and plunder retrieved from fierce; I will contend with those who contend with you, and your children I will save. I will make your oppressors eat their own flesh; they will be drunk on their own blood, as with wine. Then all mankind will know that, I the Lord, I Am your Savior, your Redeemer, the Mighty One of Jacob."

CHAPTER 34

THE FAMILY IS IN THE
HANDS OF GOD

In 2012 we move back to the city that we used to live, and my daughter met the daughter of our new neighbor and they became good friends. Her friends have been coming to our house many times, and one day my daughter invited her and her sisters to come to our house, so I had a chance to meet them. I love the children. They were very nice and polite. I tried to feed them and whatever I have I give it to them.

One day, they came to the house and I was not home. One of the sisters saw my letters on the table that has my name on it. For the first time, they found out about my last name. They were amazed how God brought us together knowing that we have the same last name. We were amazed because they came from the Dominican Republic and I am from the Philippines. I feel joy and love knowing that even though I don't have a family here in America. But for me meeting them I felt like I have a new family. We became good friends. I met their mother briefly, but at that time we did not have a chance to talk a lot.

One day, she mentioned to me about how their mother is going to leave them in their house by themselves without an adult. She will start taking care of her two younger sisters by herself. Dana was very sad as she continued sharing with me what is going to take place in their lives: that their mother is about to get married and that her mother will leave her two sisters with her to take care of them, and her mother will be marrying the man that does not want the children.

As I was listening to her story, my heart was broken. I don't want to see the children being by themselves without their mother. So I prayed to the Lord, and I heard the voice of the Lord saying, "Their mother will come back home." So I told to Dana what God was saying to me about their situation. I told her what God is saying to me that their Mother is "coming back home" and she will never be the same person again because God will change her completely to live righteousness before Him. I told her that when her mother comes back, she will have to forgive her Mother. When I told that to Dana, she was just looking at me with unbelief. Dana does not want to believe me because what I was trying to tell her sounded impossible. I still continued sharing with her about what God was saying to me for them, that she should not be worried about everything but to have joy and to trust God instead.

One day, I had a chance to talk to her Mother. Her mother was very excited to see me. Her mother was sharing to me about the man that just bought her a beautiful ring and was engaged with her and she just bought a beautiful wedding dress for her wedding. As she was sharing those things to me, I heard the voice of God saying that she will come back home, but then at the same time, the way it looked like and sounded like, it seemed that she was not planning to come back home.

So I started to talk to God, and I asked Him, "Lord, I know what You told me before." I asked God if He changed His mind about the mother coming back with her children. God answered me, and He said to me, that He does not change His mind, that God will bring the mother back home to the children. After God told me that, I felt peace. I have faith that God will perform miracles for the family.

When the mother was sharing to me her story, I tried to change the topic. Instead I was sharing and encouraging her to have a better understanding about how to love God and how to be a better parent. She loved it when we talk about God.

One week later, I noticed that they were moving her furniture from her bedroom and bringing them to her fiancé's house. I was concerned about the children that I decided to come to their house to see if the mother is really moving. When I get there, I saw her bedroom furniture and her clothes were already gone. Some of the furniture and her clothes were in the living room getting ready to be brought to her fiancé's house. I was so concerned about the children. As I was looking at the house, not believing what I was seeing, I believe God and what He says is true. As I was looking at her stuff at the living room, Dana came up to me and she told me that, "I told you so," that her mother is really leaving them. Dana does not believe me when I told her that her mother is coming back home. I smiled at her and I gave her encouraging words from God that she must trust God. I saw her being sad with what is going on in their lives that her mother will actually be leaving them for good. My heart was troubled. I tried my best and continued sharing with her the word of God. I shared with her that a good thing is about to take place in their lives, that God is getting ready to bless them, restore them, and deliver them.

Dana was just smiling with unbelief. She knew this time her mother will never come back for good because she is marrying the man, that she will never see her mother again. As she was saying those things to me, I started to feel sad for her and her sisters. But at the back of my mind, the word of God stayed with me. I believe God and what He was saying to me was true. I have confidence in God. There is nothing I saw and heard at that moment that will move my faith in God. I knew without any doubt that God will rescue and will make a way for the family. I pressed in to share with her with confidence that God is faithful and He will perform miracles for them. Even though what I saw was so hard to understand because in the natural, her mother is moving out, but in the spiritual realm, her mother is coming back home. At that time, I felt like an eagle soaring and going up to the air and looking down and seeing everything. I was very strong about my faith in the Lord, that I can see what is going to happen to them. That will restore them and bless them.

The mother had left and gone, and the children were alone and do not know what is going to happen to them next. So I kept checking the children. I'll make sure they have food to eat and sometimes they all come to my house and spend the night and we will pray and I order pizza for everybody, and they will all come with us to church. God is doing a good thing for them.

Two weeks later, I noticed that her mother's car is parked at the driveway. I started praying for them and I asked God as to what is the meaning of all those things with her car being parked at her driveway. God spoke to me with a clear voice and He said, "IAM sending her back home." I have full of joy after I heard that from Him.

Three days later, I visited their house and her mother asked me to go for a ride in her car. I got the chance to talk to the mother. I was sharing to her what God is saying to me concerning her and her family. I told her that God is going to bless them and protect them, and also God is going to heal them. Her mother was blessed for me to share the good thing about God. She felt the love of God and decided to open up with me. I am so glad that God opened the door for her to share her experience with me while she was away.

She started to share with me about everything what had happened to her life. She experienced hardship and she was trying to find life in God. Because of all those chaotic things that were happening to her, God opened her eyes to see the light in her life. God sent her back home with her children. The whole family was filled with joy and laughter in the house because they knew that God is real and alive and God is with them. Dana started to believe in God. She knows everything I told her is true from God, and she was thanking God for everything.

The children gave their lives to Jesus Christ, and they got baptized and later on the mother gave her life to Jesus. Everybody was feeling the presence of God. The family is being revived, renewed, refreshed, and reborn. God is moving in their lives mightily. God gave me a word about the salvation that everyone will come to Him and worship Him. The family did worship God.

Joel 3:17

Then you will know that I the Lord your God, dwell in Zion, Holy hill. Jerusalem will be Holy: never again will foreigners invade her.

Again God revealed Himself to me that there is nothing impossible for Him. He has the power to change things around. He wants me to put my confidence and trust in Him.

One day, their mother and I were talking and she was mentioning to me that she needed a job to support the children. I heard the voice of God saying that He was getting ready to bless them mightily. I mentioned to them about the pictures that they have in front of the fireplace. I told her that the pictures have the statues of Pharaoh's soldiers and the Pharaoh's soldier hurt and enslaved Israelites. I heard the voice of God saying that the picture is not from God but instead is from the enemy of God. And God told me that God wants her to break the picture and not to sell it or to give it away. If they will do that, God will bless them mightily and God is going to rescue them. They will not feel like they are slaves by the enemies. At that time they needed money. Dana does not want her mother to break the picture; instead she wants her to sell it so that they will have money. They want to sell the pictures for about three hundred dollars. I told them what God is about to do for them and it is greater than three hundred dollars. I told them that God is going to bless them mightily. I told her mother to pray about it and see what God is saying concerning the picture.

One month later, after praying to the Lord of what she needed to do, she came back to me and she decided to break the picture. She believed what I was trying to tell her is true. The mother and I started to pick up the picture and take the picture outside where the trash is. Her younger daughter gave her the hammer and she started breaking the picture into little pieces, as if she was hammering the works of the enemies in their lives. While she was breaking the picture, I decided to sing the song, "There Is Power in the Name of Jesus." I continued singing that song until there is nothing left in the picture. The whole picture was broken to pieces. But Dana was not very happy for the picture to be broken. She was very upset with the whole situation. Dana has doubt that God can make a way and be able to bless them.

Two weeks later, God gave her mother a job. And they decided to go back to their old house and the mortgage payment for that house was twelve hundred dollars every month. God moved among them and performed miracles for them. God allowed them to stay at that house without making payment for four years. God protected them, healed them, and restored them and bless them. God is faithful and He will do what He says He will do.

PSALM 91:14

Because He loves Me, says the Lord, I will rescue Him; I will protect Him, for He acknowledges My name. He will call upon Me, and I will answer Him; I will be with Him in trouble, I will deliver Him and honor Him. With long life will I satisfy Him and show Him My salvation.

Due to circumstances, I lost contact with the family for many years. On March 11, 2017, God spoke to me to contact them again. I was so glad that I found her old number. One day I called her to see how they were doing. When she picked up the phone, I was so happy to hear from her. She is also even glad to hear from me, and she told her daughter that everything will be right in their lives since they have heard from me again.

I was so glad that God told me to call them, because they are in the situation of distress at that moment. She told me that she moved out from her old house after living there for so many years. They told me that they have moved far away, and they were renting a house. They were so glad that I came back in their lives again because I came at the right place and at the right time. The mother mentioned to me that she cannot pay the house that they were renting at that time and she already received the noticed from the landlord for eviction and also they have a bakery store and the landlord was suing them for not making payment. But they don't have any money to pay her house rent and also the bakery store's rent. They found themselves with no way out and no hope. They were having a hard time. I promised to her that I will pray for her, for her family, for the bakery store, and for them to have a new home. I believe that there is nothing impossible with God.

On March 14, 2017, we decided to see each other and meet at the church after dropping off her children from the school. When we saw each other, we were so happy to see each other. On the way back to her house, which is almost two hours from the church, on the way to the city where she lives, she was sharing with me about the house that she wants to buy for them, but she was concerned that she may not be able to buy the house because she doesn't have any money and also she was concerned about her credit. She showed me the house and when I saw the house, God spoke to me that the house is already ordained for them to have, knowing she is not sure if she even qualified to buy it.

But I believed God for them, when we get to the house that she wants to buy. I started to pray, declaring and proclaiming that God already gave them the house for her and for her family. After praying for the house, she brought me to the bakery store, and I started praying for the bakery store for miracles also. I believed God wants to bless them mightily.

On March 17, 2017, her landlord already put her stuff out on the street. Since it was already getting late, she did not have enough time to get a truck. She decided to stay in the car and the children stayed in the bakery. She was trying to get a truck, but the truck was not available for them at that time. She decided to sleep in her car close to her stuff so that she can watch her stuff and no one will try to get them. The following morning, I talked to her and she told me that all of their stuff got wet because it rained the whole night before. She told me that they finally have the truck, but that morning when they were trying to put their stuff to the truck, she fell from the truck and she was badly hurt and the children took her to the hospital. My friend was losing hope and she was losing courage. She thought that God was not with them. I encouraged her to let her know that God is on her side. I told her that God is fighting for them. At that moment, I cannot lose my faith either. I believed God wants to bless them mightily, because that is the promise of the Lord for them. I refused the principalities and high place that were trying to show me the confusion that can move my faith in the Lord.

I believed God will make a way for her and her family. All I can do is to pray for them. Even though they were having a hard time at that moment, I believed in miracles for them that God will make a way in their lives, that they will have home and God will bless them and give them peace.

They are very distressed and they are desperate, needing help. I was feeling concerned for her and the children. I noticed myself praying harder even more to the Lord for their situation. I believed that God will perform miracles for them, and I knew it sooner than I could even imagine. I trusted God that He will perform miracles for them. I want to see that "God will rend the heaven and come down" for their situation. In that moment I was relying and trusting God for them.

On March 21, 2017, in that morning, she picked me up again at the church so I can pray for them. Instead of her bringing me to her bakery store, she brought me to the realtor first, hoping that I will pray and she will get the house. When we get there, I told her that we should pray first before we go inside the building. The Bible said that if "there is two or three gathering together in His name, there's God in the midst." I knew without any doubt that God will perform miracles for her that day. I prayed to God to give her favor that the house that she was trying to buy already belongs to them and also bakery.

After I prayed, we went inside the building and I have confidence in God that God already performed miracles for her. That God already gave her the house. I saw her talking to the realtor, and lo and behold, God did perform a miracle for them. The realtor was holding the key for the house and I saw the joy and peace on her face that came over her, knowing she and her children will have a place to live. The realtor gave her the keys for the house. And God performed miracle for her by giving them a new house for her and her children.

When we were are on the way to go to the bakery, the landlord of the bakery store called her and told her that the landlord will drop the charges if she will pay the landlord the whole amount of what she owes them. The landlord wants her to pay the whole amount she owes them that same day so that they don't have to go to the court. When she heard that she was even more afraid, knowing she doesn't have any money to give to the bakery landlord that day. She was so concerned that if she did not pay them, she will lose everything in the bakery store. The mother does not have a regular job. She was just depending on the bakery store for everything they needed for them to survive. She didn't have enough money to pay for the bakery. She really needed God at that moment. But I am not concerned because I knew that God will make a way for them. I knew God will perform miracles for her again. I prayed for her and with my confidence with God, I told her that she will get the bakery store back. She was having anxiety and distress. She wants to believe me that God wants to perform miracles for her, but at the same time she had a little bit doubt on her part. I was there to encourage her and for her eyes to be open to see God's love and His power over her life and her family.

I was confident to speak life over her life, and she started to believe God. At the same time, I was continuing to pray for God to release the bakery for them. After the prayer, on the way to the bakery store, everybody was calling her to give her a lot of money. Before the bakery store's landlord called and asked for the money they owed, my friend already had all the money that the landlord needs. Through prayer, confidence, trust in God that God will perform miracles for them, she received the breakthrough. She received the miracles of God. She had the house and the bakery at the same time and all the miracles happened within three hours. God is a God of signs, wonders, and miracles. Who can compare to Him?

Prayer is the key of the breakthrough. Trusting God, having confidence in Him and being patient to wait upon the Lord to open the door for God's glory.

TRUST IN THE LORD

JEREMIAH 17:7–8

But blessed is the one who trusts in the Lord, whose confidence is in Him. They will be like a tree planted by the water that sends out its roots by the stream. It does not fear when heat comes; its leaves are always green. It has no worries in a year of drought and never fails to bear fruit.

PROVERBS 3:5–6

Trust in the Lord with all your heart and lean not on your own understanding; in all your ways submit to Him, and He will make your paths straight.

1 CORINTHIANS 16:13

Be on your guard; stand firm in the faith; be courageous; be strong.

1 JOHN 5:14

This is the confidence we have in approaching God: That if we ask anything according to His will, He hears us.

JAMES 1:6

But when you ask, you must believe and not doubt, because the one who doubts is like a wave of the sea, blown and tossed by the wind.

2 CORINTHIANS 5:7

For we live by faith, not by sight

PSALM 16:8

I have set the Lord always before Me. I will not be shaken.

PRAYER

Dear Heavenly Father,

When there's situation, challenges, fear and anxiety threatening over us, You, O Lord, overtake us with your power, kindness, and goodness in our life. You give us Your love, joy, and faith, You bring riches and wealth in our life. You give us hope, courage, boldness, and strength to do our duty of the things that You want us to do. Lord, You are our strong tower, our guidance, our teacher and truth within us. Lord, You are our Baptizer of the Holy Spirit who walk with us, our Tree of Life that transforms us. Lord, You are our God, the river, and Your virtues flowing within us. You are our God, and Your word is alive and made flesh to reveal to us how to follow and live with You. You are our Exalted and excellent One in our life. Lord, help us to remember Your promises to be with us and every minute of our days. Help us to remember that You are the One who fights the battles for us. God, You provide, You heal and protect us. God, touch our mind, our body, and our soul. God, You are the one who completes us, You are the One whom we desire. Lord, we will gain victory, and You will trample down our enemies. We love You, In Jesus' name. Amen.

CHAPTER 35

IN AWE OF GOD

One day, the young woman's father called to tell me that he has only twenty dollars that will last him only for two weeks. He does not have a job but he was trying to find one, but for some reason the blessings of the Lord have not come his way yet. He was having anxiety, fear, and distress. His life at that moment was very hard and difficult, His car was repossessed, and his life was upside-down without any direction, nowhere to go, and no place to escape. Until one day, God spoke to me about how God is going to bless him. God said to me that if I talk to him about the Lord, He will make sure that He will provide for him.

One day, I talked to him about what God was saying to me concerning his situation. I told him about the goodness of God in his life. I told him that with God, nothing is impossible for him. I told him about the God's salvation and love, how God can bless him, and how he can trust God. I started to tell him everything that God was saying to me concerning him. As he listened to me, he felt like that there was a hope in his life. He started to humble himself before God and have a greater understanding about God. For the first time in his life, he believed that God will make a way in his life. He wants to agree with me, and in his heart he thought that he should give God a chance because in all of those times in his life, the enemy who is always the one controlling him. This time, he wants God to control him. So I told him what he needed to do for him to be able to receive the blessings from the Lord.

I told Him to pray and read the Scripture about . . .

John 3:16

For God so loved the world that He gave His One and only Son, that whoever believes in Him shall not perish but have eternal life.

I told Him to give tithes to his church for the amount of fifteen dollars and fifteen cents. Then he asked me why I chose to tell him to give fifteen dollars and fifteen cents. I told him that that's the amount of money that God told me for him to give to his church, and I told him to watch out because God is going to bless him mightily.

One week later, he called me and said that somebody gave him fifteen dollars and fifteen cents, and it was the exact amount that I told him to give to his church. He was so shocked to receive the same amount that I asked him to give to the Lord. I told him not to spend the money and to wait until he goes to church to give the money as offering to the Lord. He realized then that God is real. But God is not finished with him yet. He was waiting for God to perform miracle right away, but in those weeks, God did not answer the prayer yet and he started to get impatient.

Two weeks later, I asked him if he already read John 3:16 and his response I s very agitated because he was losing patience and at the same time he was desperate for a miracle. It just happened that he had not read the Bible yet and he was losing hope. He told me that he might as well read the Bible because he doesn't have anything to do anyway because he did not have a job. He also said that he might as well read the Bible just to see if I was telling him the truth, that if he reads the Bible, God will really bless him. And I am very confident that I heard the voice of God saying that he will bless him mightily. He tried to keep those words from God so he can be able to move on without feeling distressed.

Two days later, he called and told me about the woman giving Him the exact amount of fifteen dollars and fifteen cents again. He said that it was ironic because it was the same amount that I told him to give it to his church, and it just happened that the same amount was in his hand and the word from God confirmed it. He asked me about the meaning of it and what he needs to do. I told him to save the money until he goes to his church and give his tithes with that amount. He did use the money to give his tithes and he continued to read the Bible, hoping and believing God for his situation.

Within two weeks, I called him back and asked him if he had read the Bible, and he said yes. I told him to wait for the Lord because his blessings are already beginning to manifest. So he waited on the Lord and tried to be patient. *Two weeks later, he decided to go to the place where the miracles will take place, but when he got to the place, the person told him that he was not qualified to receive the money. He was very sad and then went toward the door, and right when he was about to walk out the door (the miracle began), another man came, called him, and told him that he was qualified to have the money.*

And they gave him three hundred dollars every week for two years. He was shocked, immediately called me, and told me that I was right, that God really did bless him. He said that he was not expecting to get the money because he knew that he was not qualified but by the grace of God, He gave him a favor and blessed him. From then on, he believed God, but he believed God greater than before. Because of God's wonders, his faith strengthened by God's favor over his life. His eyes were open and he followed God's will in his life from them on. He thanked God that His eyes are on him that God is really watching over him. He is in awe of God. I am so glad that God spoke to me concerning him, and he never put me to shame.

PRAYER:

Lord Jesus, expand my territory and enlarge my dreams and visions, for You are with me. Your love gives me strength and melts my entire being. Lord Jesus, let my ears be quick to hear your voice, let my eyes quick to see you face-to-face, let my heart be quick to trust you in every detail of my life. Lord Jesus, thank You because You lifted me up before Your throne. Lord Jesus, thank You for strengthening me. Thank You for loving me and giving me courage. I love You.

MARK 11:22–24

So Jesus answered and said to them, "Have Faith in God". For assuredly, I say to You, whoever says to this mountain, Be remove and be cast into the sea, and does not doubt in His heart, but believes that those things He says will be done, He will have whatever He says. Therefore I say to you, whatever things you ask when you pray, believe that you receive them, and you will have them.

JOHN 6:29

Jesus answered and said to them, "This is the work of God that you believe in Him whom He sent."

COLOSSIANS 2:6–7

So then, just a s you received Christ Jesus as Lord, continue to live your lives in Him, rooted and build up in Him strengthened in the faith as you were taught, and overflowing with thankfulness.

God completes you and everything you do. You are love and possessed with God's love and His power and embraced by the one who is Mighty, and His nature is fullness of signs, wonders, miracles, love, life, hope, strength, and peace. God called you to be holy, because He is Holy. God developed your nature and character to have strong faith that cannot be shaken and He captured you into His image, for you are His. He teaches you His way to have a new life for His glory. In the realm of His wonders, He took your heart and put His heart to your heart, and the heavens were opened, and God said, "You are mine." You are the reflection of God's manifesting glory, grace, and mercy. You are called the gateway from heaven to earth for His purpose and for His will in your life. You are the mouthpiece of God.

You are blessed . . .

CHAPTER 36

THE JOURNEY FROM THE WOMAN'S SHELTER

One day, the Holy Spirit spoke to me and said that I was going to be able to give land and homes to the homeless and also to the family with children struggling to make things meet, people that need home. God said to me that He wants to bless them. After God told me that, a lot of homeless people started to come to me asking me to give them a place to stay. Because God put the homeless people in my heart, I started to have compassion toward them. God put it in my heart so I may be able to help people that don't have homes, and I opened my house to the people that needed a home. I helped them, prayed for them, and even prophesied to them and miracle is happening to them. By the time they left my house, they are all blessed by God.

One day, the homeless couple had asked me if I can give them a place to live, I look at them with love, compassion and comfort and I said yes to them. The man was a professional athlete and the woman is a professional singer but through the circumstances in their lives that they lost everything. While they were living with us she had express her emotion with me by sharing with me about her children, the children does not leave with them because they cannot support them. I shared with them about the goodness of God over their life. I told them that God loves to perform miracles for them, and they believe God for their situation. "I shared with them that their children will come back to them and the blessings of the Lord will follow them wherever they go."

One week later, they had asked us if they can take us to have dinner with them, they took us to a nice restaurant and when we get there, they realize that they don't have enough money to pay for the bills, the woman check her bank account the second time, she knew that her bank account does not have the money, but she thought to try to check it again anyway. In her shocking moment, she found out that her bank account have ten thousand dollars. They remember what I told them that their "blessings of the Lord will follow them wherever they go." God bless them. The blessings that the Lord promised to them has arrive and also God bless them to have their children back with them, the same word that I told them that they will have their children back to them. The people gave them a home and pay their utilities. The couple was blessed and later on, the professional athlete man got a job as the professional athlete. The woman sings all over the world. God is upon them, and the "blessings of the Lord followed them wherever they go."`

Some homeless bought a house, and some found an apartment, and some found a place to live. I thanked God for His love, goodness, and kindness toward them.

One day, God spoke to me and told me to move out of my place and He doesn't want me to take everything with me; He wants me to leave everything behind. I was shocked to hear that from God because I don't have a place to go. But I started to pack our clothes and our pictures anyway as if we have a place to go. I stepped out of my faith that God will make a way. One day, my friend came to me and said that I can live with them. I felt joy; I knew it was from the Lord.

Three months later, due to battling cancer and me being sick all the time, the sickness did not allow me to work anymore. My daughter and I lost everything in our house, and I mean everything. The only things that we have were our clothes and our pictures. It was the exact word that God was telling me to do the whole time, that is, to leave everything behind, and to trust Him. I have to defend everything from the Lord.

I tried my best to make sure that I can pay my friend while we live in her house.

Months later, I realized that the money that I was receiving was not enough to pay for the rent and to put gas in my car. By the grace of God, I was so glad when my daughter called me and asked me if we can live with them and also to be able to take care of my grandchildren. I was so happy to find out that I can be with them, and it was the best thing that happened to us. After six months living with them and due to circumstances of our living situation, I found myself sleeping in the car. There was a time that I was tempted to call some of my friends to rescue me. But God stopped me because He wants to be the one who can help me, and He wants to be the one to be with me in my quiet place. The whole time, I was alone, and while I was lay down inside the car, God spoke to me again and said that He wants to see me face-to-face. While I was in my car, I can feel His presence at that moment. I thought that night was very special. God talked to me, comforted me, and He let me know that He is always with me no matter what the situation and obstacle are in my life. God promised me that He will give me peace. After God told me that, I trusted His word that He will make a way in my life. I stayed focused on the Lord. Later on, someone told me about the shelter; they can take me in, and I went, and I stayed in the shelter.

When I was at the women's shelter, I saw a lot of women who were lost, in despair, and carrying so much pain, anxiety, fear, lost confidence, rejection, brokenness, and sickness in their life. My heart was full of compassion for them. And also a lot of women did not have a car. After they left the shelter, they tried to go to places where they can find shelter in the morning. They end up walking in a very cold day. And I saw the opportunity to help them by taking them to the places where they needed to go. I also prayed for them, I gave them some money, and I shared the gospel to them. God is moving mightily upon His people.

FAVOR BY GOD FOR HIS PEOPLE

One night, this one woman at the shelter shared with me that she was trying to get an apartment. There was an apartment that she really likes, but when she asked the person that works in the apartment if she can rent it, He told her that she can't, because is not available anymore. She only had two days left at the shelter, and they will not let her extended her stay. She was very sad and distressed because she was not going to have a place to live and she was concerned that she will end up being on the street sleeping in her car. As I was listening to her situation, I saw her face feeling down because she was losing hope. I asked her if I can pray for her, and she said yes. I prayed that God will give her that apartment that she wants and for the Lord to give her a favor. The following night, I saw her again and she looked very radiant, like she had been touched by an angel. This time, she had good news. She shared to me that while she was at work, she received a phone call from the apartment office to let her know that the apartment that she likes was already reserved just for her, that she can have the apartment and she can move in anytime. The woman was shocked and felt joy at the same time. She knew that God was giving her a favor and God answered my prayer. After I heard the good news from the woman, I starting to have confidence and I felt joy for her.

As I was talking to her, I saw another woman with three children, and she looked very sad and distressed. I came up to her and asked if she will let me pray for her. I was so glad when she said yes to the prayer. I started to pray for the woman and her children, and while I was praying for her, I noticed her tears coming down at the back of my hands. It was like a river that won't stop; her tears just kept flowing and flowing. After I prayed for her, she found peace in her soul. She was healed, restored, delivered and blessed, and from that moment on she believed God. The following night, I did not see the woman at the shelter, because God blesses her to have home.

When the other woman that likes the apartment saw that I was praying for the woman with three children and that we were feeling the presence of the Lord, she came to me and asked me if I could pray for her again because she believes that God will perform miracles for her again. She believes that the goodness of God and the prayer will manifest in her life. Through prayers, the woman started to have confidence that God is real and He is alive in her life. And the woman was blessed.

I saw the manifestation of God in the shelter; miracles after miracles were pouring out on the women in the shelter. THE SHELTER

BECOME A HEALING ROOM for the people, God provide for the women in the shelter.

THE GATE OF HEAVEN IS OPEN

At the same time my heart was in trouble because I was like them; I didn't have a home for me to live also. I was at the shelter for four days. I was waiting for God to open the door for me and my daughter, because my daughter was staying with her dad at that time and she needs to go back to me and go back to school on Monday, but I don't have a place for us to live yet. And it was already Saturday night. I was desperate for God to make a move in our life. I kept praying to the Lord to help us. I knew that God will make a way in our life. We need the miracles of God in our life in that moment.

I was praying to the Lord to give me a favor and bless me. The more I pray, the more the enemies tried to come against me. Some people that I knew helped me, some people that I knew rejected me, some people criticized me, and some felt bad for me. At that time of my distress, I knew that my heart was crushed. I cried night and day, I asked God where He is, because I wanted to make sure that God is with me. I felt at that moment that God stripped me down to my knees. I felt like God was testing my faith at that time, in my brokenness moment, I was not sure if I passed the test. But I knew that God will lead me to His way.

I remember it was already Sunday morning and my daughter's father was going to bring her back to me that Sunday night, but I have not found a place for us to live yet. I started to cry out to the Lord, I was very desperate for God to perform a miracle for us. I started to be concerned about my situation, but at the same time I knew God will make a way for me, so I continued to trust God in my situation. That Sunday, I was supposed to go to the church because I had to pray and give prophecy to the people at my church, but at that time I was so broken that I told God that I didn't want to go to church. I told God about how can I pray for broken people when I know that I am also broken? My situation was critical for me; I didn't know where my daughter and I will stay. I only had one day left at the shelter. I asked God to help me immediately. I never stopped asking God because I knew that He is able.

As I was praying to the Lord, I heard the voice of God saying to me that, "The blessings of the Lord are in the house of God." When God told me that, I quickly dressed up and came to the church. On the way to church, God brings me back the remembrance about Jacob telling God that he will not let him go unless He bless him. When I was at the church, I asked my healing team to pray for me before I can pray for the people. I told them that I was broken and I was hanging on the cross at that moment, and they were all shocked because they have never heard that coming from my mouth before. They knew that when I speak, I speak with boldness and power. But at that moment, I was speaking with humbleness and humility instead. I humbled myself before the Lord. I was desperate for God's help for me and for my daughter.

I told to my prayer team what was happening to me. They all prayed for me and believed God for me. After they prayed for me, God touched one of the people. The person came to me with love and compassion and offered us a place to live in their house. And it just happened that her husband was with her and they both offered us their home. I jumped for joy in my heart. I thanked God, and I thanked them for letting us live with them. I thanked God that He covers us with His feathers. I knew that God loves me. God never leaves me nor forsakes me. I continue and faithfully serve God. God is never late; He is always on time to rescue me. To God be the glory. I keep asking God to help, and God helped me. He answered my prayers.

GENESIS 17:16

I will bless her and will surely give a son by her. I will bless her so that she will be the mother of Nations, Kings of peoples will come from her.

GENESIS 18:10

Then the Lord said, I will surely return to you about this time next year, and Sarah your wife will have a son.

GENESIS 21:2–3

Sarah became pregnant and bore a son to Abraham in His old age, at the very time God has promised Him. Abraham gave the name Isaac to the son Sarah bore Him.

GOD IS ALWAYS ON TIME

While I was still at the women's shelter, I met this young woman and her baby, they both needs help. I started to help her by babysitting for her baby. I have compassion for this young woman. I tried to help her in any way I can. I took her to her work and babysit for her baby. One day, she moved into this hotel and we found out that it was not a safe place; a man told us that somebody just died beside the hotel. I was so concerned for the woman and her infant baby for their safety, and so I asked her if she wants to go to another hotel. We decided that she should not stay in that hotel, so I took her to another hotel that I knew was safe and cheaper. The following morning on the way to the hotel, I prayed that God will give her favor and give her a place to live.

I picked the woman and her baby up from the hotel and took her to the safe hotel. After dropped her off, I prayed for her and her baby for protection, on the way back to pick her up, I prayed for her again for God's favor; I want her and her baby to have a place to live like me. I was running late to pick her up because of the distance; she wanted me to take her to do some errands. She met a woman at the place where I dropped her off. God touched the woman's heart; she had compassion toward her and decided to give her a place for her and her baby to live. I thanked God the whole time for giving her a favor. The woman and her baby now have a place to live. God is always on time and He answers my prayers.

After all those things that took place, I looked back and started to cry for God's love, kindness, and compassion toward me and other people. I was so glad that God gave me strength to do the task of what He wanted me to do. I thanked God for allowing me to help other people, knowing that I also needed help for myself. In my brokenness and in the darkness moment of my life, I saw God's power manifested over me and His people. To God be the glory.

JOBS 5:9–11

He performs wonders that cannot be fathomed, miracles that cannot be counted. He bestows rain on the earth, He sends water upon the countryside, the lowly He sets on high and those who mourn are lifted to safely.

PSALM 45:2–4

You are the most excellent of men and your lips have been anointed with grace, clothe yourself with splendor and majesty. In your majesty ride forth victoriously in behalf of truth, humility, and righteousness; let your right hand display awesome deeds.

The word of the Lord says to you at this moment:

Don't give up and don't give in. You have been weak you have been labored, and waited too long. You persevered through many test, trials, persecution, suffering, tribulation, challenges, and so many battles to lay down the weapon in these season of your life. You need to hold, to press in, and keep moving forward, knowing God is on your side. Fix your eyes on God, knowing that He is the answer to all your prayers. No matter what happen in your life, everything is the way God intended to be.

God's power has been revealed by dividing the Red Sea, by splitting the rock, by bringing the fire from heaven, by walking on water, by calming the storm, by making the sun still, by bringing down fire from heaven, by healing the sick, by resurrecting the dead body, and by feeding five thousand people, and nothing is impossible for Him. He will reveal His power over you; you need only to be still.

You are very strong, you persevere through all things, and you always win the victory. You are tough and you can bend without breaking. You hear from God and you humble yourself and obey Him. You have the courage to pass the fire, the winds, and the rushing river, knowing that God is with you; you can conquer all things. Continue to walk the right path with God, because He is the only one who knows your destiny and your future. He wants to take you and lead to the unseen and seen in your life.

When God makes a promise, He will always make them happen, because it's already been ordain for you to have them for your destiny and for your future. God depends on you to do the task that He ordained you to do. Through your faithfulness, obedience, and the sacrifice to the Lord, God's plan in your life have already been fulfilled.

YOU ARE THE CHILD OF GOD AND HE LOVES YOU!

PRAYERS

Dear Jesus,

Thank you for opening my eyes to see you. Your kindness and goodness for me brings comfort to my soul. You are my God that I can trust and depend on for the rest of my life. You have been giving me the blessings beyond my understanding. You are my God who leads and directs me to the path of righteousness. You have been giving me an abundance of blessings, life, health, and the unmerited favor. Lord Jesus, thank you for your victory to rule and reign from your throne over my life. Lord Jesus, I love you, in Jesus' name, Amen.

CHAPTER 37

TESTIMONIES

MATHEW 8:8

The centurion answered and said, Lord, I am not worthy that you should come under my roof. But only speak a word, and my servant will be healed.

JOSHUA 21:45

Not one of all the Lord's good promises to Israel failed; everyone was fulfilled.

AMOS 3:7

Surely the Sovereign Lord does nothing without revealing His plan to His servants the prophets.

DANIEL 2:19–23

During the night the mystery was revealed to Daniel in a vision. Then Daniel praised the God of Heaven and said: "Praise be to the name of God forever and ever; wisdom and power are His. He changes times and seasons; He deposes kings and raise up others. He gives wisdom to the wise and knowledge to the discerning. He reveals deep and hidden things; He knows what lies in darkness, and light dwells with Him. I thank and praise You, God of my ancestor: You have given me wisdom and power. You have made known to me what we asked of You, You have made known to us the dream of the king."

God is the God of the impossible and His activity flow through you. When the heaven is open the glory of God came down and manifested Himself into a massive signs, wonders, and miracles instantly before your eyes. By the word and the breath of God, things came to be. With His word, you bowed down and said, surely He is the Alpha and Omega, He is the Almighty God, He is the beginning and the end, He is the first and the last, who Is, who Was, and who Is to Come, the Almighty God. He exists since the foundation of this world. He is the same yesterday, today, and forever. He is the living God and He lives in you. YOU ARE BLESS.

PSALM 66:16–20

Come and hear, all you who fear God; let me tell you what He has done for me. I cried out to Him with my mouth; His praise was on my tongue. If I had cherished sin in my heart, the Lord would not have listened; but God has surely listened and has heard my prayer. Praise be to God, who has not rejected my prayer or withheld His love from me.

THE ANOINTED ONE

HABAKKUK 3:2

Lord, I have heard of Your fame; I stand in awe of Your deeds,

PSALM 24

The earth is the Lord's, and everything in it, the world, and all who live in it; for He founded it on the seas and established it on the waters. Who may ascend the mountain of the Lord? Who may stand in His holy place the one who has clean hands and a pure heart, who does not trust in an idol or swear by a false god. They will receive blessing from the Lord and vindication from God their Savior. Such is the generation of those who seek Him, who seek your face, God of Jacob.

Lift up your heads, you gates; be lifted up, you ancient doors, that the king of glory may come in. who is this king of glory? The Lord strong and mighty, the Lord mighty in battle. Lift up your heads, you gates; lift them up, you ancient doors, that the king of glory may come in. who is He, this king of glory? The Lord Almighty- He is the king of glory.

THE KING OF GLORY RISE UP UPON ME

As the years go by hearing the voice of God in my life, I felt His love, and His love brings boldness, courage, assurance, and confidence in my life. With His will, His love, His power, the way He leads me, the way He directs me, the way He guides me, and the way He gives me power to speak His word over His people. I saw the authority of God and the manifestation of His glory over His people. I would like to share with you some of the power and the miracles that took place on God's people in their lives as I ministered to them. And here are some people that God revealed His power and miracles to them. We saw the glory of God and His word manifested in their life accompanied with signs, wonders, and miracles. And they are all in awe of the wonders of God over their life. Every one of them worships Him. Here is the testimony from their lips.

I pray, as I share with you about their powerful testimony and the move of God upon their lives, I pray that you will also encounter God in the mighty way for His glory. I pray that the king of glory will rise up upon you. And May the Spirit of God activates His power and mighty over you and His virtues shine within your soul. I pray that you will also see the power of His glory in your life that the signs, wonders, and miracles will manifest within you.

1 THESSALONIANS 1:3

We remember before our God and Father your work produced by faith, your labor prompted by love, and your endurance inspired by hope in our Lord Jesus Christ.

JOHN 11:40

Then Jesus said, did I not tell you that if you believe, you will see the glory of God?

MATTHEW 17:20

He replied, "Because you have so little faith." Truly I tell you, if you have faith as small as a mustard seed, you can say to this mountain, move from here to there; and it will move. Nothing will be impossible for you."

REVELATION 22:16

I, Jesus, have sent my angel to give you this testimony for the churches I am the root and the offspring of David, and the bright morning star.

HOLY SPIRIT

My child, I will take you to the highest position and a new level of My glory, I will lead you higher all the way to My throne, and I will direct you higher and greater than you could ever imagine, and I will let you sit with me into the dimension of My heavenly realms. I will take you higher above the activity and the works, tactics, and schemes of the enemies in your life, and your love one's life. I will raise you up as My co-heir, My bride, My son and My daughter, I will raised you up as My soldiers, My disciples, My Chosen One, My instruments and My warriors. I will raise you up as My Eyes, My Voice, My Hands, My Feet, and My Mind. And I will raise you up as My prophet for my people. I will raise you up mightily accompany with signs, wonders, and miracles working on My behalf, My presence will go before you on the earth with My authority and My power. You shall have My power, My word, with My fire, My winds and My spirit. You will walk with power and authority and with confidence with Me on the earth. You will stand up firm, you will stand up tall, you will stand up with courage and you will stand up with boldness, and you will stand up with revelation, and you will stand up with discernment, and you will stand up with wisdom, and be able to speak My word, for the nations to kneel down in my presence. I will make My voice and your testimony to be one with Me. And to you and through you, My people will be transformed for My glory. My kingdom will be established on the earth. And my presence will move and empower you to bring justice to the nations.

In My eyes, you are beautiful, and perfect. You are My precious bride. Everything about you is Me. Everything you said is what I said. When you speak, it is the very essence of My word. Your word will be established for My glory. Signs, wonders, and miracles will take place, for you are one with Me. You are the Image of My existence. You and I are one!

I Love You,

Your Abba, Father, God

STORIES:

God blessed Carla with the car

One day, I prayed and prophesied to the woman. At that time, the woman did not have a mode of transportation; somebody always picked her up and took her to church and wherever places she had to go. *I heard the voice of God saying that He wants to bless her. God instructed her to come to the church for one week; she will come every night to spend the night with the king.* It was fascinating that God will tell her that, knowing that she doesn't have a car to come to church for the whole week, but with God, nothing is impossible. She managed to come to church for that whole week by asking her good friends to bring her to church. She believed that God will make a way in her situation and for the Lord to perform miracle for her. At that moment, she was in the lowest point of her life; she needed help.

After I shared with her what God wanted to say to her, the woman did what God said to her to do she came to church faithfully every night for one week. She prayed, worshipped, and read her Scriptures, until two weeks later I saw her full of joy and in awe of God, because she just experienced the love of God and His kindness toward her. She told me that *God used someone to bless her and give her a car.* And now she has a car to go to church and to go anywhere God wishes her to go for His kingdom.

God is good. He is truthful and faithful for everything He does.

Pastor Gabriel danced with the angel

One day, I prophesied to the pastor and *told him that I saw him dancing with an angel.* The pastor did not expect that word because he wanted to hear the blessings of the Lord over him at that moment. So the pastor went home confused by that prophecy. But that night, as *he lay in bed, he saw an angel, and the angel started to dance with him.* He was shocked, glad, and felt joy at the same time. One day, he came back to church because he wanted to share with me about what he just experienced. But he was sad to find out that I was not in church; I was gone for almost a year. One day, I came back to church. Right before I came in to the door, the pastor came up to me and told me that he was waiting for me to tell me about the prophecy that I had given to him. He was full of awe and joy that He wanted to share with me about the word that I gave him, *about the angel dancing with him.* After he shared that to me, he asked me if I can come and share the gospel and testimony to his church. I was so glad, very happy, and honored to come to their church. God was blessing his people.

God blessed Sarah with a home

One day, I was talking to a woman who told me that *she wanted to buy a house one day.* When I heard that, *I told her that she will get a house.* Less than a year later, she and *her family bought a house* that my daughter and I now live in for a while. God loves His children.

God blessed Joseph,

One Saturday morning, the man shared with me that he wants to marry his fiancée, but due to difficulty for not having enough money, *he cannot buy her a ring.*

So I asked him if he wants me to pray for him, and he said yes for the prayer. So I started praying for him; *I asked God to bless him and give him favor mightily.*

The following weekend, I saw him and shared with me about his testimony. *One Wednesday, someone had given him some money and it was $300, and on a Friday, someone gave him some money and it was $1,100.* He was so amazed by God. God loves him and he is faithful to him. God performs miracles for him. Truly, God is real and He answers prayers of the saints.

God blessed the woman with the heart of God

One day, the woman shared with me about the confusion, stress, and sadness that were happening with her. She needed a job. She used to be a teacher and she gave out her resume to seven school districts, but no one contacted her. She was losing hope. One day, she came up to me and told me what was happening to her. I gave her the word of the Lord and *"told her that from this day forward, the job she was looking for already belongs to her; she will get the job. I also I told her that she will receive blessings that will not come from her paycheck and she will also have a place to live.*

The following day, she came to me and said that somebody had given her a job as a teacher. She also found a new place to live, and months later, she received the inheritance money from her late ex-husband whom she had not seen in many years." God truly doesn't lie. He is faithful and He will not put me to shame.

Testimony from the woman;

Esther, I knew God backs you up! I've seen it time and time again. Supernaturally, *you said that you saw my husband and I moving to different states* two weeks prior to him getting interviewed, which was completely out of nowhere. It would involve us moving to other states. *My husband did end up getting a job, and we did end up actually moving again.* God backed up my Esther again. Thank you.

Sincerely yours,

Woman with the heart of God

God brought Alex's brother to America

I was having a fellowship in my house and one of the men that was in the fellowship asked me if *I can pray for his brother to come to America because he was from another country.* He showed me the picture of his brother. After looking at the picture, *I started praying for him and also for his brother to come to America.* By the grace of God, with his amazement and awe with God, *God answered the prayer. His brother arrived in America.* He praised and worshipped God.

God is good. He loves to give things to His children.

God blessed Minister Brianna with the car, but she refused it

One day, the woman shared with me that she doesn't have a car to go to work and to go to church. She told me that she had to ride with somebody. I heard the voice of God saying that God wants to bless her with a car, so I came up to her and told her about what God is saying concerning her, *that she is going to receive the car for free.* The following weekend, I saw her again. I came up to her and asked *if God gave her a car yet.* She looked at me with awe because *somebody did give her a car for free,* but she did not accept it because she wants the Mercedes Benz instead. One day she bought a new car, and lost the car at the same time. She wishes she accept the car that God gave her.

God blessed Jerome

One early morning, the man called me. While he was talking to me, *I heard the voice of the Lord commanding me to tell him that there is something that He needs from God and God was the only one who can help him.* When I told him that, he was shocked and said that he did not need anything from me until we hung up the phone. The man had three children and his ex-wife left him. The following morning, he called me again and shared with me that *his electricity got cut off* and the children needed the power in the house. He asked me if I can help him. I said yes and asked him how much he needed. Then he told me how much he needed. *I was I amazed because the amount that he was asking from me was the same amount that was in my bank account, and no matter how much I spent the money all those times to go shopping, the same amount still remained in my bank account. I gave him the money to pay for his electricity.* Years later, I asked him why he did not tell me right away when I told him that he needed my help. He said that he was embarrassed to me and he said that he was shocked and in awe of how I knew what was happening to him. He was amazed with God and he worshipped Him.

Years later, I introduced him to one of my friends. And another year later, they got married. *One morning, she called me and while she was talking to me, I heard the voice of the Lord saying that I should give everything I have in the garage, everything. I thought I was not hearing God very well because I have many stuff in my garage that it's worth so much money.* But I have to be obedient to the Lord. While she was talking, I interrupted her and told her that everything that I have in my garage is for her to take everything. They can have everything in my garage. And she knew that I have a lot of stuff and that they are worth a lot of money.

She started crying and told me that she and her husband just lost their jobs at the same day, for two weeks they didn't know how they are going to support the children in that moment. She was so glad that I am able to help them. The following weekend, they had a garage sale in my house and they made good money to take care of their children.

God is love, kind, good, and faithful to His children.

God blessed Pastor George's wife with the gifts

One day, the pastor's wife was sitting on the table and she asked if I want to sit with her, and I said yes. While I sat on the table, *I heard the voice of God telling me about the Scriptures* and I shared it with her. *I told her about Paul being in a prison and the congregation came and visited him. They brought all kinds of gifts and perfume, and it pleased God.*

I also told her that she felt like she was in prison. She was shocked and said yes, because they had just moved to their new place and there was no place for her to go. She didn't have any friends at that time and *felt like she was actually in jail.* I told her about what happened to Paul and it's the same thing that God will do for her. *I told her that the whole congregation will give her gifts and they will also bless her with money.*

One weekend later, the whole congregation gave her gifts, flowers, and envelope with money. God truly blessed her. God fulfilled His promises over her life.

One day, the pastor asked to the whole congregation if someone will come up to him and give him prophecy. I looked around and did not see anybody that will want to prophesy for him, *so I stood up and shared with him in front of congregation that he will receive a car for free. He was shocked because he needed a car. One month later, the whole congregation had given him a new car.*

God is faithful. He does wonders for His children.

Fellowship In My House

While we were having a fellowship in my house, there was a man came to me and asked me if I can pray for his brother who still in his country. His brother wants to come to America but he was having a hard time to come. The man showed me his brother's picture, I lay my hand on the picture and I start praying for him to come to America, after I prayed God blessed him, less than three months he came to America. God answered the prayer for him.

One day, the same man came to me again and asked me if I can pray for his debt, he owe ten thousand dollar to the company and he was having a hard time to pay them back. He asked me if God can be able to help him, he really needs help from God. I lay my hand on his head and I starting to pray for him for God to bless him. One day the man saw me at the church, and he shares me that the company he owed ten thousand dollar called him and told him that the money he owed is already been dismissed, he doesn't owed them anymore. We thanked God for all the blessings that He has done for the man.

God used uses the water to bring miracles, the water is a point of contact from God to them

One day, I was having a fellowship in my house. I heard the voice of God saying that I should let the people walk through the water, and I did. I borrowed a baby pool from somebody and I poured water in the baby pool and I told everybody that when they walk through the water, God will bless them. And every one of them walked through the water.

One day, I asked one of the men who walked through the water if he wants to come with me at my friend's church. My friend was a pastor in the church. The man said yes, he would like to come with me. While we were in the church, the pastor asked the congregation to put their money together, and the pastor gave all the money from the congregation to the man who walked through water.

And everybody who walked through the water was blessed.

One person who walked through the water did not have a job, after he walk through the water the man is been given a job less than one week later, he is been given a raise from His job less than a week.

Another person was given a ticket that is worth three hundred dollars after she walk through the water.

Another person who was homeless, after he walk through the water, he had a place to live within two days.

One weekend, the man brought Muslim woman's friend, after I prayed for the woman, she felt the Holy Spirit and she immediately surrender her life to Jesus Christ.

More of God's power for those who will believe, God is good. He loves to saves, heals, delivered, restore, and comforts His people.

God blessed Mark from the anointing oil God used the anointing oil as a point of contact for him

One day, Mark came to my house. *God spoke to me to give him the anointing oil.* Then I *told Mark that I want God to bless him. The following day, God bless Mark and he received $8,000.* Mark thanked me for speaking life over him. I told Him to thank God for his blessings.

God is so good, He loves His children.

The daughter is healed from the anointing oil the anointing oil is a point of contact from God to her

One day, I went to the woman's house and I gave her anointing oil. *The woman gave some anointing oil to her daughter.* Her daughter's doctor found a cyst in her breast. She came back again to the doctor to check her breast. Her daughter was very scared. She was very distressed and cried out to the Lord for help her.

She used the anointing oil all over her breast believing that God will use the anointing oil as an instrument to bring healing to her breast. Every day, she rubbed the anointing oil on her breast faithfully. Until one day, it was time for her to come back to the doctor. She rubbed the anointing oil one more time and believed that she will be healed by God. By the power of God, the doctor said to the daughter that whatever He saw before, it's miraculously disappeared. The doctor cannot find anymore cyst from her breast. The daughter was healed and bless. She had full of faith and love with God.

THE MIRACLES OF THE ANOINTING OIL

The woman came to me and told me that her friend's brother got shot on the forehead and she asked me if I can pray for her friend's brother and also she asked me if I can give her more of the anointing oil to give it to her friend's brother.

One day, I was having a Fellowship in my house, for the first time I meet her friend, and she was sharing to us about the anointing oil that I give for her brother. She told us that they were rubbing the anointing oil on her brother, the doctor were giving up on him but by the grace of God and His power, her brother still alive.

One woman shares with me also that her sister was very sick and dying, the doctor had given up on her. While she was at the hospital with her sister, she remember that she have the anointing oil that I gave to her a while back. She immediately took the anointing oil out from her purse and anointed her sister with the anointing oil. By the grace of God and His love over her sister, her sister still alive.

PEACE AND HOPE

I was one of the volunteered to give away food for the people. One day, there were new people came and they were all also volunteered, after we finished with all our work and putting all the foods to the plastic bags to give away for the people, I asked the volunteered if they would like me to prayed for them and they all said yes, after they said yes for me to pray for them, we decided to make us a circles. I asked all of them is to what would they want God to do for them? They all look at me and they were all shocked that I asked them that question. Because they were never heard that before.

One person starting to burst out crying, with peace and hope from God. She starting saying that she was broken and helpless that she needed God in her life and also she needed a job. I prayed for God to save her and to bless her, the following week God bless her and she have found hope with God and God healed her and God gave her a job. One person asked me to pray for God to give him a job and for God to help to stay out of trouble, after I prayed the following week God gave him a job, and God bless him with peace and love.

One person wants God to help him from the court issues after I prayed for him, the following week the police said to him that he will back him up. God is making away for him and blessing him.

I encourage one person about the goodness of God in his life, he was amazed by God with all the revelation that He shares with me, everything he heard concerning him was right from the heavenly throne. He was overwhelmed with awe to the Lord Jesus Christ in his life.

Artist man,

One Sunday morning, I went to the Flea market and I saw the artist man paint a beautiful portrait. I came up to him and I asked him if he can paint a portrait for me, the man with the sad face said to me that he cannot be able to paint me a portrait because he is going to jail the next day. I look at him and I told him that he is not going to jail, because he is going to paint me a beautiful portrait, and I prayed over him. The following weekend I came back to the Flea Market, and he told me that he did not have to go to jail and he can be able to paint me a beautiful portrait. He was thanking for speaking life and prayed over him, I told him that we should thank God for His faithfulness in our lives.

PSALM 107:14–16

He brought them out of darkness the utter darkness, and broke away their chains. Let them give thanks to the Lord for His unfailing love and His wonderful deeds for mankind, for He breaks down gates of bronze and cuts through bars of iron.

JOHN 2:11

What Jesus did here in Cana of Galilee was the first of the signs through which He revealed His glory; and His disciples believed in Him.

JOHN 6:40

For my Father's will is that everyone who looks to the Son and believes in Him shall have eternal life' and I will raise them up at the last day.

PSALM 40:5

Many, Lord my God, are the wonders You have done, the things you planned for us. None can compare with you: were I to speak and tell of your deeds, they would be too many to declare.

PHILIPPIANS 2:13

For it is God who works in you to will and to act in order to fulfill His good purpose.

ISAIAH 48:6–7

You have heard these things; look at them all. Will you not admit them? "From now on I will tell you of new things, of hidden things unknown to you. They are created now, and not long ago", you have not heard of them before today. So you cannot say, 'yes, I knew of them.

REVELATION 10:6–7

And He sworn by Him who lives forever and ever, who created the heavens and all that is in them, the earth and all that is in it, and the sea and all that is in it, and said "There will be no more delay! But in the days when the Seventh Angel is about to sound His trumpet, the mystery of God will be accomplished, Just as He announced to His servant the Prophets.

God loves His people and He loves you. He loves to perform miracles for you. God is the one who created you into His image. God loves to bring mystery into your being and created things that is beyond your understanding. His mystery over your life is to expand your mind into His existence. You have been chosen to carry His glory on earth. Your word has power to create and make a new thing to bring glory and joy to God who created you.

"Right now, as you read this word, the desires of your heart that God put in there have already been fulfilled. No more delay" In Jesus name. Amen.

You are blessed.

ROMANS 15:13

May the God of hope fill you with all joy and peace as you trust in Him, so that you may overflow with hope by the power of the Holy Spirit.

CHAPTER 38

THE VICTORY OF GOD OVER ME

1 CORINTHIANS 15:55–57

Where, O death, is your victory? Where, O death, is your sting? The sting of death is sin, and the power of sin is the law. But thanks be to God! He gives the victory through our Lord Jesus Christ.

As I look back about my experiences throughout my life, I knew that my stories are full of lights and also full of darkness. There were good and some were not so good. My stories are about Jesus being on the cross who takes away my sins, my pain, the hurt, the poverty, the rejection, the persecution, the hardships, the darkness, and even death in every area of my life. I was so glad that I have conquered all things through Christ who strengthens me, the One who died for me. "Jesus Christ is the One who set me free." God's hidden mind and the unthinkable ways of life is been reveals to me in the mighty way. He poured out His love for me to win the victory over my enemies.

The world became the heart of my stories, but through God's eyes, my stories became beautiful and unique. All those things that I had experienced are a part and a shadow of my past and I thank God that He allowed me to experience them all, because without the story of my past, I will not be who I am right now. I thank God for lifting me up and putting me in the "palm of His hands." I thank God that He let me be with Him for a moment in heaven to be able to see the real radiance of His brightness, His beauty, His warmness, His love over me, and I thank God for bringing me back "from death to life." I thank God that I do not lose heart that even my outward appearance was perishing, but my inward appearance is being renewed each and every day of my life. The word of God is full of truth and depth into my soul. His magnificent love and strength over me put a mark into my heart and to my whole entire being.

I thank God that I can be able to share and testify that God is real and He is alive within my soul.

THE DEMONS AND DEATH CANNOT HOLD ME DOWN. I AM STILL STANDING. GOD TRIUMPHS THE VICTORY OVER MY LIFE! I AM GOD'S TROPHY FOR HIS VICTORY AND FOR HIS KINGDOM.

I AM WHO GOD SAYS I AM, AND I AM WOTHY IN HIS EYES.

God loves you, He desires you, He delights in you, and He is pleased with you.

God is full of comfort, love, and affection toward you.

You are going forward pertaining to seen and to the unseen of the things of God.

You have been given a favor from on high for His glory.

The wisdom, knowledge, and revelation are already imparted for you by God, through God, and for God.

You have been given the gifts, life, and health for God's glory.

The riches and wealth in heaven have been released from His treasures for His will in your life.

Your character, emotions, and your attitude are full of awe with excellence and perfection in God's eyes.

You are the apple in God's eyes.

Your faith is the one that can remove God's power that came out from the Anointing One, His Son Jesus Christ.

Your word has power and it has life.

You are a blessing to the cities, communities, and to the nations.

This moment is your season to shine. So let your face shine so that they will see God in you.

CHAPTER 39

JESUS CHRIST THE ANOINTED ONE

OUR KING

REVELATION 22:13

I am the Alpha and Omega, the first and the
last, the beginning and the end

ISAIAH 53

Jesus Christ has no beauty to attract us to Him, nothing in His appearance that we should desire Him.

But yet He is our radiance of love, He is our beautiful light, He is our magnificent creator, He is our bright morning star.

Jesus Christ is despised and rejected by men, a man of sorrows, and familiar with suffering.

But He is our comfort, He is our assurance, He is our confidence, He is our all and all that we need, He is the same yesterday, today, and forever.

Jesus Christ, is the one whom men hide their faces, He was despised, and we esteemed Him not.

But yet He is our king, He is our champion, He is our hero, He is our only cause. He is our consuming fire.

Jesus Christ took our infirmities and carried our sorrows.

But yet He is our joy, He is our strength, He is our hope of glory, He is our bread of life who feeds us, He is our living water who quenches our thirst, and He is our lily in the valley who makes us brave.

Jesus Christ, whom we considered stricken by God, smitten by Him, and afflicted.

But yet He is our Savior, the one who is anointed by God, He is our omnipresent, and He is omnipotent god. He is our kingdom of light.

Jesus Christ was pierced for our transgressions, He was crushed for our iniquities.

But yet He is the lover of our soul, He is our mediator from heaven to earth, He is our affection, He is our courage, He is our future, and He is our destiny.

Jesus Christ was oppressed and afflicted, He was led like a lamb to the slaughter.

But yet He gives life, He gives hope, He revives, He renews, He refreshes, and He gives a new beginning to the broken one.

Jesus Christ was cut off from the land of the living, He was stricken for the transgressions of His people,

But yet He is our lion on the tribe of Judah, He is our warrior who makes war on our behalf, He is the one who is, who was, and who is to come, the Almighty God.

Jesus Christ was assigned a grave with the wicked, and the rich in His death.

But yet He is our King who conquered death, He is the one who can raise the dead, He is the one who holds the keys of Death and Hades, and He is the one who is seated at the right hand of the Father.

PSALM 22:15

Jesus Christ, His strength is dried up like potsherd, and His tongue sticks to the roof of His mouth; He laid in the dust of death.

But yet He is our resurrection power, He is our healer, He is our restorer, He is our deliverer, He is our Provider, He is our way maker, and He is our shield and buckler.

JESUS CHRIST OUR SAVIOR

Hebrews 1:3

Jesus Christ, whom He appointed heir of all things, and through whom He made the universe.

Jesus Christ is the radiance of God's glory and the exact representation of His being, sustaining all things by His powerful word.

Jesus Christ, after He had provided purification for sins, He sat down at the right hand of the Majesty in heaven.

COLOSSIANS 1:15–20

Jesus Christ is the image of the invisible God, the first born of all creation.

Jesus Christ, for by Him all things were created: things in heaven and on earth, visible and invisible, whether thrones or powers or rulers or authorities; all things were created by Him and for Him.

Jesus Christ, He is before all things, and in Him all things hold together.

Jesus Christ, He is the head of the body, the church.

Jesus Christ, He is the beginning and the first born among the dead, so that in everything He might have the supremacy.

Jesus Christ, for God was pleased to have all His fullness dwell in Him, and through Him to reconcile to Himself all things, whether things on earth or things in heaven, by making peace through His blood, shed on the cross.

THE GOD ALMIGHTY

I called you "My child"

I love you My precious child, everything about Me, everything about who I AM, and everything about what I AM and everything about where I AM is a mark of treasures in your heart from Me. Before I formed you in your mother's womb, I knew you. Before you were born, I set you apart and I appointed you as My Prophet to the Nations. The moment I saw you My heart filled with joy, I embraced you and kiss you and I called you My Image. I made you fearfully and wonderfully made. You did not choose me, but I chose you before the foundation of this world. The minute I have eye contact with you I got hold of you and I put you in my warm heart, the minute you were born you become mine. When I saw you from your mother's womb, My heart jumped for joy and I embraced and comforted you with My tender heart. You are My precious Jewel, and you are very important to Me. I want to lavish you with everything I AM. I AM quick to hear your voice as you whisper into My ears. You are the one whom I cherish, I desire, I delight, and I behold. You have Me in your "hearth." The minute you called Me, I came immediately to rescue you and to be with you. You are beautiful in My eyes and I love every detail about you. I love the way you speak, the way you move and the way you listen to Me. You are unique, perfect, special, and peculiar child that I created with My own bare hands, and you are the one who completes Me. I have made My Son known to you, I love you My child.

When I saw your heart being beaten, torn, crushed, shattered and broken, I immediately touched you with my tears falling down my face. My heart is troubled and broken as I see you crying out for Me. I wiped your tears with My love. In your deep pain and sorrow, I was there to give you My love, My peace and My hope. When people hurt and failed you, I was there as your bridegroom to lift you up high and take you higher in My realms. When you worry, I was there to strengthen you and give you comfort. When you are in danger, I was there to protect and rescue you with My body, My blood, and My resurrection. When you are hungry, I was there to feed you with My breads and My fruits. When you are thirsty I was there to give My living water.

When you fall, I was there to get you back up and show you the way of my salvation. When you are sick, I was there to heal you and cover you with My blood and My wings. When you are anxious, I was there to calm you down and give you My strength and peace. When you are losing hope, I was there to guide and direct you. When you felt like there is no way out, I was there to give you the path of my existence. When you felt isolated, I was there beside you, carrying you with Me in my hidden place. When you are distressed, I was there to hold you in my arms. When you are having fear, I was there to rescue you. When there's war trying to cripple you in, I send my mighty angels fighting the battles for you. When you are alone, my presence is with you. When there is death trying to call you, I'AM there to give you My life.

You are my precious child. I will never leave you nor forsake you. You are who I'AM, you are My Image, My existence and you and I are One,

your "ABBAH," YOUR "FATHER."

CHAPTER 40

FAITH

GALATIANS 2:20

I have been crucified with Christ and I no longer live, but Christ lives in me. The life I now live in the body, I live by faith in the Son of God, who loved me and gave Himself for me.

EPHESIANS 2:8

For it is by grace you have been saved through faith, and this is not from yourselves, it is the gift of God.

HEBREWS 11:1–3

Now faith is the confidence in what we hope for and assurance about what we do not see. This is what the ancients were commended for. By faith we understand that the universe was formed at God's command, so that what is seen was not made out of what was visible.

EPHESIANS 3:16 17

I pray that out of His glorious riches He may strengthen you with power through His Spirit in your inner being, so that Christ may dwell in your hearts through faith. And I pray that you, being rooted and established in love.

MATTHEW 21:21–22

Jesus replied, "Truly I tell you, if you have faith and do not doubt, not only can you do what was done to the fig tree, but also you can say to this mountain, 'Go, throw yourself into the sea, and it will be done. If you believe, you will receive whatever you ask for in prayer.

ROMANS 15:13

May the God of hope fill you with all joy and peace as you trust in Him, so that you may overflow with hope by the power of the Holy Spirit.

MATTHEW 17:20

He replied, "Because you have so little faith. Truly I tell you, if you have faith as small as a mustard seed, you cay to this mountain, 'Move from here to there,' and it will move. Nothing will be impossible for you."

ROMANS 1:17

For in the Gospel the righteousness of God is revealed—a righteousness that is by faith from first to last, just as it is written: "The righteous will live by faith."

MARK 11:24

Therefore I tell you, whatever you ask for in prayer, believe that you have received it, and it will be yours.

MARK 10:52

"Go," said Jesus, "your faith has healed you." Immediately He received His sight and followed Jesus along the road.

JOHN 7:38

Whoever believes in Me as Scriptures has said, rivers of living water will flow from within them.

I want to ask you, how do you know that you have faith? Faith is not about what you think and what you feel.

Faith is about you choosing God that you believe Him for the impossible and trust His leadership over your life.

Faith is the mind and the confirmation of what you hope and what you believe in.

Faith is about being bold, courage, assurance and confidence to the One who created all.

Faith is to have the clarity and open to the word of God that has spoken over you, and for God's word to manifest in your life.

Faith is seeing His love, faithfulness, passion, dedication, beauty, and light in your heart when all you have in front of you is cloudy, foggy, uncertainty, and darkness in your eyes.

Faith is seeing the ocean being parted from where you are, and where the ocean of passion and light from the hiding place God is taking you.

Faith means committing and trusting yourself with all your heart, mind, and soul to God for everything, and pouring out your heart to Him until He accomplishes them.

Faith is the power, confidence, assurance, boldness, and stronger feeling in your heart, and never giving up no matter what.

Faith is when the falling world went up before your feet, and God lifted the whole world higher from the earth and released His love, peace, power and strength over you.

Faith is the invisible God, by His word, He spoke it and it came to be.

Faith is to know that you can count on God, for everything that is impossible.

Faith is about trusting God to make a way from open heaven for your life and manifest His glory over you.

Without faith, it is impossible to please God. It is a sin not to have faith. The Scripture said, sin separates us from God.

When you are having challenges and situation in your life, you can count on God that He will make away, if you have faith, belief, and confidence in Him, He will come like a tsunami accompany with His lightning bolt from heaven. With God, nothing is impossible for Him. With His one finger, God will manifest His power, goodness, and kindness over you, and you will see God face-to-face.

Your faith can move the mountain out of the way and bring you to the place where He is.

With God, you will never put to shame. He is here to always back you up.

No matter how big is the mountain in your life, I want you to know that God is greater than all of them. God said to speak to the mountain to get out of the way so that God can act and move for your destiny and for your future.

FAITH MEANS THERE IS MORE OF HIM.

1 CORINTHIANS 2:5

So that your faith might not rest on human wisdom, but on God's power.

CHAPTER 41

HEALING

Nothing is impossible for God. He is your healer, He is your restorer, He is your Redeemer, He is you deliverer, He is your Provider, He is your refuge, and He is your way maker. If you have sickness and disease and even death, you can call on God and believe that He will heal you, restore you, deliver you, and even to bring back your dead body.

When the soldiers were beating Jesus, His blood was gushing all over His body, and the blood that came out of His body is part of your healing miracles. With one drop of His blood, you will live and be set free. Have faith, trust, and believe in Him. He is your way to have a greater health, He is your only physician, and He is your only medicine. He is the only healing for your mind, body, and soul, and you can depend on Him.

With God, you do not have to fear, to be confused, or to be shaken with sickness and disease, because God will touch you and heal you, and that is His promise to you. Through your faith and the Holy Spirit on you, the miracles are already at work within your soul. The miracle from God is "love," and that love is now your healing. From the drop of His blood, you are now "healed." In Jesus' name, amen

ISAIAH 53:5

But He pierced for our transgressions, He was crushed for our iniquities; the punishment that brought us peace was on Him, and by His wounds we are healed.

MARK 10:52

"Go," said Jesus, "your faith has healed you." Immediately He received His sight and followed Jesus along the road.

MARK 11:24

Therefore I tell you, whatever you ask for in prayer, believe that you have received it, and it will be yours.

PSALM 107:19–20

Then they cried to the Lord in their trouble, and He saved them from distress. He sent out His word and healed them; He rescued them from the grave. Let them give thanks to the Lord for His unfailing love and His wonderful deeds for mankind.

EXODUS 23:25-26

Worship the Lord your God, and His blessings will be on your food and water. I will take away sickness from among you. And none will miscarry or be barren in your land. I will give you a full life span.

PSALM 30:2

Lord my God, I called to you for help, and you healed me.

DEUTERONOMY 7:15

The Lord will keep you free from every disease. He will not inflict on you the horrible disease you knew in Egypt, but He will inflict them on all who hate you.

DEUTERONOMY 8:1

Be careful to follow every command I am giving you today, so that you may live and increase and may enter and possess the land that the Lord promised on oath to your forefathers.

God is the God of miracles; I believe and trust Him.

PRAYER:

Lord Jesus, you are my healer, You are my medicine, and You are my Great Physician. Thank You for touching my body and heal me completely. Thank You for your cross, for Your tomb, and for Your resurrection that changed my life. Your fire brings freedom into my soul. You are my God who sees me and nothing from Your sight You cannot reveal. Your love and comfort toward me bring confidence into my soul.

Lord Jesus, thank You for healing my body, my mind, and my soul. It is done it is finish on the cross.

In Jesus mighty name amen.

THE HEART OF YOUR HEAVENLY
FATHER TO YOUR HEART

LUKE 4:14–20

Jesus returned to Galilee in the power of the Spirit, and news about Him spread through the whole countryside. He was teaching in their synagogues, and everyone praised Him. He went to Nazareth where He had been brought up, and on the Sabbath day He went to the synagogue, as was His custom. And He stood up to read. The scroll of the prophet Isaiah was handed to Him. Unrolling it, He found the place where it is written:

The Spirit of the Lord is upon me because He has anointed me to preach good news to the poor. He has sent me to proclaim freedom for the prisoners and recovery of sight for the blind, to release the oppressed, and to proclaim the year of the Lord's favor. Then He rolled up the scroll, gave it back to the attendant, and sat down. The eyes of everyone in the synagogue were fastened on Him, and He began by saying to them, "Today, this Scripture is fulfilled in your hearing."

HEBREWS 2:14–18

Since the children have flesh and blood, He too shared in their humanity so that by His death He might destroy Him who holds the power of death— that is, the devil—and free those who all their lives were held in slavery by their fear of death. For surely, it is not angels He helps, but Abraham's descendants. For this reason, He had to be made like His brothers in every way in order that He might become a merciful and faithful high priest in service to God, and that He might make atonement for the sins of the people. Because He himself suffered when He was tempted, He is able to help those who are being tempted.

HABAKKUK 3:2

Lord, I have heard of Your fame; I stand in awe of Your deeds. Repeat them in our day.

REVELATION 22:6

The angel said to me, "These words are trustworthy and true. The Lord, the God of the Spirits of the Prophets, sent His angel to show His servants the things that must soon take place."

REVELATION 22:17

The Spirit and the bride say, "Come!" And let him who hears say." "Come!" Whoever thirsty, let him come; and whoever wishes, let him take the free gift of the water of life.

REVELATION 22:20-21

He who testifies to these things says, "Yes, I AM COMING SOON." Amen. Come, Lord Jesus.

The grace of the Lord Jesus be with God's people. Amen.